Student Solutions Manual

MATHEMATICS:
WITH APPLICATIONS IN
MANAGEMENT AND ECONOMICS

Sixth Edition

Earl K. Bowen
Gordon D. Prichett
John C. Saber
all of
Babson College

Manual prepared by
George Recck
Babson College

1987

IRWIN

Homewood, Illinois 60430

TABLE OF CONTENTS

Page

1.

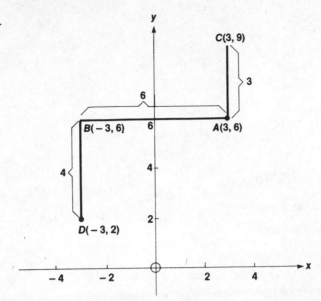

$$AB = |(-3) - 3| = 6$$
$$AC = |9 - 6| \quad = 3$$
$$DB = |2 - 6| \quad = 4$$

4. P_1P_2 will be horizontal if $y_1 = y_2$ and P_1P_3 will be perpendicular to P_1P_2 if $x_1 = x_3$

7. a) Sales increase $= 30 - 14 = \$16$

   b) Sales expense increase $= 22 - 10 = \$12$

   c)

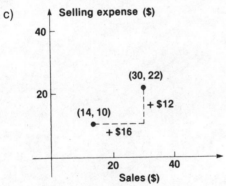

1.5 Problem Set 1-2

2. a) $\sqrt{(11 - 5)^2 + (18 - 10)^2} = \sqrt{36 + 64} = 10$

   b) $\sqrt{(9 - 0)^2 + (12 - 0)^2} = \sqrt{81 + 144} = 15$

   c) $\sqrt{(3 - (-2))^2 + (-4 - (-5))^2} = \sqrt{25 + 1} = 5.1$

   d) $\sqrt{(6 - (-2))^2 + (9 - 3)^2} = \sqrt{64 + 36} = 10$

   e) $\sqrt{(6 - 3)^2 + (-5 - (-5))^2} = \sqrt{9 + 0} = 3$

   f) $\sqrt{(4 - 4)^2 + (9 - 7)^2} = \sqrt{0 + 4} = 2$

5.

a) $x_c = \dfrac{100 - 0}{2} = 50$ $y_c = \dfrac{50 - 0}{2} = 25$ (50, 25)

b) $\sqrt{(50 - 0)^2 + (25 - 0)^2} = \sqrt{2{,}500 + 625} = 55.9$ feet

c) $\sqrt{(40 - 10)^2 + (45 - 5)^2} = \sqrt{900 + 1{,}600} = 50$ feet

1.7   Problem Set 1-3

1. a) rise $= y_2 - y_1$ b) run $= x_2 - x_1$

3. Slope $= \dfrac{\text{rise}}{\text{run}} = \dfrac{8}{12} = 2/3$

6. (50, 500)(100, 900)

   a) Slope $= \dfrac{900 - 500}{100 - 50} = \dfrac{400}{50} = 8$ b) \$8

8. Slope $= \dfrac{2 - 0}{2 - 0} = \dfrac{2}{2} = 1$

18. Slope $= \dfrac{6 - (-5)}{3 - 12} = \dfrac{11}{-9} = \dfrac{-11}{9}$

23. $\dfrac{-b - (-2)}{3 - a} = \dfrac{2 - b}{3 - a}$ or $\dfrac{b - 2}{a - 3}$

1.14   Problem Set 1-4

1. $y = mx + b$

   $4 = 3(3) + b$

   $b = -5$

   $y = 3x - 5$

13. Slope $= m$

   $\dfrac{7 - 6}{-3 - 4} = m$

   $\dfrac{1}{-7} = m$

   $m = \dfrac{-1}{7}$

   using $m = \dfrac{-1}{7}$ and (4, 6)

   $y = mx + b$

2

$$6 = 4\left(\frac{-1}{7}\right) + b$$

$$b = \frac{46}{7}$$

$$y = \frac{-1}{7}x + \frac{46}{7}$$

27. Slope $= \dfrac{6 - 3}{-5 - 2}$

$$= \frac{-3}{7}$$

using $m = \dfrac{-3}{7}$ and (2, 3)

$$y = mx + b$$

$$3 = \frac{-3}{7}(2) + b$$

$$b = \frac{27}{7}$$

$$y = \frac{-3}{7}x + \frac{27}{7}$$

$$x = 17$$

$$y = \frac{-3}{7}(17) + \frac{27}{7}$$

$$y = \frac{-24}{7}$$

32. Two points are (100, 75) and (400, 150)

Slope $= \dfrac{150 - 75}{400 - 100}$

$$= \frac{75}{300}$$

$$= \frac{1}{4}$$

using (100, 75)

$$75 = \frac{1}{4}(100) + b$$

$$b = 50$$

Selling expense $= \dfrac{1}{4}$(sales) $+ 50$

35. a) $y = .8m + .5$
    b) $E = .1V + 50$

42. When $x = 0$ intercept $= (0, 6)$
    When $y = 0$ intercept $= (6, 0)$

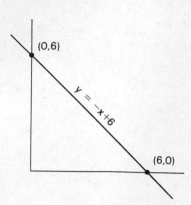

or

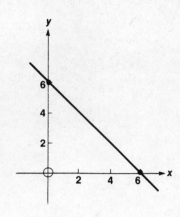

47. $(-3x) + 3x - 2y = 7(-3x)$

$$\left(-\frac{1}{2}\right) - 2y = (-3x + 7)\left(-\frac{1}{2}\right)$$

$$y = \frac{3}{2}x - \frac{7}{2}$$

$$\text{Slope} = \frac{3}{2}$$

51. a) $8A + 12B = 96$

b) $8A = -12B + 96$

$A = -1.5B + 12$

1.5 pounds of A per pound of B

c) $12B = -8A + 96$

$$4 = \frac{-2}{3}A + 8$$

2/3 pounds of B per pound of A

55. Use point slope form

a) $y - 7 = 1.5(x - 2)$

$y - 7 = 1.5x - 3$

$y = 1.5x + 4$

b) find slope of new line

$$\frac{-1}{1/3} = -3$$

next use point-slope form

$y - (-6) = -3(x - (-2))$

$y + 6 = -3x - 6$

$y = -3x - 12$

60. Equation of existing pipeline

$$\frac{0 - 5}{8 - 0} = \frac{-5}{8} = \text{slope}$$

$$y = \frac{-5}{8}x + 5 \longrightarrow y\text{-intercept}$$

slope of new line

$$\frac{-1}{-5/8} = \frac{8}{5}$$

4

use point slope form

$$y - 6 = \frac{8}{5}(x - 5)$$

$$y - 6 = \frac{8}{5}x - 8$$

$$y = \frac{8}{5}x - 2$$

B exists at $y = 0$

$$0 = \frac{8}{5}x - 2$$

$$2 = \frac{8}{5}x$$

$$\frac{5}{4} = x \quad \text{or}$$

$$B = \left(\frac{5}{4}, 0\right)$$

1.16   Problem Set 1-5

11. a)   variable cost $= 3(50) = 150$

  b)   total cost $= 3(50) + 20 = 170$

  c)   variable cost per unit $= \dfrac{\text{variable cost}}{\text{total units}}$

$$\frac{150}{50} = 3$$

  d)   average cost per unit $= \dfrac{\text{total cost}}{\text{total units}}$

$$\frac{170}{50} = 3.4$$

  e)   marginal cost of 50th unit = total cost of 50 units − total cost of 49 units
$$[3(50) + 20] - [3(49) + 20] = 3$$

13. Slope $= \dfrac{15,000 - 7,500}{2,500 - 1,000}$

$$\frac{7,500}{1,500} = 5$$

$$y = 5x + b$$

  a)   using $(1,000, 7,500)$

$$7,500 = 5(1,000) + b$$
$$b = 2,500$$
$$y = 5x + 2,500$$

  b)   variable cost $=$ (slope)($\#$ units produced)
$$= (5)(2,000)$$
$$= \$10,000$$

c) fixed cost = y intercept = $2,500

d) variable cost per unit = slope = $5

e) $\dfrac{\text{total cost}}{\#\text{ units}} = \dfrac{10,000 + 2,500}{2,000} = \$6.25$

f) marginal cost = slope = $5

1.21 Problem Set 1-6

13. a) $R = 5q \qquad C = 2q + 60,000$

b) $P = R - C \qquad R = 5(25,000) = 125,000$

$C = 2(25,000) + 60,000 = 110,000$

$P = 125,000 - 110,000 = \$15,000$

c) $R = 5(10,000) = 50,000 \qquad C = 2(10,000) + 60,000 = 80,000$

$P = 50,000 - 80,000 = -30,000$ or loss of $30,000

d) $q_e = \dfrac{F}{p - v} = \dfrac{60,000}{5 - 2} = 20,000$ units

e) $R = 5(20,000) = \$100,000$

f) Revenue cost ($000)

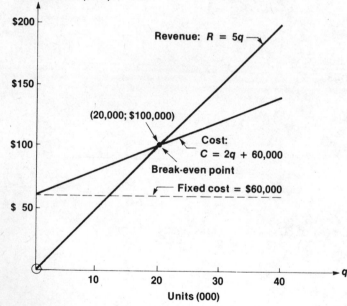

15. $q_e = \dfrac{F}{p - v} = \dfrac{200,000}{180 - 100}$

$= 2,500$ units

29. a) $x_e = \dfrac{b}{1 - m}$

$= \dfrac{22,800}{1 - (.45 + .17)}$

$= \$60,000$

6

b) $y = .62x + 22,800$

c) $P = R - C$

$P = 75,000 - [.62(75,000) + 22,800]$

$ = 75,000 - 69,300$

$ = \$5,700$

d)

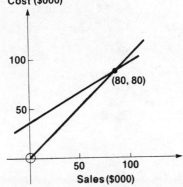

Cost ($000)

(80, 80)

Sales ($000)

31. a) variable cost per $1 sales = $0.47

b) fixed cost = $29,786

c) total cost = $y = .47(72,000) + 29,786$

$ = \$63,626$

d) $x_e = \dfrac{29,786}{1 - .47} = \$56,200$

e) $P = 80,000 - [.47(80,000) + 29,786]$

$ = \$12,614$

35. Horizontal shift is 50 to the left because horizontal intercept for

$$DD: \quad 0 = -.1q + 40 \text{ is } 400$$
$$D'D': \quad 0 = -.1q + 35 \text{ is } 350$$

or demand is 50 units less at every price level
Vertical shift is 5 downward (40 to 35)
50 price is $5 per unit less at every level of demand.

7

1. a) $AC = |-2 - (-4)| = |+2| = 2$

    b) $BC = |3 - 5| = |-2| = 2$

    c) $AB = \sqrt{(5 - 3)^2 + (-2(-4))^2} = \sqrt{2^2 + 2^2} = \sqrt{8} = 2.83$

3. a)   Given $(0, 0)$ and $(3, 4)$, the other corners are $(0, 4)$ and $(3, 0)$.
        The diagonal has length $\sqrt{(3 - 0)^2 + (0 - 4)^2} = \sqrt{9 + 16} = \sqrt{25} = 5$

    b)   Given $(-1, 2)$ and $(8, 14)$, the other corners are $(-1, 14)$ and $(8, 2)$.
        The diagonal has length $\sqrt{(8 - (-1))^2 + (2 - 14)^2} = \sqrt{81 + 144} = \sqrt{225} = 15.$

    c)   Given $(1, 2)$ and $(3, 4)$, the other corners are $(1, 4)$ and $(3, 2)$.
        The diagonal has length $\sqrt{(3 - 1)^2 + (2 - 4)^2} = \sqrt{4 + 4} = \sqrt{8} = 2.83.$

5. a)   Let city A have coordinates $(0, 0)$ and let city B have coordinates $(5, 12)$, then

    $$\text{distance } AB = \sqrt{(5 - 0)^2 + (12 - 0)^2}$$
    $$= \sqrt{25 + 144}$$
    $$= \sqrt{169}$$
    $$= 13 \text{ miles.}$$

    b)   5 blocks from 2nd St. to 7th St. and 12 blocks from 7th Ave. to 19th Ave. $5 + 12 = 17$ blocks.

    c) $\sqrt{(7 - 2)^2 + (19 - 7)^2} = \sqrt{25 + 144} = \sqrt{169} = 13$ blocks.
        13 blocks $\times$ 400 feet/block $= 5{,}200$ feet.

7. a) $(100(S_2 - S_1))/S_1$

    b)   A negative result means that sales decreased.

9. a) $m = \dfrac{3 - 7}{-1 - (-4)} = \dfrac{-4}{3}$

    using $(-4, 7)$,

    $b = 7 - \left(-\dfrac{4}{3}\right)(-4) = 7 - \dfrac{16}{3} = \dfrac{5}{3}$

    $y = -\dfrac{4}{3}x + \dfrac{5}{3}$

    b) $m = \dfrac{6 - 2}{5 - 1} = \dfrac{4}{4} = 1$

    using $(1, 2)$, $b = 2 - (1)(1) = 2 - 1 = 1$

    $y = x + 1$

    c) $m = \dfrac{5 - 0}{0 - 0} = \dfrac{5}{0}$ Undefined slope, $x = 0$, a vertical line.

    d) $m = \dfrac{-1 - (-1)}{10 - 5} = \dfrac{0}{5} = 0$, $y = -1$, a horizontal line.

    e) $m = \dfrac{3 - 0}{5 - 5} = \dfrac{3}{0}$ Undefined slope, $x = 5$, a vertical line.

8

f) $m = \dfrac{-4 - (-1)}{2 - (-2)} = \dfrac{-3}{4}$

using $(-2, -1)$

$b = -1 - \left(-\dfrac{3}{4}\right)(-2) = -1 - \dfrac{3}{2} = -\dfrac{5}{2}$

$y = -\dfrac{3}{4}x - \dfrac{5}{2}$

g) $m = \dfrac{-1 - (-3)}{4 - 1} = \dfrac{2}{3}$

using $(1, -3)$,

$b = -3 - \left(\dfrac{2}{3}\right)(1) = -\dfrac{11}{3}$

$y = \dfrac{2}{3}x - \dfrac{11}{3}$

h) $m = \dfrac{5 - 5}{3 - (-2)} = \dfrac{0}{5} = 0$

using $(-2, 5)$, $b = 5 - (0)(-2) = 5$

$y = 5$

11. $y = -5$

13. Selling expense ($)

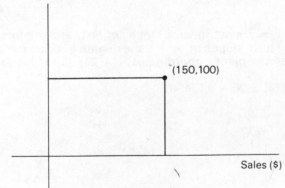

$m = \dfrac{\text{Change in Selling Expense}}{\text{Change in Sales}} = \dfrac{1}{3}$

$b = 100 - \left(\dfrac{1}{3}\right)(150) = 100 - 50 = 50$

$y = \dfrac{1}{3}x + 50$

Selling Expense is fifty dollars more than one third of the total sales.

15. For $y = -6$, $m = 0$. The negative reciprocal of zero is undefined and the line $x = 15$ has an undefined slope, hence the two lines are perpendicular.

9

17.

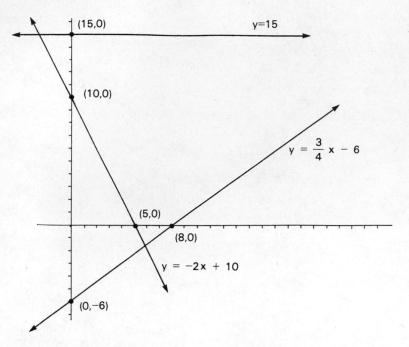

19. $y = -\dfrac{2}{3}x - 4$

21. a) $m = -2$, the negative reciprocal of 1/2.

$b = 15 - (-2)(-1) = 15 - 2 = 13$

$y = -2x + 13$

b) Since $y = mx + b$, the pipeline described by $\overset{\frown}{x = y}$ must have a slope, $m = 1$, and y-intersect, $b = 0$. All lines perpendicular to the pipeline will have slopes $m = -1$, the negative reciprocal of 1. To find the equation of the plant's pipeline, use the plant's coordinates, (14, 26) and solve for b.

$$b = 26 - (-1)(14) = 26 + 14 = 40$$

So, the plant's pipeline is described by $y = -x + 40$.

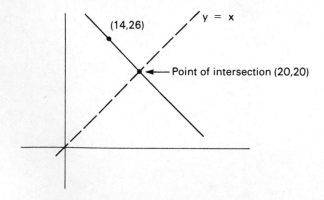

To find the length of the plant's pipeline, first determine the coordinates of the connecting point. Since that point lies on the existing pipeline, y must be equal to x therefore you can substitute x for y in the equation for the plant's pipeline.

10

$$x = -x + 40$$
$$2x = 40$$
$$x = 20$$

$$\text{Length} = \sqrt{(26 - 20)^2 + (14 - 20)^2} = \sqrt{6^2 + (-6)^2} = \sqrt{72} = 8.5$$

23. $R = 4x$ is a line through the origin and it means that $0 of revenue is received when 0 units are sold.

25. productivity = output/labor-hour.

productivity $= \dfrac{y}{x} = 5$. The ratio of output to labor-hours is constantly 5.

27. $y = 2x + 40$ describes the total cost of making x units.

a) variable cost = cost per unit times the number of units.

$$= 2(100)$$
$$= \$200$$

b) total cost $= 2(100) + 40$
$$= \$240$$

c) The variable cost per unit is $2.

d) The average cost per unit is the total cost divided by the number of units produced.

$$\text{Av. cost} = 240/100 = \$2.40$$

e) The marginal cost is the variable cost per unit, $2.00.

f) In a straight line model, marginal cost is constant and is equal to the slope of the line. The marginal cost for every unit is $2.00.

29. a) $C = 7q + 75{,}000$

$R = 10q$

b) Profit = Revenue − Cost

$$= 10(40{,}000) - (7(40{,}000) + 75{,}000)$$
$$= 400{,}000 - 355{,}000$$
$$= \$45{,}000$$

c) Profit $= 10(20{,}000) - (7(20{,}000) + 75{,}000)$

$$= 200{,}000 - 215{,}000$$
$$= -15{,}000 \ (\text{A loss of } \$15{,}000)$$

d) Profit is zero at the break-even point.

$$q_e = \frac{75{,}000}{10 - 7}$$

$$q_e = \frac{75{,}000}{3}$$

$$q_e = 25{,}000 \text{ units}$$

e) If 25,000 units must be produced to break even, and each unit brings in $10 of revenue, then Break-even dollar volume = $10(25,000) = $250,000.

f)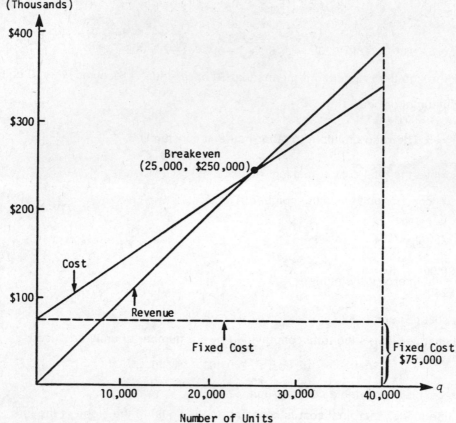

Dollars of
Cost and Revenue
(Thousands)

Breakeven
(25,000, $250,000)

Cost

Revenue

Fixed Cost

Fixed Cost
$75,000

Number of Units

31. $C = 80,000 + 12q$

$R = 13.25q$

.a) At break-even quantity, Revenue − Costs = 0

$$q_e = \frac{80,000}{13.25 - 12}$$

$$q_e = \frac{80,000}{1.25}$$

$$q_e = 64,000$$

b) Loss of $80,000.

c) Revenues from 10,000 units = $13.25(10,000) = $132,500.

Cost from 10,000 units = 80,000 + 12(10,000) = $200,000.

So, at 10,000 units, they will lose $67,500 dollars, which is a smaller loss than if they shut down. Therefore, they would not shut down.

33. $y = 10,500 + 0.58x$

a) fixed cost = $10,500

b) total cost = 10,500 + 0.58(60,000) = $45,300

12

c) The break-even point occurs when sales equals total cost.

$$x_e = \frac{b}{1 - m}$$

$$= \frac{10,500}{1 - .58}$$

$$= \frac{10,500}{.42}$$

$$= \$25,000$$

d) Net profit = Sales − total cost

$$= 65,000 - (10,500 + .58(65,000))$$

$$= 65,000 - 48,200 = \$16,800$$

35. *DD*: $p = -0.2q + 50$

vertical-intercept = 50

find horizontal-intercept by letting $p = 0$.

$$0 = (-0.2)q + 50$$

$$\frac{-50}{-0.2} = q = 250$$

D′D′: $p = (-0.2)q + 60$

vertical-intercept = 60

horizontal-intercept $\frac{-60}{-0.2} = 300$

Vertical shift = 60 − 50 = 10. Thus, the price per unit is $10 higher at every level of demand.

Horizontal shift = 300 − 250 = 50. Thus, the demand is 50 million pounds greater at every level of price.

1. e_1: $x + y = 5$

   e_2: $2x + y = 7$

   $e_1 - e_2$

$$\begin{array}{r} x + y = 5 \\ -(2x + y = 7) \\ \hline -x = -2 \end{array}$$

$$x = 2$$

   substitute $x = 2$ in e_1

   $2 + y = 5$

   $y = 3$

   $(2, 3)$

7. e_1: $x + y = 1{,}000$

   e_2: $\dfrac{.5x + .66y}{1{,}000} = .6$

                  or

   $.5x + .66y = 600$

   $e_1 - 2(e_2)$

$$\begin{array}{r} x + y = 1{,}000 \\ -(x + 1.32y = 1{,}200) \\ \hline -.32y = -200 \end{array}$$

$$y = 625$$

   $x + 625 = 1{,}000$

   $x = 375$

   375 liters of regular and 625 liters of unleaded

10. e_1: $10x + 5y = 300$

   e_2: $20x + 8y = 500$

   $2(e_1) - e_2$

$$\begin{array}{r} 20x + 10y = 600 \\ -(20x + 8y = 500) \\ \hline 2y = 100 \end{array}$$

$$y = 50$$

   $10x + 5(50) = 300$

   $10x = 50$

   $x = 5$

   5 captain's and 50 regular chairs

1. a)

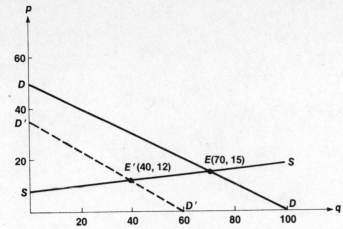

b)   *SS − DD*

$$p = .1q + 8$$
$$-(p = -.5q + 50)$$
$$\overline{0 = .6q - 42}$$
$$q = 70$$
$$p = .1(70) + 8$$
$$p = 15$$

E(70, 15)

c)   See figure A

d)   *SS − DD′*

$$p = .1q + 8$$
$$-(p = -.6q + 36)$$
$$\overline{0 = .7q - 28}$$
$$q = 40$$
$$p = .1(40) + 8$$
$$p = 12$$

E′(40, 12)

e)   The decrease in demand was accompanied by a lower demand and a lower price per unit at equilibrium.

5.   The demand function shifted to the right. At the new equilibrium, both demand and price are higher.

9.   The supply function shifted to the right because a right shift of a supply function leads to a new equilibrium in which supply is higher but price is lower.

2.11 Problem Set 2-3

1. e_1: $2x - 3y = 5$

    e_2: $6x - 9y = 8$

    $3(e_1) - e_2$

    $$6x - 9y = 15$$
    $$\underline{-(6x - 9y = 24)}$$
    $$0 = -9$$

    Parallel lines; no solution

5. e_1: $3x + 12y = -9$

    e_2: $-2x - 8y = 6$

    $2(e_1) + 3(e_2)$

    $$6x + 24y = -18$$
    $$\underline{+(-6x - 24y = 18)}$$
    $$0 = 0$$

    Unlimited number of solutions; the lines are the same

2.14 Problem Set 2-4

2. Let x be arbitrary and solve for y

    a) $3x + 4y = 3$; $4y = 3 - 3x$; $y = \dfrac{3}{4} - \dfrac{3}{4}x$

    b) Let y and z be arbitrary and solve for x

    $x + 2y - 4z = 15$; $x = 15 - 2y + 4z$

5. a)

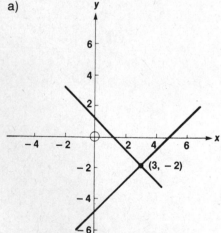

b)

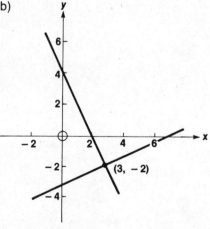

c)

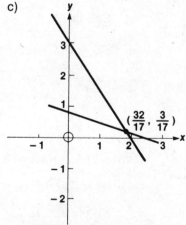

7. e_1: $2x + y + 22 = 5$

    e_2: $x + y - 2 = 0$

    e_3: $3x - 2y + 2 = 1$

    a) Solve for x in e_3

    $x = -y + 2$

16

b) Substitute $x = -y + 2$ in e_1 and e_3

e_1: $2(-y + 2) + y + 2z = 5$

$-y + 4z = 5$

e_3: $3(-y + 2) - 2y + 2 = 1$

$-5y + 4z = 1$

c) $e_1 - e_3$

$-y + 4z = 5$

$\underline{-(-5y + 4z = 1)}$

$4y \qquad = 4$

$y = 1$

using e_1

$-(1) + 4z = 5$

$z = 1.5$

using e_2

$x + 1 - 1.5 = 0$

$x = .5$

final answer

$(.5, 1, 1.5)$

11. e_1: $x + y + z = 10$

e_2: $3x - y + 2z = 14$

e_3: $2x - 2y + z = 8$

solve for x in e_1

$x = 10 - y - z$

substitute $x = 10 - y - z$ in e_2 and e_3

e_2: $3(10 - y - z) - y + 2z = 14$

$-4y - z = -16$

e_3: $2(10 - y - z) - 2y + z = 8$

$-4y - z = -12$

$e_2 - e_3$

$-4y - z = -16$

$\underline{-(-4y - z = -12)}$

$0 = -4$

e_2 and e_3 are parallel planes thus there are no solutions.

2.17 Problem Set 2-5

1. e_1: $x + y + z = 45$

e_2: $2x + 3y + z = 85$

e_3: $x + 2y + 4z = 120$

e_4: $4x + 2y + 3z = 130$

from e_1

$x = 45 - y - z$

substitute $x = 45 - y - z$ into e_2 and e_3

e_2: $2(45 - y - z) + 3y + z = 85$

$$y - z = -5$$

e_3: $(45 - y - z) + 2y + 4z = 120$

$$y + 32 = 75$$

$e_2 - e_3$

$$y - z = -5$$
$$-(y + 3z = 75)$$
$$-4z = -80$$
$$z = 20$$

using e_3

$y - 20 = -5$

$$y = 15$$

using e_1

$x + 15 + 20 = 45$

$$x = 10$$

check on e_4

$4(10) + 2(15) + 3(20) = 130$

$$130 = 130$$

6. a) e_1: $\quad a + b + 9c = 75$

$\quad e_2$: $\quad a + 3b + 7c = 65$

$\quad e_3$: $2a + 7b + 13c = 125$

solve e_1 for a

$a = 75 - b - 9c$

substitute $a = 75 - b - 2c$ in e_2 and e_3

e_2: $(75 - b - 9c) + 3b + 7c = 65$

$$2b - 2c = -10$$

e_3: $2(75 - b - 9c) + 7b + 13c = 125$

$$5b - 5c = -25$$

$5e_2 - 2e_3$

$$10b - 10c = -50$$
$$-(10b - 10c = -50)$$
$$0 = 0$$

let c be arbitrary then $b = c - 5$ and using e_1, $a = 75 - (c - 5) - 9c = 80 - 10c$

b) The profit mixture is:

$$p = 20a + 30b + 40c$$

18

taking any solution from part (a)

$$c \text{ arbitrary}, a = 80 - 10c$$
$$b = c - 5$$

$p = 20(80 - 10c) + 30(c - 5) + 40c$

$p = 1600 - 200c + 30c - 150 + 40c$

$p = 1450 - 130c$

since profit decreases as c increases use minimum value for $c = 5$

$c = 5$

$a = 80 - 10(5) = 30$

$b = 5 - 5 = 0$

therefore

$$p = 20(30) + 30(0) + 40(5)$$
$$= \$800$$

8. a) Set demand = supply for p_1 to get e_1

$1,000 - 5q_1 - 4q_2 = 90 + 2q_1 + 3q_2$

e_1: $910 \qquad\qquad = 7q_1 + 7q_2$

Set demand = supply for p_2 to get e_2

$900 - 2q_1 - 5q_2 = 120 + q_1 + 4q_2$

e_2: $780 \qquad\qquad = 3q_1 + 9q_2$

$3e_1 - 7e_2$

$\qquad 2,730 = 21q_1 + 21q_2$

$\underline{-(5,460 = 21q_1 + 63q_2)}$

$\quad -2,730 = \qquad\quad -42q_2$

$\qquad\quad 65 = \qquad\qquad q_2$

using e_1

$910 = 7q_1 + 7(65)$

$\;65 = q_1$

using $q_1 = 65$ and $q_2 = 65$

$p_1 = 1,000 - 5(65) - 4(65) \qquad p_2 = 900 - 2(65) - 5(65)$

$p_1 = \$415 \qquad\qquad\qquad\qquad p_2 = \$445$

b) Set demand = supply for p_1 to get e_1

$1,210 - 5q_1 - 4q_2 = 90 + 2q_1 + 3q_2$

e_1: $1,120 \qquad\qquad = 7q_1 + 7q_2$

Set demand = supply for p_2 to get e_2

$984 - 2q_1 - 5q_1 = 120 + q_1 + 4q_2$

e_2: $864 \qquad\qquad = 3q_1 + 9q_2$

$3e_1 = 7e_2$

$$3{,}360 = 21q_1 + 21q_2$$
$$\underline{-(6{,}048 = 21q_1 + 63q_2)}$$
$$-2{,}688 = \quad\quad -42q_2$$
$$64 = \quad\quad q_2$$

using e_1

$$1{,}120 = 7q_1 + 7(64)$$
$$96 = q_1$$

using $q_1 = 96$ and $q_2 = 64$

$$p_1 = 1{,}210 - 5(96) - 4(64) \quad\quad p_2 = 984 - 2(96) - 5(64)$$
$$p_1 = \$474 \quad\quad\quad\quad\quad\quad p_2 = \$472$$

2.21 Problem Set 2-6

1.

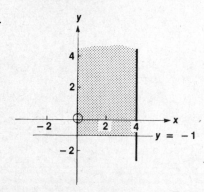

6. first solve equality and sketch

e_1: $2x + 3y = 12$

e_2: $x - 2y = 2$

$e_1 - 2e_2$

$$2x + 3y = 12$$
$$\underline{-(2x - 4y = 4)}$$
$$7y = 8$$

$$y = \frac{8}{7}$$

using e_2

$$x - 2\left(\frac{8}{7}\right) = 2$$

$$x = \frac{30}{7}$$

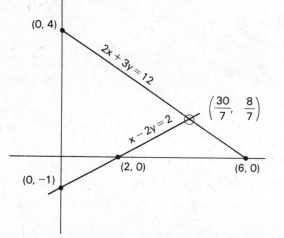

If $2 \leq x \leq \dfrac{30}{7}$ then

$$0 \leq y \leq \frac{x - 2}{2}$$

which is i_2 solved for y.

20

If $\dfrac{30}{7} \leq x \leq 6$ then

$$0 \leq y \leq \frac{12 - 2x}{3}$$

which is i_2 solved for y

10. a) $L + 2w + 2h \leq 108$

      $L + 2(16) + 2h \leq 108$

           $2h \leq 108 - 32 - L$

            $h \leq \dfrac{76 - L}{2}$ where $0 < L < 76$

   b) $L + 4x \leq 108$

        $4x \leq 108 - L$

          $x \leq \dfrac{108 - L}{4}$ where $0 < L < 108$

14. a) $0 \leq x \leq 2$

       $0 \leq y \leq 5 - x$

       $2 \leq x \leq \dfrac{7}{2}$

       $0 \leq y \leq 7 - 2x$

   b)   If $x =$ y can be

       0   0, 1, 2, 3, 4, 5
       1   0, 1, 2, 3, 4
       2   0, 1, 2, 3
       3   0, 1

17.   First sketch the equalities

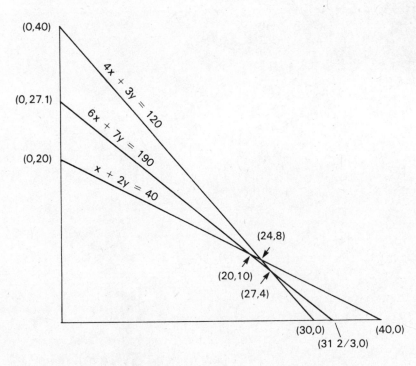

21

If $0 \leq x \leq 20$

then $0 \leq y \leq \dfrac{40 - x}{2}$

which is $x + 2y \leq 40$ solved for y.

If $20 \leq x \leq 27$ then

$$0 \leq y \leq \dfrac{190 - 6x}{7}$$

which is $6x + 7y = 190$ solved for y.

If $27 \leq x \leq 30$

then $0 \leq y \leq \dfrac{120 - 4x}{3}$

which is $4x + 3y \leq 120$ solved for y.

1. $3e_1 - e_2$

$$3x + 30y = 75$$
$$\underline{-(3x - 7y = 1)}$$
$$37y = 74$$
$$y = 2$$

using e_1

$$x + 10(2) = 25$$
$$x = 5$$

3. Using e_1 to get $x = 11 - 2y + 3z$ we can get

e_2: $3(11 - 2y + 3z) + 2y + z = 1;$
$$-4y + 10z = -32$$

e_3: $2(11 - 2y + 3z) + y - 5z = 11;$
$$-3y + z = -11$$

$e_1 - 10e_2$

$$-4y + 10z = -32$$
$$\underline{-(-30y + 10z = -110)}$$
$$26y = 78$$
$$y = 3$$

using e_3

$$-3(3) + z = -11$$
$$z = 2$$

using e_1

$$x + 2(3) - 3(-2) = 11$$
$$x = -1$$

final answer

$(-1, 3, -2)$

5. $e_2 + e_3$

$$3y + 2z = 6$$
$$\underline{+(4x - 3y = 2)}$$
$$4x + 2z = 8$$
$$\underline{-(4x + 2z = 8)} \quad \longleftarrow \quad \text{subtract } 2e_1$$
$$0 = 0$$

In e_1, let x be arbitrary, then $z = 4 - 2z$

Get y in terms of x by substituting $z = 4 - 2x$ in e_2.

Thus:

$$3y + 2(4 - 2z) = 6$$
$$3y + 8 - 4z = 6$$
$$3y = 4x - 2$$
$$y = \frac{4x - 2}{3}$$

x arbitrary, $y = \dfrac{4x - 2}{3}$, $z = 4 - 2x$.

7. Let x, y and z be the number of pounds of cashews, walnuts and almonds respectively.

e_1: $2x + y + z = 9$

e_2: $3x + 2y + z = 13$

e_3: $x + y = 4$

$e_2 - e_1$

$$3x + 2y + z = 13$$
$$\underline{-(2x + y + z = 9)}$$
e_4: $x + y \quad\quad = 4$

$e_3 - e_4$

$$x + y = 4$$
$$\underline{-(x + y = 4)}$$
$$0 = 0$$

Let x be arbitrary, then $y = 4 - x$. Using e_1

$$z = 9 - 2x - (4 - x)$$
$$z = 5 - x \quad\quad \text{then}$$

x arbitrary

$$y = 4 - x$$
$$z = 5 - x$$

Next, change $y = 4 - x$ to $x = 4 - y$

using e_1

$$z = 9 - 2(4 - y) - y = 1 + y$$

y arbitrary

$$x = 4 - y$$
$$z = 1 + y$$

Then from above we can arrive at:

z arbitrary

$$x = 5 - z$$
$$y = z - 1$$

9. a) e_1: $x + y + z = 1{,}000$

e_2: $84x + 92y + 100z = 90(1{,}000)$

$100e_1 - e_2$ yields e_3: $16x + 8y = 10{,}000$

so that $y = 1{,}250 - 2x$

from e_1: $z = 1{,}000 - x - y$

$$z = 1{,}000 - x - (1{,}250 - 2x)$$
$$z = x - 250$$

24

x arbitrary

$$y = 1,250 - 2x$$
$$z = x - 250$$

b) from part (a), we find that x cannot be less than 250 nor greater than 625.

$$c = .5x + .55y + .65x$$

substituting from part (a)

$$c = .5x + .55(1,250 - 2x) + .65(x - 250)$$
$$c = .05x + 525$$

since x must be at least 250, the minimum cost is

$$c = .05(250) + 525 = \$537.50$$

Thus

$$x = 250$$
$$y = 1,250 - 2(250) = 750$$
$$z = 250 - 250 = 0$$

11. a) $1,700 - 3q_1 - q_2 = 100 + 2q_1 + q_2$

e_1: $\qquad 1,600 = 5q_1 + 2q_2$

$1,650 - q_1 - 2q_2 = 50 + q_1 + 2q_2$

e_2: $\qquad 1,600 = 2q_1 + 4q_2$

$2e_1 - e_2$

$\quad 3,200 = 10q_1 + 4q_2$

$\underline{(1,600 = \quad 2q_1 + 4q_2)}$

$\quad 1,600 = \quad 8q_1$

$\qquad q_1 = 200$

using e_1:

$$1,600 = 5(200) + 2q_2$$
$$300 = q_2$$

$p_1 = 1,700 - 3(200) - 300$

$\quad = 800$

$p_2 = 1,650 - 200 - 2(300)$

$\quad = 850$

b) $1,720 - 3q_1 - q_2 = 100 + 2q_1 + q_2$

e_1: $\qquad 1,620 = 5q_1 + 2q_2$

$1,710 - q_1 - 2q_2 = 50 + q_1 + 2q_2$

e_2: $\qquad 1,650 = 2q_1 + 4q_2$

$2e_1 - e_2$

$\quad 3240 = 10q_1 + 4q_2$

$\underline{(1660 = 2q_1 + 4q_2)}$

$\quad 1580 = 8q_1$

$\quad 197.5 = q_1$

using e_2

$\quad 1,660 = 2(197.5) + 4q_2$

$\quad 1,265 = 4q_2$

$\quad 316.25 = q_2$

13.

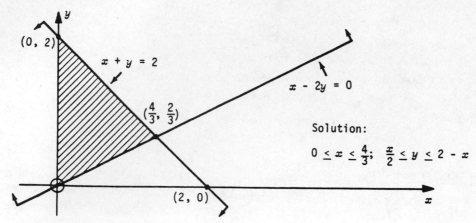

Solution:

$0 \le x \le \frac{4}{3}$; $\frac{x}{2} \le y \le 2 - x$

15.

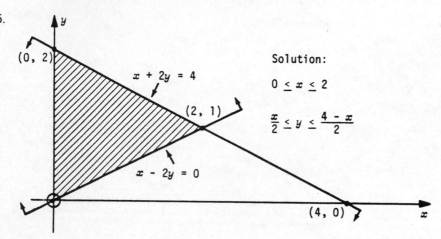

Solution:

$0 \le x \le 2$

$\frac{x}{2} \le y \le \frac{4 - x}{2}$

17.

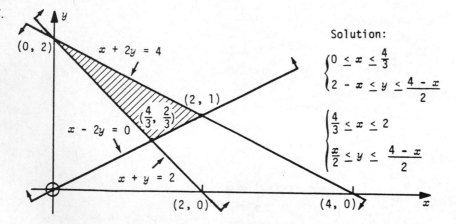

Solution:

$\begin{cases} 0 \le x \le \frac{4}{3} \\ 2 - x \le y \le \frac{4 - x}{2} \end{cases}$

$\begin{cases} \frac{4}{3} \le x \le 2 \\ \frac{x}{2} \le y \le \frac{4 - x}{2} \end{cases}$

19. a) $.06x + iy \ge .08(x + y)$

$iy \ge .02x + .08y$

$i \ge \frac{.02x + .08y}{y}, \quad x \ge 0 \quad y \ge 0$

b) $i = \frac{.02(2,000) + .08(1,000)}{1,000} = \frac{120}{1,000} = .12$ or 12%

26

21. The conditions are

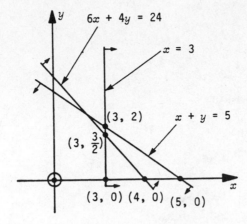

i_1: $x + y \leq 5$

i_2: $6x + 4y \geq 24$

i_3: $x \geq 3$

If $3 \leq x \leq 4$ then $\dfrac{24 - 6x}{4} \leq y \leq 5 - x$ which is found by solving i_2 and i_1 for y, respectively.

If $4 \leq x \leq 5$ then $0 \leq y \leq 5 - x$ which is found by solving i_1 for y.

23. Let x be low and y be high quality batches then,

i_1: $x + 3y \leq 70$

i_2: $3x + 4y \leq 110$

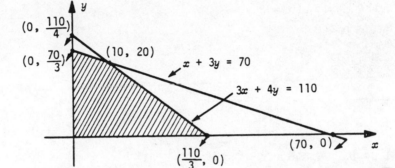

If $0 \leq x \leq 10$ then $0 \leq y \leq \dfrac{70 - x}{3}$ which is i_1 solved for y.

If $10 \leq x \leq \dfrac{110}{3}$ then $0 \leq y \leq \dfrac{110 - 3x}{4}$ which is i_2 solved for y.

25. Total output is $x + y$. The new condition says that $y \geq .05(x + y)$ or dividing by .05

$20 \geq x + y$ or $x - 19y \leq 0$

The last condition is shown as a dashed line on the graph. This space can be described as

$\dfrac{5}{3} \leq y \leq 5$

$\dfrac{65 - y}{2} \leq x \leq \dfrac{110 - 4y}{3}$

Note: The constraint $x + 3y \leq 70$ is no longer binding.

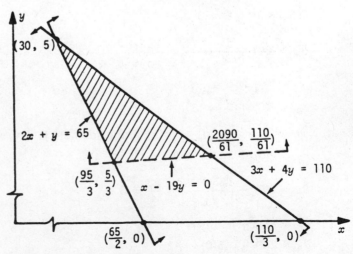

27

1.
corner	coordinates
A	(0, 0)
B	(0, 11/2)
C	(3, 4)
D	(6, 0)

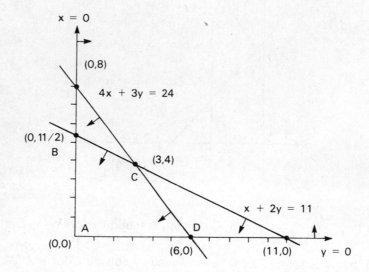

a) $\theta = x + y$, $\theta_{max} = 7$ at $x = 3$, $y = 4$

$\theta_A = 0 + 0 = 0$

$\theta_B = 0 + \dfrac{11}{2} = \dfrac{11}{2} = 5.5$

$\theta_C = 3 + 4 = 7$

$\theta_D = 6 + 0 = 6$

b) $\theta = x + 3y$, $\theta_{max} = 16.5$ at $x = 0$, $y = \dfrac{11}{2}$

$\theta_A = 0 + 3(0) = 0$

$\theta_B = 0 + 3\left(\dfrac{11}{2}\right) = \dfrac{33}{2} = 16.5$

$\theta_C = 3 + 3(4) = 15$

$\theta_D = 6 + 3(0) = 6$

c) $\theta = 3x + y$, $\theta_{max} = 18$ at $x = 6$, $y = 0$

$\theta_A = 3(0) + 0 = 0$

$\theta_B = 3(0) + \dfrac{11}{2} = \dfrac{11}{2} = 5.5$

$\theta_C = 3(3) + 4 = 13$

$\theta_D = 3(6) + 0 = 18$

d) $\theta = 2x + 1.5y$, $\theta_{max} = 12$ on line segment joining $x = 3$, $y = 4$ and at $x = 6$, $y = 0$

$\theta_A = 2(0) + 1.5(0) = 0$

$\theta_B = 2(0) + \left(\dfrac{3}{2}\right)\left(\dfrac{11}{2}\right) = \dfrac{33}{4} = 8.25$

$\theta_C = 2(3) + 1.5(4) = 12$

$\theta_D = 2(6) + 1.5(0) = 12$

28

5.

corner	coordinates
A	(0, 0)
B	(0, 4)
C	(1, 4)
D	(2, 3)
E	(3, 0)

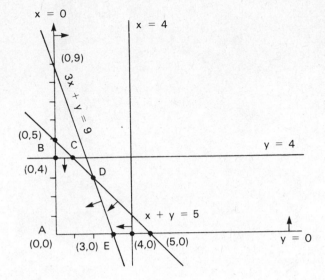

a) $\theta = 0.3x + 0.5y$ $\quad$ $\theta_{max} = 2.3$ at $x = 1$, $y = 4$

b) $\theta = 2x + y$ $\quad$ $\theta_{max} = 7$ at $x = 2$, $y = 3$

c) $\theta = 5x + y$ $\quad$ $\theta_{max} = 15$ at $x = 3$, $y = 0$

d) $\theta = 3x + 3y$ $\quad$ $\theta_{max} = 15$ on line segment joining $x = 1$, $y = 4$ and at $x = 2$, $y = 3$

9.

corner	coordinates	$\theta = 10x + 8y$
A	(0, 0)	0
B	(0, 4)	32
C	(9, 2)	106
D	(21/2, 0)	105

$\theta_{max} = 106$ at $x = 9$, $y = 2$

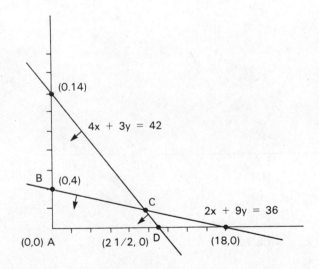

13.

corner	coordinates	$\theta = (59 - 50)x + (48 - 41)y = 9x + 7y$
A	(0, 0)	0
B	(0, 12)	84
C	(8, 8)	128
D	(13, 4)	145
E	(15, 0)	135

$\theta_{max} = 145$ at $x = 13$, $y = 4$

Machine B is not fully utilized.

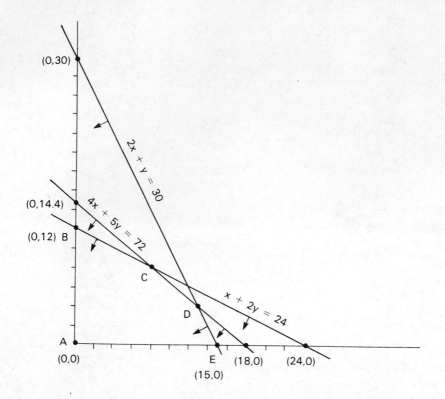

Problem Set 3-2

1. $x \geq 0$

   $y \geq 0$

   $2x + y \geq 8$

   $6x + 10y \leq 60$

$2x + y = 8$

x	y
0	8
4	0

$6x + 10y = 60$

x	y
0	6
10	0

corner	coordinates
A	(4, 0)
B	(10/7, 36/7)
C	(10, 0)

a) $\theta = 3x + 2y$, $\theta_{min} = 12$ at $x = 4$, $y = 0$

b) $\theta = 10x + y$, $\theta_{min} = 136/7 = 19.4$ at $x = 10/7$, $y = 36/7$

5. $x \geq 0$

$y \geq 0$

$2x + 4y \geq 36$

$x + y \leq 12$

$x - 2y \leq 0$

$2x + 4y = 36$

x	y
0	9
18	0

$x + y = 12$

x	y
12	0
0	12

$x - 2y = 0$

x	y
0	0
4	2

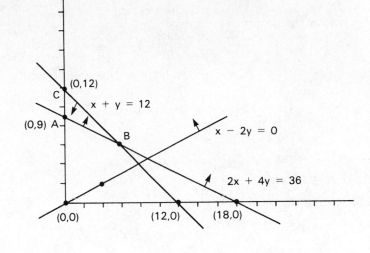

corner	coordinates
A	(0, 9)
B	(6, 6)
C	(0, 12)

a) $\theta = 3x + 5y$, $\theta_{max} = 60$ at (0, 12), $\theta_{min} = 45$ at (0, 9)

b) $\theta = 6x + 2y$, $\theta_{max} = 48$ at (6, 6), $\theta_{min} = 18$ at (0, 9)

c) $\theta = 3x + 3y$, $\theta_{max} = 36$ on line segment joining (6, 6) and (0, 12), $\theta_{min} = 27$ at (0, 9)

9. $x \geq 0$

$y \geq 0$

$x + 3y \leq 24$

$x + y \geq 10$

$2x + y = 18$

$5x + y = 20$

$x + 3y = 24$

x	y
0	8
24	0

$x + y = 10$

x	y
0	10
10	0

$2x + y = 18$

x	y
0	18
9	0

$5x + y = 20$

x	y
0	20
4	0

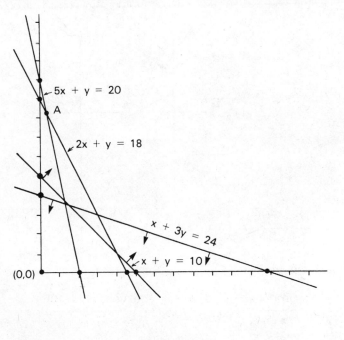

Empty feasible solution set.

Point A, at (2/3, 16 2/3) is the only point that satisfies both $2x + y = 18$ and $5x + y = 20$, however, this point does not satisfy $x + 3y \leq 24$. Thus, this problem has no maximum or minimum.

31

11.

MILL	days	tons of AAA	tons of AA	tons of A
I	x	1,000	3,000	5,000
F	y	2,000	2,000	2,000

constraints:

$x \geq 0$

$y \geq 0$

$x \leq 10$

$y \leq 10$

$1,000x + 2,000y \geq 24,000$

$3,000x + 2,000y \geq 32,000$

$5,000x + 2,000y \geq 40,000$

$1,000x + 2,000y = 24,000$

x	y
0	12
24	0

$3,000x + 2,000y = 32,000$

x	y
0	16
10 2/3	0

$5,000x + 2,000y = 40,000$

x	y
0	20
8	0

corners	coordinates
A	(4, 10)
B	(10, 10)
C	(10, 7)

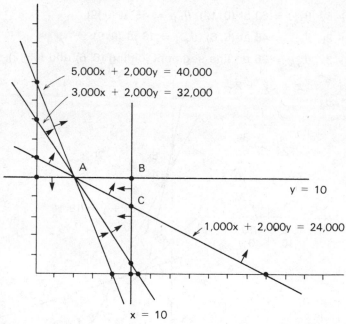

5,000x + 2,000y = 40,000

3,000x + 2,000y = 32,000

y = 10

1,000x + 2,000y = 24,000

x = 10

a) $\theta = 1,400x + 1,000y$, $\theta_{min} = 15,600$ at (4, 10)

	produced	desired	excess at (4, 10)
AAA	24,000	24,000	none
AA	32,000	32,000	none
A	40,000	40,000	none

b) $\theta = 1,500x + 3,000y$, $\theta_{min} = 36,000$ on line segment joining (4, 10) and at (10, 7)

There is no excess steel at (4, 10) but at all other points we have excess production; for example, at (10, 7)

	produced	desired	excess at (10, 7)
AAA	24,000	24,000	none
AA	44,000	32,000	12,000 tons
A	64,000	40,000	24,000 tons

32

14.

	number of quarts	price per quart	ounces of T per quart
SODA A	x	$0.20	1
SODA B	y	$0.30	3

constraints:

$x \geq 0$

$y \geq 0$

$y - x \leq 0$

$x + y = 4$

$1x + 3y \geq 6$

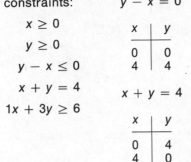

$y - x = 0$

x	y
0	0
4	4

$x + y = 4$

x	y
0	4
4	0

$x + 3y = 6$

x	y
0	2
6	0

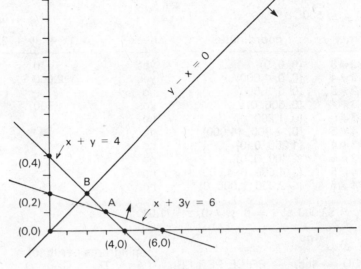

corners	coordinates
A	(3, 1)
B	(2, 2)

$\theta = 0.20x + 0.30y$, $\theta_{min} = \$0.90$ at (3, 1)

Problem Set 3-3

1. constraints:

(1) $x \geq 0$

(2) $y \geq 0$

(3) $z \geq 0$

(4) $x + 4y + 3z \leq 1,800$

(5) $2x + 3y + z \leq 2,000$

corner	coordinates	check	maximize $\theta = .5x + y + .2z$
1#2#3	(0, 0, 0)	yes	0
1#2#4	(0, 0, 600)	yes	120
1#2#5	(0, 0, 2000)	no	
1#3#4	(0, 450, 0)	yes	450
1#3#5	(0, 2000/3, 0)	no	
1#4#5	(0, 840, −520)	no	
2#3#4	(1800, 0, 0)	no	
2#3#5	(1000, 0, 0)	yes	500
2#4#5	(840, 0, 320)	yes	484
3#4#5	(520, 320, 0)	yes	580

$\theta_{max} = 580$ at $x = 520$, $y = 320$, $z = 0$

5.

MERCHANDISE	units of each	price per unit	profit per unit	required storage (ft)
A	x	$4	$1	4
B	y	$10	$3	8
C	z	$5	$2	6

33

constraints:

(1) $x \geq 0$

(2) $y \geq 0$

(3) $z \geq 0$

(4) $4x + 10y + 5z \leq 5000$

(5) $4x + 8y + 6z \leq 9600$

  $x \leq 500$

corner	coordinates	check	$\theta = 1x + 3y + 2z$
1#2#3	(0, 0, 0)	yes	0
1#2#4	(0, 0, 1,000)	yes	2,000
1#2#5	(0, 0, 1,600)	no	
1#3#4	(0, 500, 0)	yes	1,500
1#3#5	(0, 1,200, 0)	no	
1#4#5	(0, −900, 14,000)	no	
2#3#4	(1,250, 0, 0)	no	
2#3#5	(2,400, 0, 0)	no	
2#4#5	(−4,500, 0, 4,600)	no	
3#4#5	(−2,300, 7,000, 0)	no	

$\theta_{max} = \$2,000$ at $x = 0$, $y = 0$, $z = 1,000$

9.

FOOD	no. of lbs.	PRICE PER LB.	miligrams per lb. of			
			A	B	C	D
X	x	$1.50	2	4	1	6
Y	y	$2.50	9	3	4	2
Z	z	$2.00	7	2	8	1

constraints:

(1) $x \geq 0$

(2) $y \geq 0$

(3) $z \geq 0$

(4) $2x + 9y + 7z \geq 66$

(5) $4x + 3y + 2z \geq 48$

(6) $x + 4y + 8z \geq 40$

(7) $6x + 2y + z \geq 58$

The objective function is $\theta = 1.5x + 2.5y + 2.0z$, which should be maximized.

The solution space for this 7-by-3 system contains 35 possible corners which will result in a maximum of $26 @ (8, 4, 2)

Problem Set 3-4

1.

	no. of minutes	viewers per minute
Program (I.M.H.)	x	15,000
Commercial	y	−150

constraints:

(1) $x \geq 0$

(2) $y \geq 0$

(3) $y - 0.25x \leq 0$

(4) $y - 0.2x \geq 0$ or $-y + 0.2x \leq 0$

(5) $x + y = 90$

corner	coordinates	check	$\theta = 15{,}000x - 150y$
1#2	(0, 0)	yes	0
1#3	(0, 0)	yes	0
1#4	(0, 0)	yes	0
1#5	(0, 90)	no	
2#3	(0, 0)	yes	0
2#4	(0, 0)	yes	0
2#5	(90, 0)	no	
3#4	(0, 0)	yes	0
3#5	(72, 18)	yes	$1{,}080{,}000 - 2{,}700 = 1{,}077{,}300$
4#5	(75, 15)	yes	$1{,}125{,}000 - 2{,}250 = 1{,}122{,}750$

The optimum stategy is to allot 75 minutes to Hilarious and 15 minutes to commercials. This will reach the maximum number of viewers which is 1,122,750.

5.

CATEGORY	no. of QUESTIONS	points per QUESTION	no. at QUESTS ANSWERED
T/F	50	1	x
M/C	50	2	y
S/E	10	4	z

constraints:

(1) $x \geq 0$

(2) $-x + y \geq 1$ (thus $y \geq 0$)

(3) $z \geq 5$ (thus $z \geq 0$)

(4) $x + y + z \geq 40$

(5) $x + y + z \leq 60$

(6) $z \leq 10$

(7) $y \leq 50$

(8) $-x + y - 2z \geq 10$

The objective function is $\theta = 2x + y + 4z$

The solution space for this 8-by-3 system contains 56 possible corners.

11.

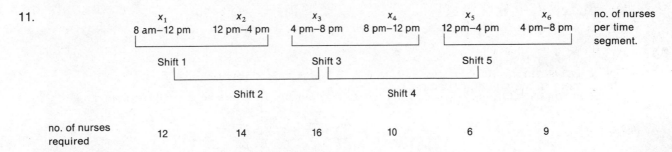

	x_1 8 am–12 pm	x_2 12 pm–4 pm	x_3 4 pm–8 pm	x_4 8 pm–12 pm	x_5 12 pm–4 pm	x_6 4 pm–8 pm	no. of nurses per time segment.
no. of nurses required	12	14	16	10	6	9	

constraints:

$x_1 + x_6 \geq 12$

$x_1 + x_2 \geq 14$

$x_2 + x_3 \geq 16$

$x_3 + x_4 \geq 10$

$x_4 + x_5 \geq 6$

$x_5 + x_6 \geq 9$

all $x_i \geq 0$

The objective function to be minimized is $x_1 + x_2 + x_3 + x_4 + x_5 + x_6$

1.   Given $x + 2y \leq 40$ and $3x + y \leq 45$ find the corners of the solution space.

x-intercept:

$0 + 2y \leq 40$

$y \leq 20$

y-intercept:

$x + 2(0) \leq 40$

$x \leq 40$

x-intercept:

$0 + y \leq 45$

$y \leq 45$

y-intercept:

$3x + 0 \leq 45$

$x \leq 15$

point of intersection:

$\left. \begin{array}{l} x + 2y \leq 40 \\ 3x + y \leq 45 \end{array} \right\}$

$\begin{array}{rl} 3x + 6y &\leq 120 \\ -3x + y &\leq 45 \\ \hline 5y &\leq 75 \\ y &\leq 15 \end{array}$

Solving for x:

$$x + 2(15) \leq 40$$
$$x \leq 10$$

Since we are looking for a maximum, our solution space is bound by: (0, 20), (10, 15), and (15, 0).

a) $\theta = 2x + 3y$

   $\theta_{max} = 65$

   @ $x = 10$, $y = 15$

   $\theta_{(0, 20)} = 2(0) + 3(20) = 60$

   $\theta_{(10, 15)} = 2(10) + 3(15) = 65$

   $\theta_{(15, 0)} = 2(15) + 3(0) = 30$

b) $\theta = 6x + 2y$

   $\theta_{max} = 90$ on line segment joining

   @ $x = 10$, $y = 15$

   $\theta_{(0, 20)} = 6(0) + 2(20) = 40$

   $\theta_{(10, 15)} = 6(10) + 2(15) = 90$

   $\theta_{(15, 0)} = 6(15) + 2(0) = 90$

and

@ $x = 15$, $y = 0$

3.   The corners of the solution space are (3, 4), (5, 1), and (1, 2). With $\theta = 2x + y$, we have

$$\theta_{(3, 4)} = 2(3) + 4 = 10$$
$$\theta_{(5, 1)} = 2(5) + 1 = 11$$
$$\theta_{(1, 2)} = 2(1) + 2 = 4$$

thus $\theta_{max} = 11$ at $x = 5$, $y = 1$

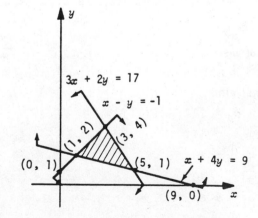

5.   The corners of the solution space are (2, 5), (4, 3) and (8, 0). With $\theta = 3x + 2y$ we have $\theta_{min} = 16$ at $x = 2$, $y = 5$.

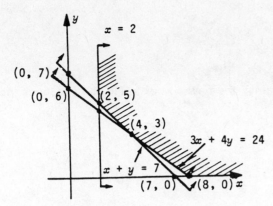

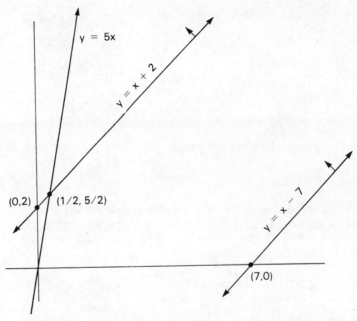

7. $\theta_{\min} = 3(1/2) + 4(5/2) = \frac{23}{2} = 11.5$
   at $x = \frac{1}{2}$, $y = \frac{5}{2}$

9.

	Price	Nutrient I	Nutrient II
Food A	$1 per lb.	2 ounces	4 ounces
Food B	$2 per lb.	3 ounces	1 ounce

minimize $\theta = 1x + 2y$ where x = pounds of Food A

y = pounds of Food B

constraints:

$2x + 3y \geq 90$

$4x + y \geq 80$

$\theta_{\min} = \$45$ at 45 lbs of A and
0 lbs of B

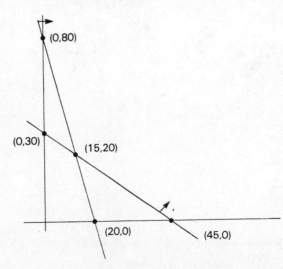

11. Adding the constraint $y \geq .8(x + y)$.

$$5y \geq 4x + 4y$$

$$y \geq 4x$$

When $y \geq 4x$ is graphed along with the previous constraints, the new corner at (10, 40) produces the minimum value for the objective function, $\theta_{min} = \$90$.

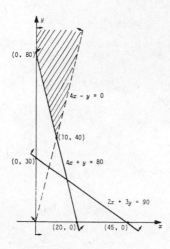

13. Adding the constraint $x \geq y$, creates a new corner (not shown on the graph) at (1,200/7, 1,200/7) where $x \geq y$ and $3x + 4y = 1,200$ intersect. However, at this corner, the value of the objective function is 2,400/7 which is less than \$350. Thus $\theta_{max} = 350$ remains.

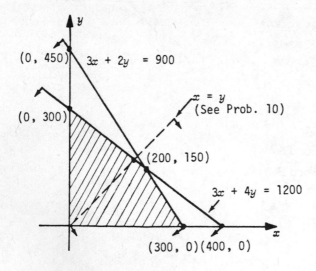

15. The five constraints of the problem are:

(1) $x \geq 0$

(2) $y \geq 0$

(3) $z \geq 0$

(4) $4x + 8y + z \leq 52$

(5) $8x + 28y + 3z \leq 168$

The 10 corners possible in this 5-by-3 system are listed in the following table, along with values of the objective function at permissible corners.

corner	coordinates	check	$\theta = 3x + 9y + z$
1#2#3	(0, 0, 0)	yes	0
1#2#4	(0, 0, 52)	yes	52
1#2#5	(0, 0, 56)	no	
1#3#4	(0, 52/8, 0)	no	
1#3#5	(0, 6, 0)	yes	54
1#4#5	(0, 3, 28)	yes	55
2#3#4	(13, 0, 0)	yes	39
2#3#5	(21, 0, 0)	no	
2#4#5	(−3, 0, 64)	no	
3#4#5	(7/3, 16/3, 0)	yes	55

$\theta_{max} = 55$ on line segment joining $x = 0$, $y = 3$, $z = 28$ and $x = 7/3$, $y = 16/3$, $z = 0$

17. The six constraints of this problem are

(1) $x \geq 0$

(2) $y \geq 0$

(3) $z \geq 0$

(4) $x + 2y + 7z \leq 21$

(5) $5x + 17y + 28z \leq 140$

(6) $x + 9y + 10z \leq 66$

The 20 corners in this 6-by-3 system are listed in the following table, along with values of the objective function at permissible corners.

corner	coordinates	check	$\theta = x + 3y + 7z$
1#2#3	(0, 0, 0)	yes	0
1#2#4	(0, 0, 3)	yes	21
1#2#5	(0, 0, 5)	no	
1#2#6	(0, 0, 33/5)	no	
1#3#4	(0, 21/2, 0)	no	
1#3#5	(0, 140/17, 0)	no	
1#3#6	(0, 22/3, 0)	yes	22
1#4#5	(0, 56/9, 11/9)	no	
1#4#6	(0, 252/43, 57/43)	yes	1,155/43
1#5#6	(0, 224/41, 69/41)	no	
2#3#4	(21, 0, 0)	yes	21
2#3#5	(28, 0, 0)	no	
2#3#6	(66, 0, 0)	no	
2#4#5	(56, 0, −5)	no	
2#4#6	(−84, 0, 15)	no	
2#5#6	(−224/11, 0, 95/11)	no	
3#4#5	(11, 5, 0)	yes	26
3#4#6	(57/7, 45/7, 0)	no	
3#5#6	(69/14, 95/14, 0)	yes	354/14
4#5#6	(2, 6, 1)	yes	27

$\theta_{max} = 27$ at $x = 2$, $y = 6$, $z = 1$

19. The five constraints in this problem are

(1) $x \geq 0$

(2) $y \geq 0$

(3) $z \geq 0$

(4) $x + 2y + 3z \leq 25$

(5) $x + 3y + 2z \leq 30$

The ten possible corners in this 5-by-3 system are listed in the following table, along with the values of the objective function at permissible corners.

corner	coordinates	check	$\theta = x + 3y + 2z$
1#2#3	(0, 0, 0)	yes	0
1#2#4	(0, 0, 25/3)	yes	50/3
1#2#5	(0, 0, 15)	no	
1#3#4	(0, 25/2, 0)	no	
1#3#5	(0, 10, 0)	yes	30
1#4#5	(0, 8, 3)	yes	30
2#3#4	(25, 0, 0)	yes	25
2#3#5	(30, 0, 0)	no	
2#4#5	(40, 0, −5)	no	
3#4#5	(15, 5, 0)	yes	30

$\theta_{max} = 30$ at triangle joining $x = 0$, $y = 10$, $z = 0$ and $x = 0$, $y = 8$, $z = 3$, and $x = 15$, $y = 5$, $z = 0$.

21. The seven constraints in this problem are:

(1) $x \geq 0$

(2) $y \geq 0$

(3) $z \geq 0$

(4) $x + 2y + 3z \leq 50$

(5) $x + 3y + 2z \leq 60$

(6) $2x + 3y + 5z \leq 110$

(7) $4x + 8y + 10z \leq 220$

There are 35 possible corners in this 7-by-3 system. There are three solutions to $\theta_{max} = 20x + 60y + 40z$. $\theta_{max} = 1200$ at

  $x = 0$, $y = 20$, $z = 0$

         and

  $x = 30$, $y = 10$, $z = 0$

         and

  $x = 0$, $y = 16$, $z = 6$

23.

mill	cost/day	number of days	tons/day of $AAAA$	tons/day of AAA	tons/day of AA	tons/day of A
I	1,400	x	4,000	1,000	3,000	10,000
F	1,000	y	3,000	2,000	2,000	4,000
S	1,200	z	2,000	4,000	1,000	3,000

$$\theta = 1,400x + 1,000y + 1,200z$$

The seven constraints for this problem are:

(1) $x \geq 0$

(2) $y \geq 0$

(3) $z \geq 0$

(4) $4,000x + 3,000y + 2,000z \geq 35,000$

(5) $1,000x + 2,000y + 4,000z \geq 29,000$

(6) $3,000x + 2,000y + 1,000z \geq 23,000$

(7) $10,000x + 4,000y + 3,000z \geq 62,000$

The 35 possible corners in this 7-by-3 system are listed in the following table, along with the values of the objective function at permissible corners.

25. x_1 = the number of Executive desks produced at PLANT 1
x_2 = the number of Executive desks produced at PLANT 2
y_1 = the number of Sec./Sten. desks produced at PLANT 1
y_2 = the number of Sec./Sten. desks produced at PLANT 2

PLANT	TOTAL PRODUCTION TIME
1	80 hrs.
2	50 hrs.

Revenues $= 350(x_1 + x_2) + 275(y_1 + y_2)$

Profit = Revenues − Costs

$$\theta = (350 - 250)x_1 + (350 - 260)x_2 + (275 - 200)y_1 + (275 - 180)y_2$$

$$\theta = 100x_1 + 90x_2 + 75y_1 + 95y_2$$

Maximize θ under the following eight constraints:

(1) $x_1 \geq 0$

(2) $x_2 \geq 0$

(3) $y_1 \geq 0$

(4) $y_2 \geq 0$

(5) $250x_1 + 260x_2 \leq 2,000$

(6) $200y_1 + 180y_2 \leq 2,200$

(7) $7.0x_1 + 4.0y_1 \leq 80$

(8) $6.0x_2 + 5.0y_2 \leq 50$

This 8-by-4 system has 70 possible corners.

CHAPTER 4

Problem Set 4-1

1. $(2 \quad 3 \quad 4) + (1 \quad -2 \quad 3) = (3 \quad 1 \quad 7)$

7. $(2 \quad 7)\begin{pmatrix} 3 \\ 5 \end{pmatrix} = 41$

11. $4\begin{pmatrix} 1 & -3 & 2 \\ 5 & 1 & -3 \end{pmatrix} - 3\begin{pmatrix} 2 & 5 & -3 \\ 1 & 2 & -1 \end{pmatrix} = \begin{pmatrix} 4 & -12 & 8 \\ 20 & 4 & -12 \end{pmatrix} - \begin{pmatrix} 6 & 15 & -9 \\ 3 & 6 & -3 \end{pmatrix} = \begin{pmatrix} -2 & -27 & 17 \\ 17 & -2 & -9 \end{pmatrix}$

15. $\begin{pmatrix} 2 & 1 & 1 & 0 \\ 1 & 3 & 0 & 2 \\ -1 & -2 & 1 & 4 \end{pmatrix}\begin{pmatrix} 5 & 6 \\ 1 & 1 \\ 2 & 3 \\ 0 & -1 \end{pmatrix} = \begin{pmatrix} 13 & 16 \\ 8 & 7 \\ -5 & -9 \end{pmatrix}$

$e_{11} = 2(5) + 1(1) + 1(2) + 0(0) = 10 + 1 + 2 + 0 = 13$

$e_{12} = 2(6) + 1(1) + 1(3) + 0(-1) = 12 + 1 + 3 + 0 = 16$

$e_{21} = 1(5) + 3(1) + 0(2) + 2(0) = 5 + 3 + 0 + 0 = 8$

$e_{22} = 1(6) + 3(1) + 0(3) + 2(-1) = 6 + 3 + 0 - 2 = 7$

$e_{31} = (-1)(5) + (-2)(1) + 1(2) + 4(0) = (-5) - 2 + 2 + 0 = -5$

$e_{32} = (-1)(6) + (-2)(1) + 1(3) + 4(-1) = (-6) - 2 + 3 - 4 = -9$

20. $(10 \quad 20) \cdot \begin{pmatrix} 8 & 2 & 5 \\ 4 & 8 & 3 \end{pmatrix} = (160 \quad 180 \quad 110)$

To make 10 batches of Superior and 20 batches of Regular 160 pounds of beef, 180 pounds of pork, and 110 pounds of lamb will be required.

Problem Set 4-2

1. $\begin{pmatrix} 2 & 3 \\ 1 & 2 \end{pmatrix}\begin{pmatrix} x_1 \\ x_2 \end{pmatrix} = \begin{pmatrix} 5 \\ 3 \end{pmatrix}$

4. $3x_1 + x_2 + 2x_3 = 5$

$x_1 + 4x_2 + x_3 = 4$

8. $2x_1 + x_2 + 5x_3 + y_1 = 10$

$4x_1 + 6x_2 + 2x_3 + y_2 = 5$

Problem Set 4-3

1. a) The number 0.6 means that 60 percent of those buying Technics products buy Technics products next time and the number 0.4 means that 40 percent of those buying Technics products buy Soneton products next time. Similarly, 50 percent of those who buy Soneton products will buy Soneton products again next time and 50 percent will change and buy Technics products.

   b) The beginning state matrix is given to be (0.5 0.5).

$$(0.5 \quad 0.5)\begin{pmatrix} 0.6 & 0.4 \\ 0.5 & 0.5 \end{pmatrix} = (0.55 \quad 0.45) \qquad \text{after week \#1}$$

$$(0.55 \quad 0.45)\begin{pmatrix} 0.6 & 0.4 \\ 0.5 & 0.5 \end{pmatrix} = (0.555 \quad 0.445) \qquad \text{after week \#2}$$

   c) $(v_1 \quad v_2)\begin{pmatrix} 0.6 & 0.4 \\ 0.5 & 0.5 \end{pmatrix} = (v_1 \quad v_2)$

e_1: $0.6v_1 + 0.5v_2 = v_1$ or $-0.4v_1 + 0.5v_2 = 0$

e_2: $0.4v_1 + 0.5v_2 = v_2$ or $0.4v_1 - 0.5v_2 = 0$

e_3: $v_1 + v_2 = 1$

Using e_1 and e_3 we get
the equation e_4: $0.9v_2 = 0.4$

$$-0.4v_1 + 0.5v_2 = 0$$
$$\underline{0.4v_1 + 0.4v_2 = 0.4}$$
$$.9v_2 = 0.4$$

Thus $v_2 = 0.\overline{4}$ and $v_1 = 0.555556$. The steady state market shares are $44 4/9\%$ for Soneton and $55 5/9\%$ for Technics.

4. a) The state matrix is given to be

	owners	non-owners
	(0.2	0.8)

The transition matrix is:

	own	not own
owners	0.9999	0.0001
non owners	0.01	0.99

$$(0.2 \quad 0.8)\begin{pmatrix} 0.9999 & 0.0001 \\ 0.01 & 0.99 \end{pmatrix} = (0.20798 \quad 0.79202)$$

Thus next year, 20.8% of the population will own micro computers and 79.2% will not.

7. (0.6   0.3   0.1)

(0.3   0.1   0.6)

(0.1   0.6   0.3)

(0.6   0.3   0.1)

Problem Set 4-4

1. $\begin{pmatrix} 7 & 3 & | & 1 & 0 \\ 2 & 1 & | & 0 & 1 \end{pmatrix}$

Add -3 times row 2 to row 1.

$\begin{pmatrix} 1 & 0 & | & 1 & -3 \\ 2 & 1 & | & 0 & 1 \end{pmatrix}$

Then, add -2 times row 1 to row 2.

$\begin{pmatrix} 1 & 0 & | & 1 & -3 \\ 0 & 1 & | & -2 & 7 \end{pmatrix}$

Thus the inverse is:

$$\begin{pmatrix} 1 & -3 \\ -2 & 7 \end{pmatrix}$$

11. $\begin{pmatrix} 1 & 2 & 1 \\ 4 & 5 & -3 \\ 3 & 4 & -2 \end{pmatrix}$

17. a) Since we know that $AI = IA$, one matrix that commutes multiplicatively with A is the identity matrix of order 3.

$$\begin{pmatrix} 1 & 0 & 0 \\ 0 & 1 & 0 \\ 0 & 0 & 1 \end{pmatrix}$$

b) A matrix which does not commute multiplicatively with A is the matrix $\begin{pmatrix} 1 & 1 & 1 \\ 1 & 1 & 1 \\ 1 & 1 & 1 \end{pmatrix}$

Problem Set 4-5

1. a) A is the coefficient matrix $\begin{pmatrix} 8 & 5 \\ 3 & 2 \end{pmatrix}$

x is the solution vector $\begin{pmatrix} x_1 \\ x_2 \end{pmatrix}$

b is the vector of constants $\begin{pmatrix} 2 \\ 1 \end{pmatrix}$

b) $\left(\begin{array}{cc|c} 8 & 5 & 2 \\ 3 & 2 & 1 \end{array} \right)$

Multiply row 2 by 1/3 then interchange it with row 1.

$\left(\begin{array}{cc|c} 1 & \frac{2}{3} & \frac{1}{3} \\ 8 & 5 & 2 \end{array} \right)$

Add -8 times row 1 to row 2.

$\left(\begin{array}{cc|c} 1 & \frac{2}{3} & \frac{1}{3} \\ 0 & -\frac{1}{3} & -\frac{2}{3} \end{array} \right)$

Add 2 times row 2 to row 1.

$\left(\begin{array}{cc|c} 1 & 0 & -1 \\ 0 & -\frac{1}{3} & -\frac{2}{3} \end{array} \right)$

Multiply row 2 by -3.

$\left(\begin{array}{cc|c} 1 & 0 & -1 \\ 0 & 1 & 2 \end{array} \right)$

Thus $x_1 = -1, x_2 = 2$.

c) $\begin{pmatrix} 8 & 5 & | & 1 & 0 \\ 3 & 2 & | & 0 & 1 \end{pmatrix}$

Multiply row 2 by 1/3 then interchange it with row 1.

$\begin{pmatrix} 1 & \dfrac{2}{3} & | & 0 & \dfrac{1}{3} \\ 8 & 5 & | & 1 & 0 \end{pmatrix}$

Add -8 times row 1 to row 2.

$\begin{pmatrix} 1 & \dfrac{2}{3} & | & 0 & \dfrac{1}{3} \\ 0 & -\dfrac{1}{3} & | & 1 & -\dfrac{8}{3} \end{pmatrix}$

Add 2 times row 2 to row 1.

$\begin{pmatrix} 1 & 0 & | & 2 & -5 \\ 0 & -\dfrac{1}{3} & | & 1 & -\dfrac{8}{3} \end{pmatrix}$

Multiply row 2 by -3.

$\begin{pmatrix} 1 & 0 & | & 2 & -5 \\ 0 & 1 & | & -3 & 8 \end{pmatrix}$

Thus $A^{-1} = \begin{pmatrix} 2 & -5 \\ -3 & 8 \end{pmatrix}$

d) $\begin{pmatrix} x_1 \\ x_2 \end{pmatrix} = \begin{pmatrix} 2 & -5 \\ -3 & 8 \end{pmatrix} \cdot \begin{pmatrix} 2 \\ 1 \end{pmatrix}$

e) $x_1 = (2) \cdot (2) + (-5)(1) = 4 - 5 = -1$
$x_2 = (-3)(2) + (8)(1) = -6 + 8 = 2$

f) 1. $x_1 = (2)(1) + (-5)(0) = 2$
$x_2 = (-3)(1) + (8)(0) = -3$

2. $x_1 = (2)(0) + (-5)(1) = 0 - 5 = -5$
$x_2 = (-3)(0) + (8)(1) = 0 + 8 = 8$

3. $x_1 = (2)(1) + (-5)(1) = 2 - 5 = -3$
$x_2 = (-3)(1) + (8)(1) = -3 + 8 = -5$

4. $x_1 = (2)(3) + (-5)(4) = 6 - 20 = -14$
$x_2 = (-3)(3) + (8)(4) = -9 + 32 = 23$

5. $x_1 = (2)(-3) + (-5)(1) = -6 + -5 = -11$
$x_2 = (-3)(-3) + (8)(1) = 9 + 8 = 17$

4. $\begin{pmatrix} x_1 \\ x_2 \end{pmatrix} = \begin{pmatrix} 1 & \dfrac{7}{5} \\ 1 & \dfrac{8}{5} \end{pmatrix} \begin{pmatrix} b_1 \\ b_2 \end{pmatrix}$

8. a) Show that the following equation is true.

$$\begin{pmatrix} -\dfrac{2}{3} & \dfrac{4}{3} & -\dfrac{1}{3} \\[6pt] \dfrac{1}{3} & \dfrac{1}{3} & -\dfrac{1}{3} \\[6pt] 1 & -2 & 1 \end{pmatrix} \cdot \begin{pmatrix} 1 & 2 & 1 \\ 2 & 1 & 1 \\ 3 & 0 & 2 \end{pmatrix} = \begin{pmatrix} 1 & 0 & 0 \\ 0 & 1 & 0 \\ 0 & 0 & 1 \end{pmatrix}$$

$\left(-\dfrac{2}{3}\right)(1) + \left(\dfrac{4}{3}\right)(2) + \left(-\dfrac{1}{3}\right)(3) = -\dfrac{2}{3} + \dfrac{8}{3} - \dfrac{3}{3} = 1$ ✓

$\left(-\dfrac{2}{3}\right)(2) + \left(\dfrac{4}{3}\right)(1) + \left(-\dfrac{1}{3}\right)(0) = -\dfrac{4}{3} + \dfrac{4}{3} + 0 = 0$ ✓

$\left(-\dfrac{2}{3}\right)(1) + \left(\dfrac{4}{3}\right)(1) + \left(-\dfrac{1}{3}\right)(2) = -\dfrac{2}{3} + \dfrac{4}{3} - \dfrac{2}{3} = 0$ ✓

$\left(\dfrac{1}{3}\right)(1) + \left(\dfrac{1}{3}\right)(2) + \left(-\dfrac{1}{3}\right)(3) = \dfrac{1}{3} + \dfrac{2}{3} - \dfrac{3}{3} = 0$ ✓

$\left(\dfrac{1}{3}\right)(2) + \left(\dfrac{1}{3}\right)(1) + \left(-\dfrac{1}{3}\right)(0) = \dfrac{2}{3} + \dfrac{1}{3} + 0 = 1$ ✓

$\left(\dfrac{1}{3}\right)(1) + \left(\dfrac{1}{3}\right)(1) + \left(-\dfrac{1}{3}\right)(2) = \dfrac{1}{3} + \dfrac{1}{3} - \dfrac{2}{3} = 0$ ✓

$(1)(1) + (-2)(2) + (1)(3) = 1 - 4 + 3 = 0$ ✓
$(1)(2) + (-2)(1) + (1)(0) = 2 - 2 + 0 = 0$ ✓
$(1)(1) + (-2)(1) + (1)(2) = 1 - 2 + 2 = 1$ ✓

b) 1. $x_1 = \left(-\dfrac{2}{3}\right)(3) + \left(\dfrac{4}{3}\right)(0) + \left(-\dfrac{1}{3}\right)(3) = -\dfrac{6}{3} + 0 - \dfrac{3}{3} = -\dfrac{9}{3} = -3$

$x_2 = \left(\dfrac{1}{3}\right)(3) + \left(\dfrac{1}{3}\right)(0) + \left(-\dfrac{1}{3}\right)(3) = \dfrac{3}{3} + 0 - \dfrac{3}{3} = 0$

$x_3 = (1)(3) + (-2)(0) + (1)(3) = 3 - 0 + 3 = 6$

2. $x_1 = \left(-\dfrac{2}{3}\right)(6) + \left(\dfrac{4}{3}\right)(3) + \left(-\dfrac{1}{3}\right)(0) = -\dfrac{12}{3} + \dfrac{12}{3} - 0 = 0$

$x_2 = \left(\dfrac{1}{3}\right)(6) + \left(\dfrac{1}{3}\right)(3) + \left(-\dfrac{1}{3}\right)(0) = \dfrac{6}{3} + \dfrac{3}{3} - 0 = \dfrac{9}{3} = 3$

$x_3 = (1)(6) + (-2)(3) + (1)(0) = 6 - 6 + 0 = 0$

11. $\begin{pmatrix} 2 & -3 & | & 5 \\ 6 & -9 & | & 8 \end{pmatrix}$

Add -3 times row 1 to row 2.

$\begin{pmatrix} 2 & -3 & | & 5 \\ 0 & 0 & | & -7 \end{pmatrix}$

Multiply row 1 by 1/2.

$\begin{pmatrix} 1 & -\dfrac{3}{2} & | & \dfrac{5}{2} \\[6pt] 0 & 0 & | & -7 \end{pmatrix}$

Because the matrix has a row that contains all zeros except in the constant column, this system has no solutions.

17.
$$\begin{pmatrix} 2 & 3 & \bigm| & 15 \\ \dfrac{8}{3} & 4 & \bigm| & 20 \end{pmatrix}$$

Multiply row 2 by 3.

$$\begin{pmatrix} 2 & 3 & \bigm| & 15 \\ 8 & 12 & \bigm| & 60 \end{pmatrix}$$

Add -4 times row 1 to row 2.

$$\begin{pmatrix} 2 & 3 & \bigm| & 15 \\ 0 & 0 & \bigm| & 0 \end{pmatrix}$$

Multiply row 1 by 1/2.

$$\begin{pmatrix} 1 & \dfrac{3}{2} & \bigm| & \dfrac{15}{2} \\ 0 & 0 & \bigm| & 0 \end{pmatrix}$$

Because this matrix has a row that contains all zeros, this system has infinitely many solutions.

Problem Set 4-6

1.
$$\begin{pmatrix} 2 & -3 & \bigm| & 6 \\ 1 & 5 & \bigm| & 29 \\ 3 & -4 & \bigm| & 11 \end{pmatrix}$$

Interchange row 1 and row 2.

$$\begin{pmatrix} 1 & 5 & \bigm| & 29 \\ 2 & -3 & \bigm| & 6 \\ 3 & -4 & \bigm| & 11 \end{pmatrix}$$

Add $-2 \times$ row 1 to row 2 and -3 times row 1 to row 3.

$$\begin{pmatrix} 1 & 5 & \bigm| & 29 \\ 0 & -13 & \bigm| & -52 \\ 0 & -19 & \bigm| & -76 \end{pmatrix}$$

Multiply row 2 by $-1/13$.

$$\begin{pmatrix} 1 & 5 & \bigm| & 29 \\ 0 & 1 & \bigm| & 4 \\ 0 & -19 & \bigm| & -76 \end{pmatrix}$$

Add -5 times row 2 to row 1 and $19 \times$ row 2 to row 3.

$$\begin{pmatrix} 1 & 0 & \bigm| & 9 \\ 0 & 1 & \bigm| & 4 \\ 0 & 0 & \bigm| & 0 \end{pmatrix}$$

$x_1 = 9$ and $x_2 = 4$

7.
$$\begin{pmatrix} 3 & 4 & -6 & \bigm| & 10 \\ 12 & 16 & -24 & \bigm| & 7 \\ 1 & 2 & 3 & \bigm| & 8 \\ 5 & 3 & 2 & \bigm| & 12 \end{pmatrix}$$

47

Interchange rows.

$$\begin{pmatrix} 1 & 2 & 3 & 8 \\ 3 & 4 & -6 & 10 \\ 5 & 3 & 2 & 12 \\ 12 & 16 & -24 & 7 \end{pmatrix}$$

Add multiples of row 1 to rows 2, 3, and 4.

$$\begin{pmatrix} 1 & 2 & 3 & 8 \\ 0 & -2 & -15 & -22 \\ 0 & -7 & -13 & -28 \\ 0 & -8 & -60 & -89 \end{pmatrix}$$

Add multiples of row 2 to the other rows.

$$\begin{pmatrix} 1 & 0 & -12 & -14 \\ 0 & -2 & -15 & -22 \\ 0 & 1 & 47 & 60 \\ 0 & 0 & 0 & -1 \end{pmatrix}$$

At this point we can say that this system will have no solutions because at least one row contains all zeros except in the constants column.

11.
$$\begin{pmatrix} -3 & 1 & -2 & 9 \\ -5 & \dfrac{5}{3} & -\dfrac{10}{3} & 15 \\ -2 & \dfrac{2}{3} & -\dfrac{4}{3} & 18 \\ -7 & \dfrac{7}{3} & -\dfrac{14}{3} & 21 \\ 4 & -\dfrac{4}{3} & \dfrac{8}{3} & -12 \end{pmatrix}$$

Add 1 × row 5 to row 1.

$$\begin{pmatrix} 1 & -\dfrac{1}{3} & \dfrac{2}{3} & -3 \\ -5 & \dfrac{5}{3} & -\dfrac{10}{3} & 15 \\ -2 & \dfrac{2}{3} & -\dfrac{4}{3} & 18 \\ -7 & \dfrac{7}{3} & -\dfrac{14}{3} & 21 \\ 4 & -\dfrac{4}{3} & \dfrac{8}{3} & -12 \end{pmatrix}$$

Add multiples of row 1 to rows 2, 3, 4, and 5.

$$\begin{pmatrix} 1 & -\dfrac{1}{3} & \dfrac{2}{3} & -3 \\ 0 & 0 & 0 & 0 \\ 0 & 0 & 0 & 12 \\ 0 & 0 & 0 & 0 \\ 0 & 0 & 0 & 0 \end{pmatrix}$$

At this point we can conclude that this system has no solution because in row 3 we have all zeros except in the constants column.

17.

candy	number of dozens	gallons of milk per dozen	pounds of butter per dozen	pints of cream per dozen
Luscious	x_1	1	2	1
Delicious	x_2	3	1	1

The system to be solved is described by the following matrix.

$$\begin{pmatrix} 1 & 3 & | & 24 \\ 2 & 1 & | & 13 \\ 1 & 1 & | & 10 \end{pmatrix}$$

Add multiples of row 1 to row 2 and row 3.

$$\begin{pmatrix} 1 & 3 & | & 24 \\ 0 & -5 & | & -35 \\ 0 & -2 & | & -14 \end{pmatrix}$$

Multiply row 2 by $-1/5$ and row 3 by $-1/2$.

$$\begin{pmatrix} 1 & 3 & | & 24 \\ 0 & 1 & | & 7 \\ 0 & 1 & | & 7 \end{pmatrix}$$

Add multiples of row 2 to rows 1 and 3.

$$\begin{pmatrix} 1 & 0 & | & 3 \\ 0 & 1 & | & 7 \\ 0 & 0 & | & 0 \end{pmatrix}$$

Thus the solution is to make 3 dozen Luscious candies and make 7 dozen Delicious candies.

Problem Set 4-7

1. $\displaystyle\sum_{p=4}^{7} p = 4 + 5 + 6 + 7 = 22$

5. $\displaystyle\sum_{p=1}^{3} p^3 = 1^3 + 2^3 + 3^3 = 1 + 8 + 27 = 36$

7. $\displaystyle\sum_{i=1}^{10} i^2$

9. $\displaystyle\sum_{i=1}^{4} (i + 2)$

Problem Set 4-8

1. $\displaystyle\sum_{j=1}^{5} y_j = y_1 + y_2 + y_3 + y_4 + y_5$

5. $\displaystyle\sum_{j=1}^{n} a_j x_j = a_1 x_1 + a_2 + x_2 + \cdots + a_n x_n = c$

9. $\displaystyle\sum_{i=1}^{q} a_i x_i$

Problem Set 4-9

1. $a_{11}x_1 + a_{12}x_2 + a_{13}x_3 + a_{14}x_4 = b_1$

   $a_{21}x_1 + a_{22}x_2 + a_{23}x_3 + a_{24}x_4 = b_2$

5. $\sum\limits_{j=1}^{8} a_{ij}x_j = b_i \qquad i = 1, 2, \ldots, 6$

7. a) $d_1x_1 + d_2x_2 + d_3x_3 + d_4x_4 + d_5x_5 + d_6x_6 + d_7x_7 + d_8x_8 + d_9x_9 + d_{10}x_{10}$

   b) $\sum\limits_{i=1}^{10} d_ix_i$

Problem Set 4-10

3. $\sum\limits_{i=1}^{5} (x_i - a) = \sum\limits_{i=1}^{5} x_i - 5a = x_1 + x_2 + x_3 + x_4 + x_5 - 5a$

9. $\sum\limits_{i=1}^{10} x_i^2 - \dfrac{1}{10}\left(\sum\limits_{i=1}^{10} x_i\right)^2 = 385 - (1/10)(15)^2 = 385 - 22.5 = 362.5$

x_i	x_i^2
2	4
11	121
−4	16
5	25
8	64
3	9
−5	25
−2	4
6	36
−9	81
15	385

1. $(1 \quad 46) + (3 \quad -1 \quad 0) - 5(3 \quad 5 \quad -4) = (-11 \quad -22 \quad 26)$

3. a) $\begin{pmatrix} p_1 \\ p_2 \end{pmatrix} x + \begin{pmatrix} q_1 \\ q_2 \end{pmatrix} y = \begin{pmatrix} 0 \\ 0 \end{pmatrix}$

   b) $p_1 x + q_1 y = 0$

   $p_2 x + q_2 y = 0$

5. a) $\begin{pmatrix} x_1 \\ x_2 \\ x_3 \\ x_4 \end{pmatrix} \geq \begin{pmatrix} 0 \\ 0 \\ 0 \\ 0 \end{pmatrix}$

   b) $x_1 \geq 0$

   $x_2 \geq 0$

   $x_3 \geq 0$

   $x_4 \geq 0$

7. $\begin{pmatrix} 3 & -2 \\ 1 & 7 \end{pmatrix} - \begin{pmatrix} -3 & 4 \\ 6 & 0 \end{pmatrix} - \begin{pmatrix} 3 & 6 \\ 3 & 9 \end{pmatrix} + \begin{pmatrix} 5 & -5 \\ -10 & 10 \end{pmatrix} = \begin{pmatrix} 8 & -17 \\ -18 & 8 \end{pmatrix}$

9. $(1)(2) + (3)(-1) + (2)(3) = 2 - 3 + 6 = 5$ $\qquad \begin{pmatrix} 5 & 7 & 14 \\ 7 & 5 & 13 \\ 5 & 0 & 10 \end{pmatrix}$

   $(1)(3) + (3)(2) + (2)(-1) = 3 + 6 - 2 = 7$

   $(1)(4) + (3)(0) + (2)(5) = 4 + 0 + 10 = 14$

   $(2)(2) + (0)(-1) + (1)(3) = 4 - 0 + 3 = 7$

   $(2)(3) + (0)(2) + (1)(-1) = 6 + 0 - 1 = 5$

   $(2)(4) + (0)(0) + (1)(5) = 8 + 0 + 5 = 13$

   $(0)(2) + (1)(-1) + (2)(3) = 0 - 1 + 6 = 5$

   $(0)(3) + (1)(2) + (2)(-1) = 0 + 2 - 2 = 0$

   $(0)(4) + (1)(0) + (2)(5) = 0 + 0 + 10 = 10$

11. $(4)(0) + (1)(1) + (-1)(-1) = 0 + 1 + 1 = 2$ $\qquad \begin{pmatrix} 2 & 3 & -5 \\ -3 & 2 & 1 \\ -6 & 2 & 4 \end{pmatrix}$

    $(4)(1) + (1)(-1) + (-1)(0) = 4 - 1 - 0 = 3$

    $(4)(-1) + (1)(0) + (-1)(1) = -4 + 0 - 1 = -5$

    $(2)(0) + (0)(1) + (3)(-1) = 0 + 0 - 3 = -3$

    $(2)(1) + (0)(-1) + (3)(0) = 2 - 0 + 0 = 2$

    $(2)(-1) + (0)(0) + (3)(1) = -2 + 0 + 3 = 1$

    $(0)(0) + (-2)(1) + (4)(-1) = 0 - 2 - 4 = -6$

    $(0)(1) + (-2)(-1) + (4)(0) = 0 + 2 + 0 = 2$

    $(0)(-1) + (-2)(0) + (4)(1) = 0 - 0 + 4 = 4$

13. $\begin{pmatrix} 1 & 2 & 0 & 1 \\ 0 & 3 & -1 & 2 \\ 5 & -1 & 1 & -1 \end{pmatrix} \begin{pmatrix} x_1 \\ x_2 \\ x_3 \\ x_4 \end{pmatrix} = \begin{pmatrix} 12 \\ 6 \\ 7 \end{pmatrix}$

15. $\begin{pmatrix} 1 & 2 \\ 1 & 3 \end{pmatrix} \begin{pmatrix} x_1 \\ x_2 \end{pmatrix} + \begin{pmatrix} 1 \\ 1 \end{pmatrix} \begin{pmatrix} s_1 \\ s_2 \end{pmatrix} = \begin{pmatrix} 10 \\ 15 \end{pmatrix}$

17. $3x_1 + \quad + x_3 \le 14$

$\quad\quad 2x_2 + 4x_3 \le 10$

$2x_1 + 3x_2 \quad\quad \le 12$

19. Transition matrix $T = \begin{pmatrix} 0.8 & 0.2 \\ 0.4 & 0.6 \end{pmatrix}$

a) $(0.35 \quad 0.65) \cdot T = (0.54 \quad 0.46)$

Thus, 54% urban and 46% rural after one year.

b) $(0.54 \quad 0.46) \cdot T = (0.616 \quad 0.384)$

Thus 61.6% urban and 38.4% rural after two years.

c) $(0.616 \quad 0.384) \cdot T = (0.6464 \quad 0.3536)$

Thus 64.64% urban and 35.36% rural after three years.

d) $(v_1 \quad v_2)\begin{pmatrix} 0.8 & 0.2 \\ 0.4 & 0.6 \end{pmatrix} = (v_1 \quad v_2)$

e_1: $\quad 0.8v_1 + 0.4v_2 = v_1 \quad$ or $\quad -0.2v_1 + 0.4v_2 = 0$

e_2: $\quad 0.2v_1 + 0.6v_2 = v_2$

e_3: $\quad v_1 + v_2 = 1$

Using e_1 and e_3 we get $\quad\quad -0.2v_1 + 0.4v_2 = 0$

e_4: $\quad 0.6v_2 = 0.2 \quad\quad\quad \dfrac{+0.2v_1 + 0.2v_2 = 0.2}{0.6v_2 = 0.2}$

Thus $v_2 = 1/3$ and $v_1 = 2/3$

which means 66 2/3% urban and 33 1/3% rural.

21. $\begin{pmatrix} 0 & 1 & | & 1 & 0 \\ 1 & 0 & | & 0 & 1 \end{pmatrix}$ Add II to I to obtain a proper form. Rewrite.

$\begin{pmatrix} 1 & 1 & | & 1 & 1 \\ 1 & 0 & | & 0 & 1 \end{pmatrix}$ Multiply I by -1 and add to II. Rewrite.

$\begin{pmatrix} 1 & 1 & | & 1 & 1 \\ 0 & -1 & | & -1 & 0 \end{pmatrix}$ Divide II by -1 and rewrite.

$\begin{pmatrix} 1 & 1 & | & 1 & 1 \\ 0 & 1 & | & 1 & 0 \end{pmatrix}$ Multiply II by -1 and add to I. Rewrite.

$\begin{pmatrix} 1 & 0 & | & 0 & 1 \\ 0 & 1 & | & 1 & 0 \end{pmatrix}$ The desired inverse is $\begin{pmatrix} 0 & 1 \\ 1 & 0 \end{pmatrix}$.

23. $\begin{pmatrix} 1 & 2 & | & 1 & 0 \\ 3 & 3 & | & 0 & 1 \end{pmatrix}$ Multiply I by -3 and add to II. Rewrite.

$\begin{pmatrix} 1 & 2 & | & 1 & 0 \\ 0 & -3 & | & -3 & 1 \end{pmatrix}$ Divide II by -3 and rewrite.

$\begin{pmatrix} 1 & 2 & | & 1 & 0 \\ 0 & 1 & | & 1 & \frac{-1}{3} \end{pmatrix}$ Multiply II by -2 and add to I. Rewrite.

$$\begin{pmatrix} 1 & 0 & \bigm| & -1 & \frac{2}{3} \\[2mm] 0 & 1 & \bigm| & 1 & \frac{-1}{3} \end{pmatrix}$$

The desired inverse is $\begin{pmatrix} -1 & \frac{2}{3} \\[2mm] 1 & \frac{-1}{3} \end{pmatrix}$.

25. $\begin{array}{l} \text{I} \\ \text{II} \end{array} \begin{pmatrix} 5 & 3 & \bigm| & 1 & 0 \\ 2 & 2 & \bigm| & 0 & 1 \end{pmatrix}$ Divide I by 5 and rewrite.

$$\begin{pmatrix} 1 & \frac{3}{5} & \bigm| & \frac{1}{5} & 0 \\[2mm] 2 & 2 & \bigm| & 0 & 1 \end{pmatrix}$$ Multiply I by -2 and add to II. Rewrite.

$$\begin{pmatrix} 1 & \frac{3}{5} & \bigm| & \frac{1}{5} & 0 \\[2mm] 0 & \frac{4}{5} & \bigm| & \frac{-2}{5} & 1 \end{pmatrix}$$ Divide II by 4/5 and rewrite.

$$\begin{pmatrix} 1 & \frac{3}{5} & \bigm| & \frac{1}{5} & 0 \\[2mm] 0 & 1 & \bigm| & \frac{-1}{2} & \frac{5}{4} \end{pmatrix}$$ Multiply II by $-3/5$ and add to 1. Rewrite.

$$\begin{pmatrix} 1 & 0 & \bigm| & \frac{1}{2} & \frac{-3}{4} \\[2mm] 0 & 1 & \bigm| & \frac{-1}{2} & \frac{5}{4} \end{pmatrix}$$ The desired inverse is $\begin{pmatrix} \frac{1}{2} & \frac{-3}{4} \\[2mm] \frac{-1}{2} & \frac{5}{4} \end{pmatrix}$.

27. $\begin{array}{l} \text{I} \\ \text{II} \\ \text{III} \end{array} \begin{pmatrix} 1 & 0 & 1 & \bigm| & 1 & 0 & 0 \\ 0 & 1 & 2 & \bigm| & 0 & 1 & 0 \\ 2 & 3 & 0 & \bigm| & 0 & 0 & 1 \end{pmatrix}$ Multiply I by -2 and add to III. Rewrite.

$$\begin{pmatrix} 1 & 0 & 1 & \bigm| & 1 & 0 & 0 \\ 0 & 1 & 2 & \bigm| & 0 & 1 & 0 \\ 0 & 3 & -2 & \bigm| & -2 & 0 & 1 \end{pmatrix}$$ Multiply II by -3 and add to III. Rewrite.

$$\begin{pmatrix} 1 & 0 & 1 & \bigm| & 1 & 0 & 0 \\ 0 & 1 & 2 & \bigm| & 0 & 1 & 0 \\ 0 & 0 & -8 & \bigm| & -2 & -3 & 1 \end{pmatrix}$$ Divide III by -8 and rewrite.

$$\begin{pmatrix} 1 & 0 & 1 & \bigm| & 1 & 0 & 0 \\ 0 & 1 & 2 & \bigm| & 0 & 1 & 0 \\ 0 & 0 & 1 & \bigm| & \frac{1}{4} & \frac{3}{8} & \frac{-1}{8} \end{pmatrix}$$ Multiply III by -2 and add to II. Multiply III by -1 and add to I. Rewrite.

$$\begin{pmatrix} 1 & 0 & 1 & \bigm| & \frac{-1}{4} & \frac{-3}{8} & \frac{1}{8} \\[2mm] 0 & 1 & 0 & \bigm| & \frac{-1}{2} & \frac{1}{4} & \frac{1}{4} \\[2mm] 0 & 0 & 1 & \bigm| & \frac{1}{4} & \frac{3}{8} & \frac{-1}{8} \end{pmatrix}$$ The desired matrix is the one at the right of the last pair.

29. $\begin{array}{l} \text{I} \\ \text{II} \\ \text{III} \end{array} \begin{pmatrix} 1 & 0 & 2 & \bigm| & 1 & 0 & 0 \\ 0 & 1 & 3 & \bigm| & 0 & 1 & 0 \\ 1 & 2 & 0 & \bigm| & 0 & 0 & 1 \end{pmatrix}$ Multiply I by -1 and add to III. Rewrite.

$$\begin{pmatrix} 1 & 0 & 2 & | & 1 & 0 & 0 \\ 0 & 1 & 3 & | & 0 & 1 & 0 \\ 0 & 2 & -2 & | & -1 & 0 & 1 \end{pmatrix}$$

Multiply II by −2 and add to III. Rewrite.

$$\begin{pmatrix} 1 & 0 & 2 & | & 1 & 0 & 0 \\ 0 & 1 & 3 & | & 0 & 1 & 0 \\ 0 & 0 & -8 & | & -1 & -2 & 1 \end{pmatrix}$$

Divide III by −8 and rewrite.

$$\begin{pmatrix} 1 & 0 & 2 & | & 1 & 0 & 0 \\ 0 & 1 & 3 & | & 0 & 1 & 0 \\ 0 & 0 & 1 & | & \frac{1}{8} & \frac{1}{4} & \frac{-1}{8} \end{pmatrix}$$

Multiply III by −2 and add to I. Multiply III by −3 and add to II. Rewrite.

$$\begin{pmatrix} 1 & 0 & 0 & | & \frac{3}{4} & \frac{-1}{2} & \frac{1}{4} \\ 0 & 1 & 0 & | & \frac{-3}{8} & \frac{1}{4} & \frac{3}{8} \\ 0 & 0 & 1 & | & \frac{1}{8} & \frac{1}{4} & \frac{-1}{8} \end{pmatrix}$$

The desired matrix is the one at the right in the last pair.

31.
$$\begin{matrix} \text{I} \\ \text{II} \\ \text{III} \end{matrix}\begin{pmatrix} 60 & 30 & 20 & | & 1 & 0 & 0 \\ 30 & 20 & 15 & | & 0 & 1 & 0 \\ 20 & 15 & 12 & | & 0 & 0 & 1 \end{pmatrix}$$

Divide I by 60 and rewrite.

$$\begin{pmatrix} 1 & \frac{1}{2} & \frac{1}{3} & | & \frac{1}{60} & 0 & 0 \\ 30 & 20 & 15 & | & 0 & 1 & 0 \\ 20 & 15 & 12 & | & 0 & 0 & 1 \end{pmatrix}$$

Multiply I by −30 and add to II. Multiply I by −20 and add to III. Rewrite.

$$\begin{pmatrix} 1 & \frac{1}{2} & \frac{1}{3} & | & \frac{1}{60} & 0 & 0 \\ 0 & 5 & 5 & | & \frac{-1}{2} & 1 & 0 \\ 0 & 5 & \frac{16}{3} & | & \frac{-1}{3} & 0 & 1 \end{pmatrix}$$

Divide II by 5 and rewrite.

$$\begin{pmatrix} 1 & \frac{1}{2} & \frac{1}{3} & | & \frac{1}{60} & 0 & 0 \\ 0 & 1 & 1 & | & \frac{-1}{10} & \frac{1}{5} & 0 \\ 0 & 5 & \frac{16}{3} & | & \frac{-1}{3} & 0 & 1 \end{pmatrix}$$

Multiply II by −1/2 and add to I. Multiply II by −5 and add to III. Rewrite.

$$\begin{pmatrix} 1 & 0 & \frac{-1}{6} & | & \frac{1}{15} & \frac{-1}{10} & 0 \\ 0 & 1 & 1 & | & \frac{-1}{10} & \frac{1}{5} & 0 \\ 0 & 0 & \frac{1}{3} & | & \frac{1}{6} & -1 & 1 \end{pmatrix}$$

Divide III by 1/3 and rewrite.

$$\begin{pmatrix} 1 & 0 & \frac{-1}{6} & | & \frac{1}{15} & \frac{-1}{10} & 0 \\ 0 & 1 & 1 & | & \frac{-1}{10} & \frac{1}{5} & 0 \\ 0 & 0 & 1 & | & \frac{1}{2} & -3 & 3 \end{pmatrix}$$

Multiply III by 1/6 and add to I. Multiply III by −1 and add to II. Rewrite.

$$\begin{pmatrix} 1 & 0 & 0 & \bigg| & \dfrac{3}{20} & \dfrac{-3}{5} & \dfrac{1}{2} \\[2mm] 0 & 1 & 0 & \bigg| & \dfrac{-3}{5} & \dfrac{16}{5} & -3 \\[2mm] 0 & 0 & 1 & \bigg| & \dfrac{1}{2} & -3 & 3 \end{pmatrix}$$

The desired matrix is the one at the right in the last pair.

33.

$$\begin{matrix} \text{I} \\ \text{II} \\ \text{III} \end{matrix} \begin{pmatrix} 1 & 2 & 1 & \bigg| & 1 & 0 & 0 \\ 2 & 1 & 1 & \bigg| & 0 & 1 & 0 \\ 1 & 2 & 2 & \bigg| & 0 & 0 & 1 \end{pmatrix}$$

Multiply I by −2 and add to II. Multiply I by −1 and add to III. Rewrite

$$\begin{pmatrix} 1 & 2 & 1 & \bigg| & 1 & 0 & 0 \\ 0 & -3 & -1 & \bigg| & -2 & 1 & 0 \\ 0 & 0 & 1 & \bigg| & -1 & 0 & 1 \end{pmatrix}$$

Divide II by −3 and rewrite.

$$\begin{pmatrix} 1 & 2 & 1 & \bigg| & 1 & 0 & 0 \\[2mm] 0 & 1 & \dfrac{1}{3} & \bigg| & \dfrac{2}{3} & \dfrac{-1}{3} & 0 \\[2mm] 0 & 0 & 1 & \bigg| & -1 & 0 & 1 \end{pmatrix}$$

Multiply II by −2 and add to I. Rewrite.

$$\begin{pmatrix} 1 & 0 & \dfrac{1}{3} & \bigg| & \dfrac{-1}{3} & \dfrac{2}{3} & 0 \\[2mm] 0 & 1 & \dfrac{1}{3} & \bigg| & \dfrac{2}{3} & \dfrac{-1}{3} & 0 \\[2mm] 0 & 0 & 1 & \bigg| & -1 & 0 & 1 \end{pmatrix}$$

Multiply III by −1/3 and add to I. Multiply III by −1/3 and add to II. Rewrite.

$$\begin{pmatrix} 1 & 0 & 0 & \bigg| & 0 & \dfrac{2}{3} & \dfrac{-1}{3} \\[2mm] 0 & 1 & 0 & \bigg| & 1 & \dfrac{-1}{3} & \dfrac{-1}{3} \\[2mm] 0 & 0 & 1 & \bigg| & -1 & 0 & 1 \end{pmatrix}$$

The desired matrix is the one at the right in the last pair.

35.

$$\begin{matrix} \text{I} \\ \text{II} \\ \text{III} \end{matrix} \begin{pmatrix} 2 & 0 & 1 & \bigg| & 1 & 0 & 0 \\ 3 & 1 & 3 & \bigg| & 0 & 1 & 0 \\ 0 & 1 & 4 & \bigg| & 0 & 0 & 1 \end{pmatrix}$$

Divide I by 2 and rewrite.

$$\begin{pmatrix} 1 & 0 & \dfrac{1}{2} & \bigg| & \dfrac{1}{2} & 0 & 0 \\[2mm] 3 & 1 & 3 & \bigg| & 0 & 1 & 0 \\[2mm] 0 & 1 & 4 & \bigg| & 0 & 0 & 1 \end{pmatrix}$$

Multiply I by −3 and add to II.

$$\begin{pmatrix} 1 & 0 & \dfrac{1}{2} & \bigg| & \dfrac{1}{2} & 0 & 0 \\[2mm] 0 & 1 & \dfrac{3}{2} & \bigg| & \dfrac{-3}{2} & 1 & 0 \\[2mm] 0 & 1 & 4 & \bigg| & 0 & 0 & 1 \end{pmatrix}$$

Multiply II by −1 and add to II. Rewrite.

$$\begin{pmatrix} 1 & 0 & \dfrac{1}{2} & \bigg| & \dfrac{1}{2} & 0 & 0 \\[2mm] 0 & 1 & \dfrac{3}{2} & \bigg| & \dfrac{-3}{2} & 1 & 0 \\[2mm] 0 & 0 & \dfrac{5}{2} & \bigg| & \dfrac{3}{2} & -1 & 1 \end{pmatrix}$$

Divide III by 5/2 and rewrite.

$$\begin{pmatrix} 1 & 0 & \frac{1}{2} & \bigg| & \frac{1}{2} & 0 & 0 \\ 0 & 1 & \frac{3}{2} & \bigg| & \frac{-3}{2} & 1 & 0 \\ 0 & 0 & 1 & \bigg| & \frac{3}{5} & \frac{-2}{5} & \frac{2}{5} \end{pmatrix}$$

Multiply III by $-1/2$ and add to I. Multiply III by $-3/2$ and add to II. Rewrite.

$$\begin{pmatrix} 1 & 0 & 0 & \bigg| & \frac{1}{5} & \frac{1}{5} & \frac{-1}{5} \\ 0 & 1 & 0 & \bigg| & \frac{-12}{5} & \frac{8}{5} & \frac{-3}{5} \\ 0 & 0 & 1 & \bigg| & \frac{3}{5} & \frac{-2}{5} & \frac{2}{5} \end{pmatrix}.$$

The matrix at the right in the last pair is the desired inverse. This matrix may be written with 1/5 factored out, as follows:

$$\frac{1}{5} \begin{pmatrix} 1 & 1 & -1 \\ -12 & 8 & -3 \\ 3 & -2 & 2 \end{pmatrix}.$$

37. a) $\mathbf{A} = \begin{pmatrix} 2 & 4 \\ 5 & 6 \end{pmatrix}$; $\mathbf{x} = \begin{pmatrix} x_1 \\ x_2 \end{pmatrix}$; $\mathbf{b} = \begin{pmatrix} 4 \\ 8 \end{pmatrix}$.

b) To find the inverse of **A**:

$$\begin{matrix} \text{I} \\ \text{II} \end{matrix} \begin{pmatrix} 2 & 4 & \bigg| & 1 & 0 \\ 5 & 6 & \bigg| & 0 & 1 \end{pmatrix}$$

Divide I by 2 and rewrite.

$$\begin{pmatrix} 1 & 2 & \bigg| & \frac{1}{2} & 0 \\ 5 & 6 & \bigg| & 0 & 1 \end{pmatrix}$$

Multiply I by -5 and add to II. Rewrite.

$$\begin{pmatrix} 1 & 2 & \bigg| & \frac{1}{2} & 0 \\ 0 & -4 & \bigg| & \frac{-5}{2} & 1 \end{pmatrix}$$

Divide II by -4 and rewrite.

$$\begin{pmatrix} 1 & 2 & \bigg| & \frac{1}{2} & 0 \\ 0 & 1 & \bigg| & \frac{5}{8} & \frac{-1}{4} \end{pmatrix}$$

Multiply II by -2 and add to I.

$$\begin{pmatrix} 1 & 0 & \bigg| & \frac{-3}{4} & \frac{1}{2} \\ 0 & 1 & \bigg| & \frac{5}{8} & \frac{-1}{4} \end{pmatrix}. \qquad \mathbf{A}^{-1} = \begin{pmatrix} \frac{-3}{4} & \frac{1}{2} \\ \frac{5}{8} & \frac{-1}{4} \end{pmatrix}.$$

c)
$$\begin{pmatrix} x_1 \\ x_2 \end{pmatrix} = \begin{pmatrix} \frac{-3}{4} & \frac{1}{2} \\ \frac{5}{8} & \frac{-1}{4} \end{pmatrix} \begin{pmatrix} 4 \\ 8 \end{pmatrix}.$$

d) $(1, 1/2)$.

e) (1) $(3, -1/2)$.

   (2) $(-1, 7/2)$.

   (3) $(5, 5/2)$.

   (4) $(2, -1)$.

39. **a)**
$$\mathbf{A} = \begin{pmatrix} 2 & 3 & -15 \\ -5 & -7 & 35 \\ 3 & 4 & -21 \end{pmatrix}; \qquad \mathbf{x} = \begin{pmatrix} x_1 \\ x_2 \\ x_3 \end{pmatrix}; \qquad \mathbf{b} = \begin{pmatrix} 3 \\ 2 \\ 1 \end{pmatrix}.$$

b) To find the inverse of the matrix **A**:

I, II, III
$$\begin{array}{c} \text{I} \\ \text{II} \\ \text{III} \end{array} \left(\begin{array}{ccc|ccc} 2 & 3 & -15 & 1 & 0 & 0 \\ -5 & -7 & 35 & 0 & 1 & 0 \\ 3 & 4 & -21 & 0 & 0 & 1 \end{array} \right)$$

Divide I by 2 and rewrite.

$$\left(\begin{array}{ccc|ccc} 1 & \dfrac{3}{2} & \dfrac{-15}{2} & \dfrac{1}{2} & 0 & 0 \\ -5 & -7 & 35 & 0 & 1 & 0 \\ 3 & 4 & -21 & 0 & 0 & 1 \end{array} \right)$$

Multiply I by 5 and add to II. Multiply I by -3 and add to III. Rewrite.

$$\left(\begin{array}{ccc|ccc} 1 & \dfrac{3}{2} & \dfrac{-15}{2} & \dfrac{1}{2} & 0 & 0 \\ 0 & \dfrac{1}{2} & \dfrac{-5}{2} & \dfrac{5}{2} & 1 & 0 \\ 0 & \dfrac{-1}{2} & \dfrac{3}{2} & \dfrac{-3}{2} & 0 & 1 \end{array} \right)$$

Divide II by 1/2 and rewrite.

$$\left(\begin{array}{ccc|ccc} 1 & \dfrac{3}{2} & \dfrac{-15}{2} & \dfrac{1}{2} & 0 & 0 \\ 0 & 1 & -5 & 5 & 2 & 0 \\ 0 & \dfrac{-1}{2} & \dfrac{3}{2} & \dfrac{-3}{2} & 0 & 1 \end{array} \right)$$

Multiply II by $-3/2$ and add to I. Multiply II by 1/2 and add to III.

$$\left(\begin{array}{ccc|ccc} 1 & 0 & 0 & -7 & -3 & 0 \\ 0 & 1 & -5 & 5 & 2 & 0 \\ 0 & 0 & -1 & 1 & 1 & 1 \end{array} \right)$$

Divide III by -1 and rewrite.

$$\left(\begin{array}{ccc|ccc} 1 & 0 & 0 & -7 & -3 & 0 \\ 0 & 1 & -5 & 5 & 2 & 0 \\ 0 & 0 & 1 & -1 & -1 & -1 \end{array} \right)$$

Multiply III by 5 and add to II. Rewrite.

$$\left(\begin{array}{ccc|ccc} 1 & 0 & 0 & -7 & -3 & 0 \\ 0 & 1 & 0 & 0 & -3 & -5 \\ 0 & 0 & 1 & -1 & -1 & -1 \end{array} \right). \qquad \mathbf{A}^{-1} = \begin{pmatrix} -7 & -3 & 0 \\ 0 & -3 & -5 \\ -1 & -1 & -1 \end{pmatrix}.$$

c)
$$\begin{pmatrix} x_1 \\ x_2 \\ x_3 \end{pmatrix} = \begin{pmatrix} -7 & -3 & 0 \\ 0 & -3 & -5 \\ -1 & -1 & -1 \end{pmatrix} \begin{pmatrix} 3 \\ 2 \\ 1 \end{pmatrix}.$$

d) $(-27, -11, -6)$.

e) (1) $(-10, -8, -3)$.

(2) $(-3, -8, -2)$.

(3) $(-10, -3, -2)$.

41. This missing elements are the inverse of the matrix

$$\begin{pmatrix} 3 & 2 \\ 4 & 3 \end{pmatrix}.$$

To find the inverse:

$$\begin{matrix} \text{I} \\ \text{II} \end{matrix} \begin{pmatrix} 3 & 2 & | & 1 & 0 \\ 4 & 3 & | & 0 & 1 \end{pmatrix}$$

Divide I by 3 and rewrite.

$$\begin{pmatrix} 1 & \dfrac{2}{3} & | & \dfrac{1}{3} & 0 \\ 4 & 3 & | & 0 & 1 \end{pmatrix}$$

Multiply I by -4 and add to II. Rewrite.

$$\begin{pmatrix} 1 & \dfrac{2}{3} & | & \dfrac{1}{3} & 0 \\ 0 & \dfrac{1}{3} & | & \dfrac{-4}{3} & 1 \end{pmatrix}$$

Divide II by 1/3 and rewrite.

$$\begin{pmatrix} 1 & \dfrac{2}{3} & | & \dfrac{1}{3} & 0 \\ 0 & 1 & | & -4 & 3 \end{pmatrix}$$

Multiply II by $-2/3$ and add to I. Rewrite.

$$\begin{pmatrix} 1 & 0 & | & 3 & -2 \\ 0 & 1 & | & -4 & 3 \end{pmatrix}.$$

The desired elements are $\begin{pmatrix} 3 & -2 \\ -4 & 3 \end{pmatrix}.$

43. a) Proceeding to find the inverse of the matrix of coefficients, we find:

$$\begin{matrix} \text{I} \\ \text{II} \\ \text{III} \end{matrix} \begin{pmatrix} 1 & 1 & 1 & | & 1 & 0 & 0 \\ 2 & 3 & 2 & | & 0 & 1 & 0 \\ 1 & 2 & 1 & | & 0 & 0 & 1 \end{pmatrix}$$

Multiply I by -2 and add to II. Multiply I by -1 and add to III. Rewrite.

$$\begin{pmatrix} 1 & 1 & 1 & | & 1 & 0 & 0 \\ 0 & 1 & 0 & | & -2 & 1 & 0 \\ 0 & 1 & 0 & | & -1 & 0 & 1 \end{pmatrix}$$

Multiply II by -1 and add to I. Multiply II by -1 and add to III. Rewrite.

$$\begin{pmatrix} 1 & 0 & 1 & | & 3 & -1 & 0 \\ 0 & 1 & 0 & | & -2 & 1 & 0 \\ 0 & 0 & 0 & | & 1 & -1 & 1 \end{pmatrix}.$$

The row of zeros in the left matrix of the last pair shows that the given matrix does not have an inverse.

b) e_1: $x_1 + x_2 + x_3 = 3$

e_2: $2x_1 + 3x_2 + 2x_3 = 5$

e_3: $x_1 + 2x_2 + x_3 = 2$

e_4: $x_2 = -1$ $-2e_1 + e_2$

e_5: $-x_2 = 1$ $-2e_3 + e_2$.

It follows that x_2 must be equal to -1. Substituting this value into e_1, we find

$$x_1 - 1 + x_3 = 3$$
$$x_1 = 4 - x_3.$$

Substituting $x_2 = -1$, $x_1 = 4 - x_3$ into e_2 and e_3 shows both are satisfied. Hence, the general solution (unlimited number of points) can be written

$$x_3 \text{ arbitrary}$$
$$x_1 = 4 - x_3$$
$$x_2 = -1.$$

c) (1) Changing the constant does not affect the matrix of coefficients.

(2) The derived equations e_4 and e_5 now read

$$e_4: \quad x_2 = 1$$
$$e_5: \quad -x_2 = 1.$$

The contradictory statements mean the system now has no solutions.

(3) If the coefficient matrix has no inverse, the system has either an unlimited number of solutions, or it has no solutions.

45. $2(1^2 + 2^2 + 3^2 + 4^2 + 5^2) = 2(1 + 4 + 9 + 16 + 25) = 2(55) = 110.$

47. $\displaystyle\sum_{i=1}^{100} i.$

49. $\displaystyle\sum_{i=1}^{50} (2i).$

51. $c_{10}y_{10} + c_{11}y_{11} + c_{12}y_{12} + c_{13}y_{13} + c_{14}y_{14} + c_{15}y_{15}.$

53. $a_m x_m + a_{m+1} x_{m+1} + \cdots + a_{m+n} x_{m+n}.$

55. $2x_1 + 2x_2 + 2x_3 = 7$; or $2(x_1 + x_2 + x_3) = 7.$

57. $\displaystyle\sum_{i=1}^{3} a_i x_i.$

59. $\displaystyle\sum_{i=1}^{n} a_i x_i.$

61. $m = 6$; $c = 12$; $b_1 = 5$, $b_2 = 3$; $b_3 = -1$; $b_4 = b_5 = 0$; $b_6 = 4.$

63. Maximize $c_1 x_1 + c_2 x_2$ subject to:

$$a_{11}x_1 + a_{12}x_2 \leq b_1$$
$$a_{21}x_1 + a_{22}x_2 \leq b_2$$
$$x_1 \geq 0$$
$$x_2 \geq 0.$$

65. Minimize $c_1 x_1 + c_2 x_2 + \cdots + c_{25}x_{25}$, subject to

a)
$$a_{11}x_1 + a_{12}x_2 + \cdots + a_{1,25}x_{25} \geq b_1$$
$$a_{21}x_1 + a_{22}x_2 + \cdots + a_{2,25}x_{25} \geq b_2$$
$$\vdots$$
$$a_{15,1}x_1 + a_{15,2}x_2 + \cdots + a_{15,25}x_{25} \geq b_{15}$$
$$x_1 \geq 0$$
$$x_2 \geq 0$$
$$\vdots$$
$$x_{25} \geq 0.$$

b) Minimize $\displaystyle\sum_{j=1}^{25} c_j x_j$ subject to

$$\sum_{j=1}^{25} a_{ij}x_j \geq b_i; \quad i = 1, 2, 3, \cdots, 15$$

and $x_j \geq 0$ for all j.

1. max $\theta = 3x_1 + x_2$

s.t. $4x_1 + 3x_2 \leq 24$

$x_1 + 2x_2 \leq 11$

$x_1, x_2 \geq 0$

$4x_1 + 3x_2 + s_1 + 0s_2 = 24$

$x_1 + 2x_2 + 0s_1 + s_2 = 11$

$\theta - 3x_1 - x_2 + 0s_1 + 0s_2 = 0$

preliminary
tableau:

Basic	θ	x_1	x_2	s_1	s_2	c.v.	
s_1	0	4	3	1	0	24	→
s_2	0	1	2	0	1	11	
(max) θ	1	−3	−1	0	0	0	

second
tableau:

Basic	θ	x_1	x_2	s_1	s_2	c.v.
x_1	0	1	3/4	1/4	0	6
s_2	0	0	5/4	−1/4	1	5
(max) θ	1	0	5/4	3/4	0	18

$x_1 = 6 - \frac{3}{4}x_2 - \frac{1}{4}s_1$

$s_2 = 5 - \frac{5}{4}x_2 + \frac{1}{4}s_1$

4. max $\theta = 4x_1 - x_2$

s.t. $x_1 + x_2 \leq 13$

$x_1 + 2x_2 \leq 22$

$2x_1 + x_2 \leq 20$

$x_1 \leq 4$

$x_1, x_2 \geq 0$

$x_1 + x_2 + s_1 + 0s_2 + 0s_3 + 0s_4 = 13$

$x_1 + 2x_2 + 0s_1 + s_2 + 0s_3 + 0s_4 = 22$

$2x_1 + x_2 + 0s_1 + 0s_2 + s_3 + 0s_4 = 20$

$x_1 + 0x_2 + 0s_1 + 0s_2 + 0s_3 + s_4 = 4$

$\theta - 4x_1 + x_2 + 0s_1 + 0s_2 + 0s_3 + 0s_4 = 0$

preliminary
tableau:

Basic	θ	x_1	x_2	s_1	s_2	s_3	s_4	c.v.	
s_1	0	1	1	1	0	0	0	13	
s_2	0	1	2	0	1	0	0	22	
s_3	0	2	1	0	0	1	0	20	
s_4	0	1	0	0	0	0	1	4	→
(max) θ	1	−4	1	0	0	0	0	0	

second
tableau:

Basic	θ	x_1	x_2	s_1	s_2	s_3	s_4	c.v.
s_1	0	0	1	1	0	0	−1	9
s_2	0	0	2	0	1	0	−1	18
s_3	0	0	1	0	0	1	−2	12
x_1	0	1	0	0	0	0	1	4
(max) θ	1	0	1	0	0	0	4	16

$s_1 = 9 - x_2 + s_4$

$s_2 = 18 - 2x_2 + s_4$

$s_3 = 12 - x_2 + 2s_4$

$x_1 = 4 - s_4$

7. max $\theta = 8x_1 + 6x_2 + 12x_3$

s.t. $2x_1 + 2x_2 + 5x_3 \leq 40$

$x_1 + 4x_2 + 2x_3 \leq 26$

$3x_1 + x_2 + 3x_3 \leq 27$

$x_1, x_2, x_3 \geq 0$

$2x_1 + 2x_2 + 5x_3 + s_1 + 0s_2 + 0s_3 = 40$

$x_1 + 4x_2 + 2x_3 + 0s_1 + s_2 + 0s_3 = 26$

$3x_1 + x_2 + 3x_3 + 0s_1 + 0s_2 + s_3 = 27$

$\theta - 8x_1 - 6x_2 - 12x_3 + 0s_1 + 0s_2 + 0s_3 = 0$

preliminary tableau:

Basic	θ	x_1	x_2	x_3	s_1	s_2	s_3	c.v.
s_1	0	2	2	5	1	0	0	40 $\rightarrow$
s_2	0	1	4	2	0	1	0	26
s_3	0	3	1	3	0	0	1	27
(max) θ	1	-8	-6	-12	0	0	0	0

$\uparrow$

second tableau:

Basic	θ	x_1	x_2	x_3	s_1	s_2	s_3	c.v.
x_3	0	2/5	2/5	1	1/5	0	0	8
s_2	0	1/5	16/5	0	$-2/5$	1	0	10
s_3	0	9/5	$-1/5$	0	$-3/5$	0	1	3
(max) θ	1	$-16/5$	$-6/5$	0	12/5	0	0	96

$$x_3 = 8 - \frac{2}{5}x_1 - \frac{2}{5}x_2 - \frac{1}{5}s_1$$

$$s_2 = 10 - \frac{1}{5}x_1 - \frac{16}{5}x_2 + \frac{2}{5}s_1$$

$$s_3 = 3 - \frac{9}{5}x_1 + \frac{1}{5}x_2 + \frac{3}{5}s_1$$

Problem Set 5-2

1. max $\theta = x_1 + 2x_2$

s.t. $x_1 + x_2 \leq 5$

$2x_1 + 3x_2 \leq 12$

$x_1, x_2 \geq 0$

$x_1 + x_2 + s_1 + 0s_2 = 5$

$2x_1 + 3x_2 + 0s_1 + s_2 = 12$

$\theta - x_1 - 2x_2 + 0s_1 + 0s_2 = 0$

preliminary tableau:

Basic	x_1	x_2	s_1	s_2	c.v.	
s_1	1	1	1	0	5	$5/1 = 5$
s_2	2	3	0	1	12	$12/3 = 4$ $\rightarrow$
(max) θ	-1	-2	0	0	0	

$\uparrow$

Basic	x_1	x_2	s_1	s_2	c.v.
s_1	1/3	0	1	−1/3	1
x_2	2/3	1	0	1/3	4
(max) θ	1/3	0	0	2/3	8

$x_1 = 0$, $x_2 = 4$,
$s_1 = 1$, $s_2 = 0$,
max = 8

4. max $\theta = 5x_1 + 8x_2$

s.t. $x_1 + x_2 \le 13$

$x_1 + 2x_2 \le 22$

$2x_1 + x_2 \le 20$

$x_1 \le 4$

$x_1, x_2 \ge 0$

$x_1 + x_2 + s_1 = 13$

$x_1 + 2x_2 + s_2 = 22$

$2x_1 + x_2 + s_3 = 20$

$x_1 + s_4 = 4$

$\theta - 5x_1 - 8x_2 = 0$

preliminary tableau:

Basic	x_1	x_2	s_1	s_2	s_3	s_4	c.v.	
s_1	1	1	1	0	0	0	13	$13/1 = 13$
s_2	1	2	0	1	0	0	22	$22/2 = 11 \rightarrow$
s_3	2	1	0	0	1	0	20	$20/1 = 20$
s_4	1	0	0	0	0	1	4	$4/0 = \infty$
(max) θ	−5	−8	0	0	0	0	0	

$\uparrow$

second tableau:

Basic	x_1	x_2	s_1	s_2	s_3	s_4	c.v.	
s_1	1/2	0	1	−1/2	0	0	2	$\frac{2}{1/2} = 4$
x_2	1/2	1	0	1/2	0	0	11	$\frac{11}{1/2} = 22$
s_3	3/2	0	0	−1/2	1	0	9	$\frac{9}{3/2} = 6$
s_4	1	0	0	0	0	1	4	$4/1 = 4 \rightarrow$
(max) θ	−1	0	0	4	0	0	88	

$\uparrow$

third tableau:

Basic	x_1	x_2	s_1	s_2	s_3	s_4	c.v.
s_1	0	0	1	−1/2	0	−1/2	0
x_2	0	1	0	1/2	0	−1/2	9
s_3	0	0	0	−1/2	1	−3/2	3
x_1	1	0	0	0	0	1	4
(max) θ	0	0	0	4	0	1	92

$x_1 = 4$ $s_1 = s_2 = s_4 = 0$

$x_2 = 9$ $\theta = 92$

$s_3 = 3$

8. $\max \theta = 5x_1 + 6x_2 + x_3$

s.t. $x_1 + 5x_2 + 2x_3 \le 30$

$x_1 + 7x_2 \qquad \le 40$

$2x_1 + x_2 + 3x_3 \le 70$

$x_1, x_2, x_3 \ge 0$

$x_1 + 5x_2 + 2x_3 + s_1 = 30$

$x_1 + 7x_2 \qquad + s_2 = 40$

$2x_1 + x_2 + 3x_3 + s_3 = 70$

$\theta - 1/2x_1 - 6x_2 - x_3 \qquad = 0$

preliminary tableau:

Basic	x_1	x_2	x_3	s_1	s_2	s_3	c.v.	
s_1	1	5	2	1	0	0	30	$30/5 = 6$
s_2	1	7	0	0	1	0	40	$40/7 = 5\frac{5}{7} \rightarrow$
s_3	2	1	3	0	0	1	70	$70/1 = 70$
(max) θ	$-1/2$	-6 $\uparrow$	-1	0	0	0	0	

second tableau:

Basic	x_1	x_2	x_3	s_1	s_2	s_3	c.v.	
s_1	2/7	0	2	1	$-5/7$	0	10/7	$10/7 \cdot 1/2 = 5/7 \rightarrow$
x_2	1/7	1	0	0	1/7	0	40/7	$\dfrac{40/7}{0} = \infty$
s_3	13/7	0	3	0	$-1/7$	1	450/7	$450/7 \cdot 1/3 = 150/7$
(max) θ	5/14	0	-1 $\uparrow$	0	6/7	0	240/7	

third tableau:

Basic	x_1	x_2	x_3	s_1	s_2	s_3	c.v.
x_3	1/7	0	1	1/2	$-5/14$	0	5/7
x_2	1/7	1	0	0	1/7	0	40/7
s_3	10/7	0	0	$-3/2$	17/14	1	435/7
(max) θ	1/2	0	0	1/2	1/2	0	35

$x_2 = 40/7 \qquad x_1 = s_1 = s_2 = 0$

$x_3 = 5/7 \qquad \theta = 35$

$s_3 = 435/7$

13. $\max \theta = x_1 + 2x_2 + x_3$

s.t. $2x_1 + x_2 + 3x_3 \le 12$

$x_1 + 2x_2 \qquad \le 6$

$2x_1 \qquad + x_3 \le 4$

$2x_1 + x_2 + 3x_3 + s_1 = 12$

$x_1 + 2x_2 \qquad + s_2 = 6$

$2x_1 \qquad + x_3 + s_3 = 4$

$\theta - x_1 - 2x_2 - x_3 \qquad = 0$

preliminary
tableau:

Basic	x_1	x_2	x_3	s_1	s_2	s_3	c.v.	
s_1	2	1	3	1	0	0	12	12/1 = 12
s_2	1	2	0	0	1	0	6	6/2 = 3 →
s_3	2	0	1	0	0	1	4	4/0 = ∞
(max) θ	−1	−2	−1	0	0	0	0	

second
tableau:

Basic	x_1	x_2	x_3	s_1	s_2	s_3	c.v.	
s_1	3/2	0	3	1	−1/2	0	9	9/3 = 3 →
x_2	1/2	1	0	0	1/2	0	3	3/0 = ∞
s_3	2	0	1	0	0	1	4	4/1 = 4
(max) θ	0	0	−1	0	1	0	6	

third
tableau:

Basic	x_1	x_2	x_3	s_1	s_2	s_3	c.v.
x_3	1/2	0	1	1/3	−1/6	0	3
x_2	1/2	1	0	0	1/2	0	3
s_3	3/2	0	0	−1/3	1/6	1	1
(max) θ	1/2	0	0	1/3	5/6	0	9

$x_2 = 3$ $x_1 = s_1 = s_2 = 0$

$x_3 = 3$ $\theta = 9$

$s_3 = 1$

16.

machine	A	B	C
premium (x_1)	.5	1	2
second (x_2)	.5	2	1
	6.5	22	20

$\theta = 5x_1 + 8x_2$

$\dfrac{1}{2}x_1 + \dfrac{1}{2}x_2 \leq 6.5$

$x_1 + 2x_2 \leq 22$

$2x_1 + x_2 \leq 20$

$x_2 \leq 8$

preliminary
tableau:

Basic	x_1	x_2	s_1	s_2	s_3	s_4	c.v.	
s_1	1/2	1/2	1	0	0	0	13/2	
s_2	1	2	0	1	0	0	22	
s_3	2	1	0	0	1	0	20	
s_4	0	1	0	0	0	1	8	→
(max) θ	−5	−8	0	0	0	0	0	

second tableau:	Basic	x_1	x_2	s_1	s_2	s_3	s_4	c.v.	
	s_1	1/2	0	1	0	0	−1/2	5/2	5 →
	s_2	1	0	0	1	0	−2	6	6
	s_3	2	0	0	0	1	−1	12	6
	x_2	0	1	0	0	0	1	8	8/0 = ∞
	(max) θ	−5 ↑	0	0	0	0	8	64	

third tableau:	Basic	x_1	x_2	s_1	s_2	s_3	s_4	c.v.
	x_1	1	0	2	0	0	−1	5
	s_2	0	0	−2	1	0	−1	1
	s_3	0	0	−4	0	1	1	2
	x_2	0	1	0	0	0	1	8
	(max) θ	0	0	10	0	0	3	89

$x_1 = 5$ $s_1 = s_4 = 0$
$x_2 = 8$ $s_2 = 1$
$\theta = 89$ $s_3 = 2$

machine B and C are not fully utilized

Problem Set 5-3

1. $\theta = 2x_1 - 3x_2 + 14$ (min)

s.t. $3x_1 + 7x_2 \leq 42$

$x_1 + 5x_2 \leq 22$

$x_1, x_2 \geq 0$

preliminary tableau:	Basic	x_1	x_2	s_1	s_2	c.v.	
	s_1	3	7	1	0	42	
	s_2	1	5	0	1	22	→
	(min) θ	−2	3 ↑	0	0	14	

second tableau:	Basic	x_1	x_2	s_1	s_2	c.v.
	s_1	8/5	0	1	−7/5	56/5
	x_2	1/5	1	0	1/5	22/5
	(min) θ	−13/5	0	0	−3/5	4/5

$x_1 = 0$ $s_1 = 56/5$
$x_2 = 22/5$ $s_2 = 0$
$\theta = 4/5$

4. min $\theta = 8x_1 - 12x_2 + 150$

s.t. $-x_1 + x_2 \leq 10$

$x_1 + x_2 \leq 20$

$x_2 \leq 8$

Basic	x_1	x_2	s_1	s_2	s_3	c.v.	
s_1	1	1	1	0	0	10	
s_2	1	1	0	1	0	20	
s_3	0	1	0	0	1	8	→
(min) θ	−8	12 ↑	0	0	0	150	

Basic	x_1	x_2	s_1	s_2	s_3	c.v.
s_1	−1	0	1	0	−1	2
s_2	1	0	0	1	−1	12
x_2	0	1	0	0	1	8
(min) θ	−8	0	0	0	−12	54

$x_1 = 0$ $s_1 = 2$
$x_2 = 8$ $s_2 = 12$
$\theta = 54$

65

7. $\min \theta = 3x_1 - 5x_2 + 24$

s.t. $2x_1 + 3x_2 \leq 24$

$2x_1 - x_2 \leq 8$

$-2x_1 + 3x_2 \leq 12$

Basic	x_1	x_2	s_1	s_2	s_3	c.v.	
s_1	2	3	1	0	0	24	$24/3 = 8$
s_2	2	-1	0	1	0	8	$8/-1 = -$
s_3	-2	3	0	0	1	12	$12/3 = 4 \rightarrow$
(min) θ	-3	5	0	0	0	24	

Basic	x_1	x_2	s_1	s_2	s_3	c.v.	
s_1	4	0	1	0	-1	12	$12/4 = 3 \rightarrow$
s_2	4/3	0	0	1	1/3	12	$\dfrac{12}{4/3} = 8$
x_2	-2/3	1	0	0	1/3	4	$4/-2/3 = -$
(min) θ	1/3	0	0	0	-5/3	4	

Basic	x_1	x_2	s_1	s_2	s_3	c.v.
x_1	1	0	1/4	0	-1/4	3
s_2	0	0	-1/3	1	2/3	8
x_2	0	1	1/6	0	1/6	6
(min) θ	0	0	-1/12	0	-19/12	3

$x_1 = 3,$ $s_1 = 0,$

$x_2 = 6,$ $s_2 = 8,$

$s_3 = 0$

$\min = 3$

9. let $x_1 =$ pound of gunpowder

$x_2 =$ dozen sticks of dynamite

$\min \theta = 3x_1 - 5x_2 + 24$

s.t. $2x_1 + 3x_2 \leq 24$

$2x_1 - x_2 \leq 8$

$-2x_1 + 3x_2 \leq 12$

Basic	x_2	x_2	s_1	s_2	s_3	c.v.	
s_1	2	3	1	0	0	24	
s_2	2	-1	0	1	0	8	
s_3	-2	3	0	0	1	12	$\rightarrow$
(min) θ	-3	5	0	0	0	24	

Basic	x_1	x_2	s_1	s_2	s_3	c.v.	
s_1	4	0	1	0	-1	12	$\rightarrow$
s_2	4/3	0	0	1	1/3	12	
x_2	-2/3	1	0	0	1/3	4	
(min) θ	1/3	0	0	0	-5/3	4	

66

Basic	x_1	x_2	s_1	s_2	s_3	c.v.
x_1	1	0	1/4	0	−1/4	3
s_2	0	0	−1/3	1	2/3	8
x_2	0	0	1/3	0	0	6
(min) θ	0	0	−1/12	0	−19/12	3

$x_1 = 3 \qquad s_2 = 8$

$x_2 = 6 \qquad s_1 = s_3 = 0$

$\theta = 3$

Problem Set 5-4

1. $\max \theta = 2x_1 + 2x_2$

s.t. $3x_1 + 7x_2 \le 42 \qquad 3x_1 + 7x_2 + s_1 = 42$

$x_1 + 5x_2 \le 22 \qquad x_1 + 5x_2 + s_2 = 22$

Basic	x_1	x_2	s_1	s_2	c.v.
s_1	3	7	1	0	42 $\rightarrow$
s_2	1	5	0	1	22
(max) θ	−2 ↑	−2	0	0	0

Basic	x_1	x_2	s_1	s_2	c.v.
x_1	1	7/3	1/3	0	14
s_2	0	8/3	−1/3	1	8
(max) θ	0	8/3	2/3	0	28

$x_1 = 14 \qquad s_2 = 8$

$x_2 = s_1 = 0 \qquad \theta = 28$

4. $\min \theta = -3x_1 - 4x_2 + 25$

$x_1 - 2x_2 \le 4 \qquad x_1 - 2x_2 + s_1 = 4$

$2x_1 + 3x_2 \le 15 \qquad 2x_1 + 3x_2 + s_2 = 15$

$x_2 \le 5 \qquad\qquad x_2 + s_3 = 5$

Basic	x_1	x_2	s_1	s_2	s_3	c.v.
s_1	1	−2	1	0	0	4
s_2	2	3	0	1	0	15
s_3	0	1	0	0	1	5
(min) θ	3	4 ↑	0	0	0	25

$4/-2 = -$

$15/3 = 5 \quad \rightarrow$

$5/1 = 5$

Basic	x_1	x_2	s_1	s_2	s_3	c.v.
s_1	7/3	0	1	2/3	0	14
x_2	2/3	1	0	1/3	0	5
s_3	−2/3	0	0	−1/3	1	0
(min) θ	1/3 ↑	0	0	−4/3	0	5

$14 \cdot 3/7 = 6 \quad \rightarrow$

$5 \cdot 3/2 = 15/2$

$\dfrac{0}{-2/3} = 0$

Basic	x_1	x_2	s_1	s_2	s_3	c.v.
x_1	1	0	3/7	2/7	0	6
x_2	0	1	−2/7	1/7	0	1
s_1	0	0	2/7	−1/7	1	4
(min) θ	0	0	−1/7	−10/7	0	3

$x_1 = 6 \qquad s_1 = s_2 = 0$

$x_2 = 1 \qquad s_3 = 4$

$\theta = 3$

67

9.   max $\theta = 1.5x_1 + 3.5x_2$

s.t. $3x_1 + 7x_2 \leq 42$

$x_1 + 5x_2 \leq 22$

Basic	x_1	x_2	s_1	s_2	c.v.	
s_1	3	7	1	0	42	$42/7 = 6$
s_2	1	5	0	1	22	$22/5 = 4\ 2/5 \rightarrow$
(max) θ	$-3/2$	$-7/2$	0	0	0	

(arrow under x_2 column $\uparrow$)

Basic	x_1	x_2	s_1	s_2	c.v.	
s_1	8/5	0	1	$-7/5$	56/5	$\dfrac{56/5}{8/5} = 7 \rightarrow$
x_2	1/5	1	0	1/5	22/5	$\dfrac{22/5}{1/5} = 22$
(max) θ	$-8/10$	0	0	7/10	154/10	

(arrow under x_1 column $\uparrow$)

Basic	x_1	x_2	s_1	s_2	c.v.
x_1	1	0	5/8	$-7/8$	7
x_2	0	1	$-1/8$	15/40	3
(max) θ	0	0	1/2	0	21

$x_1 = 7 \qquad s_1 = s_2 = 0$

$x_2 = 3 \qquad \theta = 21$

or bring in x_1 first to get alternate second tableau

Basic	x_1	x_2	s_1	s_2	c.v.
x_1	1	7/3	1/3	0	14
s_2	0	8/3	$-1/3$	1	8
(max) θ	0	0	1/2	0	21

$x_1 = 14 \qquad s_1 = 0$

$x_2 = 0 \qquad s_2 = 8$

$\max = 21$

Alternative optimum 21 @ (1, 3)
So line segment joining (14, 0) and (1, 3)

12.   min $\theta = 3x_1 + 3x_2 + 12x_3$

s.t. $x_1 + x_2 + 4x_3 \leq 36$

$2x_1 + 2x_2 + 3x_3 \leq 42$

Basic	x_1	x_2	x_3	s_1	s_2	c.v.
s_1	1	1	4	1	0	36
s_2	2	2	3	0	1	42
(min) θ	-3	-3	-12	0	0	0

$s_1 = 36 \qquad x_1 = x_2 = x_3 = 0$

$s_2 = 42 \qquad \theta = 0$

68

Basic	θ	x_1	x_2	x_3	s_1	s_2	c.v.	
s_1	0	1	1	4	1	0	36	$36/4 = 9 \rightarrow$
s_2	0	2	2	3	0	1	42	$42/3 = 14$
(max) θ	1	-3	-3	-12	0	0	0	

$\uparrow$

Basic	θ	x_1	x_2	x_3	s_1	s_2	c.v.
x_3	12	1/4	1/4	1	1/4	0	9
s_2	0	5/4	5/4	0	$-3/4$	1	15
(max) θ	1	0	0	0	3	0	108

$x_1 = 0 \qquad s_1 = 0$

$x_2 = 0 \qquad s_2 = 15$

$x_3 = 9 \qquad \text{max} = 108$

also optimal @ (12, 0, 6) and (12, 6, 0)
Triangle joining (0, 12, 6), (0, 0, 9), and (12, 6, 0)

Problem Set 5-5

1. max $\theta = 2x_1 + 3x_2$

s.t. $-2x_1 + x_2 \le 2$

$\qquad x_2 \le 6$

Basic	x_1	x_2	s_1	s_2	c.v.	
s_1	-2	1	1	0	2	$\rightarrow$
s_2	0	1	0	1	6	
(max) θ	-2	-3	0	0	0	

$\uparrow$

Basic	x_1	x_2	s_1	s_2	c.v.	
x_2	-2	1	1	0	2	
s_2	2	0	-1	1	4	$\rightarrow$
(max) θ	-8	0	3	0	6	

$\uparrow$

Basic	x_1	x_2	s_1	s_2	c.v.	
x_2	0	1	0	1	6	$6/0 = \infty$
x_1	1	0	$-1/2$	1/2	2	$2/(-1/2) = -4$
(max) θ	0	0	-1	4	22	

$\uparrow$

$x_1 = 2$

$x_2 = 6$

$s_1 = s_2 = 0$

$\theta = 22$

unbounded

4. $\max \theta = 20x_1 + 12x_3$

s.t. $5x_1 - x_2 + x_3 \leq \dfrac{1}{5}$

$\quad\ x_1 + x_2 + x_3 \leq \dfrac{1}{4}$

Basic	x_1	x_2	x_3	s_1	s_2	c.v.	
s_1	5	−1	1	1	0	1/5	$\dfrac{1/5}{5} = .04 \quad \rightarrow$
s_2	1	1	1	0	1	1/4	$\dfrac{1/4}{1} = .25$
(max) θ	−20	0	−12	0	0	0	

Basic	x_1	x_2	x_3	s_1	s_2	c.v.	
x_1	1	−1/5	1/5	1/5	0	1/25	$\dfrac{1/25}{1/5} = .2 \quad \rightarrow$
s_2	0	6/5	4/5	−1/5	1	21/100	$\dfrac{21/100}{4/5} = .2625$
(max) θ	0	−4	−8	4	0	4/5	

Basic	x_1	x_2	x_3	s_1	s_2	c.v.	
x_3	5	−1	1	1	0	1/5	$\dfrac{1/5}{-1} = -$
s_2	−4	2	0	−1	1	−1/20	$\dfrac{1/20}{2} = .025$
(max) θ	40	−12	0	12	0	12/5	

Basic	x_1	x_2	x_3	s_1	s_2	c.v.
x_3	3	0	1	1/2	1/2	9/40
x_2	−2	1	0	−1/2	1/2	1/40
(max) θ	16	0	0	6	6	27/10

$x_1 = 0, x_2 = 1/40, x_3 = 9/40$

$s_1 = 0, s_2 = 0 \quad \max = 27/10$

7. a) max $\theta = 9x_1 + 12x_2 + 10x_3$

   machine A: $2x_1 + 2x_2 + x_3 \leq 36$

   B: $x_1 + 3x_2 + 2x_3 \leq 30$

   C: $x_1 + x_2 + 2x_3 \leq 24$

Basic	x_1	x_2	x_3	s_1	s_2	s_3	c.v.	
s_1	2	2	1	1	0	0	36	$36/2 = 18$
s_2	1	3	2	0	1	0	30	$30/3 = 10$ →
s_3	1	1	2	0	0	1	24	$24/1 = 24$
(max) θ	−9	−12	−10	0	0	0	0	

↑

Basic	x_1	x_2	x_3	s_1	s_2	s_3	c.v.	
s_1	4/3	0	−1/3	1	−2/3	0	16	$16 \cdot 3/4 = 12$ →
x_2	1/3	1	2/3	0	1/3	0	10	$\dfrac{10}{1/3} = 30$
s_3	2/3	0	4/3	0	−1/3	1	14	$14 \cdot 3/2 = 21$
(max) θ	−5	0	−2	0	4	0	120	

↑

Basic	x_1	x_2	x_3	s_1	s_2	s_3	c.v.	
x_1	1	0	−1/4	3/4	−1/2	0	12	$12 \cdot -4 = -48$
x_2	0	1	3/4	−1/4	1/2	0	6	$6 \cdot 4/3 = 8$
s_3	0	0	3/2	−1/2	0	1	6	$6 \cdot 2/3 = 4$ →
(max) θ	0	0	−13/4	15/4	3/2	0	180	

↑

Basic	x_1	x_2	x_3	s_1	s_2	s_3	c.v.
x_1	1	0	0	2/3	−1/2	1/6	13
x_2	0	1	0	0	1/2	−1/2	3
x_3	0	0	1	−1/3	0	2/3	4
(max) θ	0	0	0	8/3	3/2	13/6	193

$x_1 = 13$ $s_1 = s_2 = s_3 = 0$

$x_2 = 3$

$x_3 = 4$

$\theta = 193$

b)   max $\theta = 9x_1 + 12x_2 + 10x_3 - s_1 + s_2 + s_3$

   s.t. $2x_1 + 2x_2 + x_3 \leq 36$

   $x_1 + 3x_2 + 2x_3 \leq 30$

   $x_1 + x_2 + 2x_3 \leq 24$

Basic	x_1	x_2	x_3	s_1	s_2	s_3	c.v.
s_1	2	2	1	1	0	0	36
s_2	1	3	2	0	1	0	30
s_3	1	1	2	0	0	1	24
(max) θ	-9	-12	-10	1	-1	-1	0

(-1) $(s_1 - \text{row})$ -2 -2 -1 -1 0 0 -36

(1) $(s_2 - \text{row})$ 1 3 2 0 1 0 30

(1) $(s_3 - \text{row})$ 1 1 2 0 0 1 24

Basic	θ	x_1	x_2	x_3	s_1	s_2	s_3	c.v.	
s_1	0	2	2	1	1	0	0	36	$36/2 = 18$
s_2	0	1	3	2	0	1	0	30	$30/3 = 10$ $\rightarrow$
s_3	0	1	1	2	0	0	1	24	$24/1 = 24$
(max) θ	1	-9	-10	-7	0	0	0	18	

$\uparrow$

Basic	θ	x_1	x_2	x_3	s_1	s_2	s_3	c.v.	
s_1	0	4/3	0	$-1/3$	1	$-2/3$	0	16	$\dfrac{16}{4/3} = 12$ $\rightarrow$
x_2	10	1/3	1	2/3	0	1/3	0	10	$\dfrac{10}{1/3} = 30$
s_3	0	2/3	0	4/3	0	$-1/3$	1	14	$\dfrac{14}{2/3} = 21$
(max) θ	1	$-12/3$	0	$-1/3$	0	10/3	0	118	

$\uparrow$

Basic	θ	x_1	x_2	x_3	s_1	s_2	s_3	c.v.	
x_1	9	1	0	$-1/4$	3/4	$-1/2$	0	12	$\dfrac{12}{-1/4} = -$
x_2	10	0	1	3/4	$-1/4$	1/2	0	6	$\dfrac{6}{3/4} = 8$
s_3	0	0	0	3/2	$-1/2$	0	1	6	$\dfrac{6}{3/2} = 4$ $\rightarrow$
(max) θ	1	0	0	$-7/4$	12/4	1/2	0	186	

$\uparrow$

72

Basic	θ	x_1	x_2	x_3	s_1	s_2	s_3	c.v.
x_1	9	1	0	0	2/3	$-1/2$	1/6	13
x_2	10	0	1	0	0	1/2	$-1/2$	3
x_3	7	0	0	1	$-1/3$	0	2/3	4
(max) θ	1	0	0	0	11/3	1/2	7/6	193

$x_1 = 13$, $x_2 = 3$, $x_3 = 4$, $s_1 = s_2 = s_3 = 0$, max 193

c)

Basic	θ	x_1	x_2	x_3	s_1	s_2	s_3	c.v.
s_1	0	2	2	1	1	0	0	36
s_2	0	1	3	2	0	1	0	30
s_3	0	1	1	2	0	0	1	24
(min) θ	-1	49	69	53	16	11	8	0

(-16)	$(s_1 -$ row$)$	-32	-32	-16	-16	0	0	-576
(-11)	$(s_2 -$ row$)$	-11	-33	-22	0	-11	0	-330
(-8)	$(s_3 -$ row$)$	-8	-8	-16	0	0	-8	-192

$15(2x_1 + 2x_2 + x_3) + 10(x_1 + 3x_2 + 2x_3) + 9(x_1 + x_2 + 2x_3) + 16s_1 + 16s_2 + 8s_3$

Basic	θ	x_1	x_2	x_3	s_1	s_2	s_3	c.v.	
s_1	0	2	2	1	1	0	0	36	$36/2 = 18$
s_2	0	1	3	2	0	1	0	30	$30/3 = 10 \rightarrow$
s_3	0	1	1	2	0	0	1	24	$24/1 = 24$
(min) θ	-1	-2	$-4\uparrow$	-1	0	0	0	$-1{,}098$	

Basic	θ	x_1	x_2	x_3	s_1	s_2	s_3	c.v.	
s_1	0	4/3	0	$-1/3$	1	$-2/3$	0	16	$\dfrac{16}{4/3} = 12 \rightarrow$
x_2	4	1/3	1	2/3	0	1/3	0	10	$\dfrac{10}{1/3} = 30$
s_3	0	2/3	0	4/3	0	$-1/3$	1	14	$\dfrac{14}{2/3} = 21$
(min) θ	-1	$-2/3\uparrow$	0	4/3	0	4/3	0	$-1{,}058$	

Basic	θ	x_1	x_2	x_3	s_1	s_2	s_3	c.v.
x_1	2	1	0	$-1/4$	3/4	$-1/2$	0	12
x_2	4	0	1	3/4	$-1/4$	1/2	0	6
s_3	0	0	0	3/2	$-1/2$	1/2	1	6
(min) θ	-1	0	0	3/2	1/2	1	0	$-1{,}050$

$x_1 = 12$, $x_2 = 6$, $x_3 = 0$, $s_1 = 0$, $s_2 = 0$, $s_3 = 6$ min @ 1050

1. $\theta = 5x_1 + 3x_2$ min

    s.t. $4x_1 + 2x_2 \geq 20$

         $6x_1 + x_2 \geq 10$

    dual: $4p_1 + 6p_2 \leq 5$

              $2p_1 + p_2 \leq 3$

    $\max \theta = 20p_1 + 10p_2$

Basic	p_1	p_2	x_1	x_2	c.v.	
x_1	4	6	1	0	5	$5/4 = 1.2$ →
x_2	2	1	0	1	3	$3/2 = 1.5$
(max) θ	−20	−10	0	0	0	

           ↑

4. $\theta = 2x_1 + 3x_2 + x_3$ min

    s.t. $x_1 + x_2 + x_3 \geq 10$

        $2x_1 + 3x_2 + x_3 \geq 15$

        $3x_1 + x_2 + 2x_3 \geq 20$

    dual: $p_1 + 2p_2 + 3p_3 \leq 2$

              $p_1 + 3p_2 + p_3 \leq 3$

              $p_1 + p_2 + 2p_3 \leq 1$

    $\max \theta = 10p_1 + 15p_2 + 20p_3$

Basic	p_1	p_2	p_3	x_1	x_2	x_3	c.v.	
x_1	1	2	3	1	0	0	2	$2/3 = .67$
x_2	1	3	1	0	1	0	3	$3/1 = 3$
x_3	1	1	2	0	0	1	1	$1/2 = .5$ →
(max) θ	−10	−15	−20	0	0	0	0	

                   ↑

7. $\theta = x_1 + x_2 + 3x_3$ min

    s.t. $x_1 + 2x_2 + 3x_3 \geq 1{,}200$

        $2x_1 + x_2 + x_3 \geq 600$

    dual: $\max \theta = 1{,}200p_1 + 600p_2$

             s.t. $p_1 + 2p_2 \leq 1$

                   $2p_1 + p_2 \leq 1$

                   $3p_1 + p_2 \leq 3$

Basic	p_1	p_2	x_1	x_2	x_3	c.v.	
x_1	1	2	1	0	0	1	$1/1 = 1$
x_2	2	1	0	1	0	1	$1/2$ →
x_3	3	1	0	0	1	3	$3/3 = 1$
(max) θ	−1,200	−600	0	0	0	0	

           ↑

Basic	p_1	p_2	x_1	x_2	x_3	c.v.
x_1	0	3/2	1	$-1/2$	0	1/2
p_1	1	1/2	0	1/2	0	1/2
x_3	0	$-1/2$	0	$-3/2$	1	3/2
(max) θ	0	0	0	600	0	600

$\theta_{min} = 600$

$p_1 = 0$

$p_2 = 0$

$x_1 = x_3 = 0$

$x_2 = 600$

10. let $x_1 = $ # tons of steel produced per day in mill I
    $x_2 = $ # tons of steel produced per day in mill F

min $\theta = 1,400x_1 + 1,000x_2$

s.t. $1,000x_1 + 2,000x_2 \geq 24,000$

$\quad 3,000x_1 + 2,000x_2 \geq 32,000$

$\quad 5,000x_1 + 2,000x_2 \geq 40,000$

dual: $\quad$ max $\theta = 24,000p_1 + 32,000p_2 + 40,000p_3$

$\qquad$ s.t. $1,000p_1 + 3,000p_2 + 5,000p_3 \leq 1,400$

$\qquad\quad 2,000p_1 + 2,000p_2 + 2,000p_3 \leq 1,000$

Basic	p_1	p_2	p_3	x_1	x_2	c.v.
x_1	1,000	3,000	5,000	1	0	1,400
x_2	2,000	2,000	2,000	0	1	1,000
(max) θ	$-24,000$	$-32,000$	$-40,000$	0	0	0

$1,400/5,000 = .28 \quad \rightarrow$
$1,000/2,000 = .5$

Basic	p_1	p_2	p_3	x_1	x_2	c.v.
p_3	1/5	3/5	1	1/5,000	0	14/50
x_2	1,600	800	0	$-2/5$	1	440
(max) θ	$-16,000$	$-8,000$	0	8	0	11,200

$14/50.5 = 1.4$
$440/1600 = .275 \quad \rightarrow$

Basic	p_1	p_2	p_3	x_1	x_2	c.v.
p_3	0	1/2	1	640,001/5,000	1/8,000	67/200
p_1	1	1/2	0	-640	1/1,600	11/40
(max) θ	0	0	0	4	10	15,600

min $\theta = 15,600$

$\quad x_1 = 4 \qquad p_1 = p_2 = p_3 = 0$

$\quad x_2 = 10$

No grades are overproduced.

1. a)

$$\text{c.v.} = \begin{bmatrix} x_1 \\ x_2 \\ s_3 \\ \overline{\theta} \end{bmatrix} = 14s_1 + 22s_2 + 20s_3 + 0 \cdot \theta$$

$$= 14\begin{bmatrix} 2 \\ -1 \\ -3 \\ \overline{2} \end{bmatrix} + 22\begin{bmatrix} -1 \\ 1 \\ 1 \\ \overline{3} \end{bmatrix} + 20\begin{bmatrix} 0 \\ 0 \\ 1 \\ \overline{0} \end{bmatrix} + 0\begin{bmatrix} 0 \\ 0 \\ 0 \\ \overline{1} \end{bmatrix}$$

$$= \begin{bmatrix} 6 \\ 8 \\ 0 \\ \overline{94} \end{bmatrix} \qquad x_1 = 6, x_2 = 8, s_1 = 0, s_2 = 0, s_3 = 0 \qquad \max = 94$$

b)

$$\text{c.v.} = \begin{bmatrix} x_1 \\ x_2 \\ s_3 \\ \overline{0} \end{bmatrix} = 13s_1 + 20s_2 + 20s_3 + 0 \cdot \theta$$

$$= 13\begin{bmatrix} 2 \\ -1 \\ -3 \\ \overline{2} \end{bmatrix} + 20\begin{bmatrix} -1 \\ 1 \\ 1 \\ \overline{3} \end{bmatrix} + 20\begin{bmatrix} 0 \\ 0 \\ 1 \\ \overline{0} \end{bmatrix} + 0\begin{bmatrix} 0 \\ 0 \\ 0 \\ \overline{1} \end{bmatrix}$$

$$= \begin{bmatrix} 6 \\ 7 \\ 1 \\ \overline{86} \end{bmatrix} \qquad x_1 = 6, x_2 = 7, s_1 = 0, s_2 = 0, s_3 = 1 \qquad \max = 86$$

c)

$$\text{c.v.} = \begin{bmatrix} x_1 \\ x_2 \\ s_3 \\ \overline{\theta} \end{bmatrix} = 13s_1 + 22s_2 + 18s_3 + 0 \cdot \theta$$

$$= 13\begin{bmatrix} 2 \\ -1 \\ -3 \\ \overline{2} \end{bmatrix} + 22\begin{bmatrix} -1 \\ 1 \\ 1 \\ \overline{3} \end{bmatrix} + 18\begin{bmatrix} 0 \\ 0 \\ 1 \\ \overline{0} \end{bmatrix} + 0\begin{bmatrix} 0 \\ 0 \\ 0 \\ \overline{1} \end{bmatrix}$$

$$= \begin{bmatrix} 4 \\ 9 \\ 1 \\ \overline{92} \end{bmatrix} \qquad x_1 = 4, x_2 = 9, s_1 = 0, s_2 = 0, s_3 = 1 \qquad \max = 92$$

5. a)

$$\text{c.v.} = \begin{bmatrix} 24 + c \\ 18 \\ \overline{0} \end{bmatrix}$$

c.v. $= (24 + c)s_1 + 18s_2 + 0 \cdot \theta$

$$= 24 + c\begin{bmatrix} \dfrac{2}{5} \\ -1/5 \\ \hline 3 \end{bmatrix} + 18\begin{bmatrix} \dfrac{-1}{5} \\ 3/5 \\ \hline 1 \end{bmatrix} + 0\begin{bmatrix} 0 \\ 0 \\ \hline 1 \end{bmatrix}$$

$$= \begin{bmatrix} 6 + \dfrac{2}{5}c \\ 6 - \dfrac{1}{5}c \\ \hline 90 + 3c \end{bmatrix}$$

$x_3 = 6 + \dfrac{2}{5}c \geq 0; \dfrac{2}{5}c \geq -6; c \geq -15$

$x_1 = 6 - \dfrac{1}{5}c \geq 0; \dfrac{-1}{5}c \geq -6; c \leq 30$

$-15 \leq c \leq 30$

Thus, the RHS for constraint #1 is 9 to 54

$$\text{c.v.} = \begin{bmatrix} 24 \\ 18 + c \\ \hline 0 \end{bmatrix}$$

c.v. $= 24s_1 + (184c)s_2 + 0 \cdot \theta$

$$= 24\begin{bmatrix} \dfrac{2}{5} \\ -1/5 \\ \hline 3 \end{bmatrix} + (184c)\begin{bmatrix} \dfrac{-1}{5} \\ 3/5 \\ \hline 1 \end{bmatrix} + 0\begin{bmatrix} 0 \\ 0 \\ \hline 1 \end{bmatrix}$$

$$= \begin{bmatrix} 6 - \dfrac{1}{5}c \\ 6 + \dfrac{3}{5}c \\ \hline 90 + c \end{bmatrix} \quad x_3 = c - \dfrac{1}{5}c \geq 0; \dfrac{-1}{5}c \geq -6; c \leq 30$$

$$x_1 = 64\dfrac{3}{5}c \geq 0; \dfrac{3}{5}c \geq -6; c \geq -10$$

$-10 \leq c \leq 30$

Thus, the RHS for constraint #2 is 8 to 48

5. b)
$$\text{c.v.} = \begin{bmatrix} x_3 \\ x_1 \\ \hline \theta \end{bmatrix} = 30s_1 + 20s_2 + 0 \cdot \theta$$

$$= 30\begin{bmatrix} \dfrac{2}{5} \\ -1/5 \\ \hline 3 \end{bmatrix} + 20\begin{bmatrix} -\dfrac{1}{5} \\ 3/5 \\ \hline 1 \end{bmatrix} + 0\begin{bmatrix} 0 \\ 0 \\ \hline 1 \end{bmatrix}$$

$$= \begin{bmatrix} 8 \\ 6 \\ \hline 110 \end{bmatrix} \quad x_1 = 6, x_2 = 0, x_3 = 8, s_1 = 0, s_2 = 0 \quad \text{max @ } 110$$

Basic	θ	x_1	x_2	x_3	s_1	s_2	s_3	c.v.	
s_1	0	1	3	2	1	0	0	48	$48/3 = 16$
s_2	0	3	10	5	0	1	0	150	$100/15 = 15$
s_3	0	1	5	5	0	0	1	70	$70/5 = 14$ →
(max) θ	1	-1	-4	-2	0	0	0	0	

Basic	θ	x_1	x_2	x_3	s_1	s_2	s_3	c.v.	
s_1	0	2/5	0	-1	1	0	$-3/5$	6	$\dfrac{6}{2/5} = 15$
s_2	0	1	0	-5	0	1	-2	10	$10/1 = 10$
x_2	4	1/5	1	1	0	0	1/5	14	$\dfrac{14}{1/5} = 70$
(max) θ	1	$-1/5$	0	2	0	0	4/5	56	

11. a)

Basic	θ	x_1	x_2	x_3	s_1	s_2	s_3	c.v.
s_1	0	0	0	1	1	$-2/5$	1/5	2
x_1	1	1	0	-5	0	1	-2	10
x_2	4	0	1	2	0	$-1/5$	3/5	12
(max) θ	1	0	0	1	0	1/5	2/5	58

$x_1 = 10$, $x_2 = 12$, $x_3 = 0$, $s_1 = 2$, $s_2 = 0$, $s_3 = 0$ max $= 58$

b) Shadow price for $s_2 = 1/5$ or $\$0.20$

$s_3 = 2/5$ or $\$0.40$

c)

$$\text{c.v.} = \begin{bmatrix} 48 \\ 150 + c \\ 70 \\ \hline 58 \end{bmatrix}$$

$\text{c.v.} = 48s_1 + (150 + c)s_2 + 70s_3 + 0 \cdot \theta$

$$= 48\begin{bmatrix} 1 \\ 0 \\ 0 \\ \hline 0 \end{bmatrix} + (150 + c)\begin{bmatrix} -\dfrac{2}{5} \\ 1 \\ -1/5 \\ \hline 1/5 \end{bmatrix} + 70\begin{bmatrix} \dfrac{1}{5} \\ -2 \\ 3/5 \\ \hline 2/5 \end{bmatrix} + 0\begin{bmatrix} 0 \\ 0 \\ 0 \\ \hline 1 \end{bmatrix}$$

$$= \begin{bmatrix} 2 - \dfrac{2}{5}c \\ 10 + c \\ 12 - 1/5c \\ \hline 58 + 1/5c \end{bmatrix}$$

$s_1 = 2 - \dfrac{2}{5}c \geq 0$; $-\dfrac{2}{5}c \geq -2$; $c \leq 5$

$x_1 = 10 + c \geq 0$; $c \geq -10$

$x_2 = 12 - \dfrac{1}{5}c \geq 0$; $-\dfrac{1}{5}c \geq -12$; $c \leq 60$

$-c \leq 5$

For s_2:

$\dfrac{2}{-2/5} = -5$

$10/1 = 10$

$\dfrac{12}{-1/5} = -60$

$150 - 10 = 140$

$150 - (-5) = 155$

For s_3:

$\dfrac{2}{1/5} = 10$

$10/-2 = -5$

$\dfrac{12}{3/5} = 20$

$70 - 10 = 60$

$70 - (-5) = 75$

The RHS for constraint #2 is 140 to 155

$$\text{c.v.} = \begin{bmatrix} 48 \\ 150 \\ \dfrac{70 + c}{0} \end{bmatrix}$$

$$\text{c.v.} = 48s_1 + 150s_2 + (70 + c)s_3 + 0 \cdot \theta$$

$$= 48\begin{bmatrix} 1 \\ 0 \\ \dfrac{0}{0} \end{bmatrix} + 150\begin{bmatrix} -\dfrac{2}{5} \\ 1 \\ \dfrac{-1/5}{1/5} \end{bmatrix} + (70 + c)\begin{bmatrix} \dfrac{1}{5} \\ -2 \\ \dfrac{3/5}{2/5} \end{bmatrix} + 0\begin{bmatrix} 0 \\ 0 \\ \dfrac{0}{1} \end{bmatrix}$$

$$= \begin{bmatrix} 2 + \dfrac{1}{5}c \\ 10 - 2c \\ \dfrac{12 + 3/5c}{58 + 2/5c} \end{bmatrix}$$

$s_1 = 2 + \dfrac{1}{5}c \geq 0; \dfrac{1}{5}c \geq -2; c \geq -10$

$x_1 = 10 - 2c \geq 0; -2c \geq -10; c \leq 5$

$x_2 = 12 + \dfrac{3}{5}c \geq 0; \dfrac{3}{5}c \geq -12; c \geq -20$

$-10 \leq c \leq 5$

The RHS for constraint #3 is 60 to 75

1.

Basic	x_1	x_2	x_3	s_1	s_2	s_3	Current Value	
s_1	1	5	10	1	0	0	150	$150/10 = 15$ →
s_2	3	20	25	0	1	0	500	$500/25 = 20$
s_3	1	15	15	0	0	1	300	$300/15 = 20$
(max) θ	−1	−6	−10	0	0	0		

Basic	x_1	x_2	x_3	s_1	s_2	s_3	Current Value	
x_3	1/10	1/2	1	1/10	0	0	15	$\dfrac{15}{1/2} = 30$
s_2	1/2	15/2	0	−5/2	1	0	125	$\dfrac{125}{15/2} = 16.67$
s_3	−1/2	15/2	0	−3/2	0	1	75	$\dfrac{75}{15/2} = 10$ →
(max) θ	0	−1	0	1	0	0	150	

Basic	x_1	x_2	x_3	s_1	s_2	s_3	Current Value	
x_3	2/15	0	1	1/5	0	−1/15	10	$\dfrac{10}{2/15} = 75$
s_2	1	0	0	−1	1	−1	50	$50/1 = 50$ →
x_2	−1/15	1	0	−1/5	0	2/15	10	$\dfrac{10}{-1/15} = -$
(max) θ	−1/15	0	0	4/5	0	2/15	160	

Basic	x_1	x_2	x_3	s_1	s_2	s_3	Current Value
x_3	0	0	1	1/3	−2/15	1/15	10/3
x_1	1	0	0	−1	1	−1	50
x_2	0	1	0	−4/15	1/15	1/15	40/3
(max) θ	0	0	0	11/15	1/15	1/15	490/3

3.

Basic	x_1	x_2	x_3	s_1	s_2	s_3	Current Value	
s_1	3	2	1	1	0	0	8	$8/2 = 4$
s_2	2	3	1	0	1	0	10	$10/3 = 3.33$ →
s_3	5	3	2	0	0	1	17	$17/3 = 5.67$
(max) θ	−2	−3	−1	0	0	0	0	

Basic	x_1	x_2	x_3	s_1	s_2	s_3	Current Value
s_1	5/3	0	1/3	1	−2/3	0	4/3
x_2	2/3	1	1/3	0	1/3	0	10/3
s_3	3	0	1	0	−1	1	7
(max) θ	0	0	0	0	1	0	10

$x_1 = 0$, $x_2 = 10/3$, $x_3 = 0$, $s_1 = 4/3$, $s_2 = 0$, $s_3 = 7$, max = 10
Also optimal at (4/5, 14/5, 0) and (0, 2, 4) on triangle

5.

Basic	x_1	x_2	x_3	s_1	s_2	s_3	Current Value	
s_1	3	1	1	1	0	0	35	$35/3 = 11.67 \rightarrow$
s_2	2	10	3	0	1	0	140	$140/2 = 70$
s_3	4	4	1	0	0	1	50	$50/4 = 12.5$
(max) θ	−3 ↑	−2	−1	0	0	0	0	

Basic	x_1	x_2	x_3	s_1	s_2	s_3	Current Value	
x_1	1	1/3	1/3	1/3	0	0	11 2/3	$\dfrac{11\ 2/3}{1/3} = 35$
s_2	0	28/3	8/3	−2/3	1	0	116 2/3	$\dfrac{116\ 2/3}{28/3} = 12.5$
s_3	0	8/3	−1/3	−4/3	0	1	3 1/3	$\dfrac{3\ 1/3}{8/3} = 1.25 \rightarrow$
(max) θ	0	−1 ↑	0	1	0	0	35	

Basic	x_1	x_2	x_3	s_1	s_2	s_3	Current Value	
x_1	1	0	3/8	1/2	0	−1/8	11 1/4	$\dfrac{11\ 1/4}{3/8} = 30$
s_2	0	0	7/2	4	1	−7/2	105	$\dfrac{105}{7/2} = 30 \rightarrow$
x_2	0	1	−1/8	−1/2	0	3/8	1 1/4	$\dfrac{1\ 1/4}{−1/8} = −$
(max) θ	0	0	−1/8 ↑	1/2	0	3/8	36.25	

Basic	x_1	x_2	x_3	s_1	s_2	s_3	Current Value
x_1	1	0	0	1/14	−3/28	1/4	0
x_3	0	0	1	8/7	2/7	−1	30
x_2	0	1	0	−5/14	1/28	1/4	5
(max) θ	0	0	0	9/14	1/28	1/4	40

$x_1 = 0$, $x_2 = 5$, $s_3 = 30$, $s_1 = s_2 = s_3 = 0$, max = 40

7.

Basic	x_1	x_2	x_3	s_1	s_2	s_3	Current Value	
s_1	1	1	2	1	0	0	8	$8/1 = 8$
s_2	2	1	1	0	1	0	10	$10/2 = 5$
s_3	3	1	3	0	0	1	15	$15/3 = 5 \quad \rightarrow$
(max) θ	-2	-1	-2	0	0	0	0	
	$\uparrow$							

Basic	x_1	x_2	x_3	s_1	s_2	s_3	Current Value	
s_1	0	2/3	1	1	0	$-1/3$	3	$\dfrac{3}{2/3} = 4.5$
s_2	0	1/3	-1	0	1	$-2/3$	0	$\dfrac{0}{1/3} = 0 \quad \rightarrow$
x_1	1	1/3	1	0	0	1/3	5	$\dfrac{5}{1/3} = 15$
(max) θ	0	$-1/3$	0	0	0	2/3	10	
		$\uparrow$						

Basic	x_1	x_2	x_3	s_1	s_2	s_3	Current Value	
s_1	0	0	3	1	-2	1	3	$3/3 = 1 \quad \rightarrow$
x_2	0	1	-3	0	3	-2	0	$0/-3 = -$
x_1	1	0	2	0	1	1	5	$5/2 = 2.5$
(max) θ	0	0	-1	0	1	0	10	
			$\uparrow$					

Basic	x_1	x_2	x_3	s_1	s_2	s_3	Current Value
x_3	0	0	1	1/3	$-2/3$	1/3	1
x_2	0	1	0	1	1	-1	3
x_1	1	0	0	$-2/3$	1/3	1/3	3
(max) θ	0	0	0	1/3	1/3	1/3	11

$x_1 = 3$, $x_2 = 3$, $x_3 = 1$, $s_1 = s_2 = s_3 = 0$, max $= 11$

9. $x_1 =$ Model E $\quad x_2 =$ Model D

Basic	x_1	x_2	s_1	s_2	s_3	Current Value	
s_1	2	1	1	0	0	30	$30/2 = 15 \quad \rightarrow$
s_2	1	2	0	1	0	24	$24/1 = 24$
s_3	4	5	0	0	1	72	$72/4 = 18$
(max) θ	-9	-7	0	0	0		
	$\uparrow$						

Basic	x_1	x_2	s_1	s_2	s_3	Current Value	
x_1	1	1/2	1/2	0	0	15	$\frac{15}{1/2} = 30$
s_2	0	3/2	$-1/2$	1	0	9	$\frac{9}{3/2} = 6$
s_3	0	3	-2	0	1	12	$12/3 = 4$ →
(max) θ	0	$-5/2$ ↑	9/2	0	0	135	

Basic	x_1	x_2	s_1	s_2	s_3	Current Value
x_1	1	0	5/6	0	$-1/6$	13
s_2	0	0	1/2	1	$-1/2$	3
x_2	0	1	$-2/3$	0	1/3	4
(max) θ	0	0	17/6	0	5/6	145

$x_1 = 13$, $x_2 = 4$, $s_1 = 0$, $s_2 = 3$, $s_3 = 0$ Profit = 145

Machine B is not fully utilized

11.

Basic	x_1	x_2	x_3	s_1	s_2	s_3	Current Value	
s_1	2	2	5	1	0	0	40	$40/5 = 8$ →
s_2	1	4	2	0	1	0	26	$26/2 = 13$
s_3	3	1	3	0	0	1	27	$27/3 = 9$
(max) θ	-8	-6	-12 ↑	0	0	0	0	

Basic	x_1	x_2	x_3	s_1	s_2	s_3	Current Value	
x_3	2/5	2/5	1	1/5	0	0	8	$\frac{8}{2/5} = 20$
s_2	1/5	3/5	0	0	1	0	10	$26/1 = 26$
s_3	9/5	$-1/5$	0	$-3/5$	0	1	3	$\frac{3}{9/5} = 1.67$ →
(max) θ	$-16/5$ ↑	$-6/5$	0	12/5	0	0	96	

Basic	x_1	x_2	x_3	s_1	s_2	s_3	Current Value	
x_3	0	4/9	1	1/3	0	$-2/9$	22/3	$\frac{22/3}{4/9} = 16.5$
s_2	0	55/9	0	1/3	1	$-5/9$	73/3	$\frac{73/3}{55/9} = 3.98$ →
x_1	1	$-1/9$	0	$-1/3$	0	5/9	5/3	$\frac{5/3}{-1/9} = -$
(max) θ	0	$-14/9$ ↑	0	4/3	0	16/9	101 1/3	

Basic	x_1	x_2	x_3	s_1	s_2	s_3	Current Value
x_3	0	0	1	17/55	−4/55	−2/11	5.56
x_2	0	1	0	3/55	9/55	−1/11	3.98
x_1	1	0	0	−18/55	1/55	6/11	2.11
(max) θ	0	0	0	78/55	14/55	18/11	107.53

$x_1 = 2.11$, $x_2 = 3.98$, $x_3 = 5.56$, $s_1 = 0$, $s_2 = 0$, $s_3 = 0$ Profit $= \$107.53$

13.

Basic	x_1	x_2	x_3	s_1	s_2	s_3	s_4	s_5	Current Value	
s_1	3	2	1	1	0	0	0	0	23	$23/3 = 7.67 \rightarrow$
s_2	1	3	2	0	1	0	0	0	26	$26/1 = 26$
s_3	2	1	2	0	0	1	0	0	19	$19/2 = 9.5$
s_4	4	5	3	0	0	0	1	0	49	$49/4 = 12.25$
s_5	3	4	4	0	0	0	0	1	45	$45/3 = 15$
(max) θ	−5 ↑	−3	−4	0	0	0	0	0	0	

Basic	x_1	x_2	x_3	s_1	s_2	s_3	s_4	s_5	Current Value	
x_1	1	2/3	1/3	1/3	0	0	0	0	23/3	$\dfrac{23/3}{1/3} = 23$
s_2	0	7/3	5/3	−1/3	1	0	0	0	55/3	$\dfrac{55/3}{5/3} = 11$
s_3	0	−1/3	4/3	−2/3	0	1	0	0	11/3	$\dfrac{11/3}{4/3} = 2.75 \rightarrow$
s_4	0	2/3	5/3	−4/3	0	0	1	0	55/3	$\dfrac{55/3}{5/3} = 11$
s_5	0	2	3	−1	0	0	0	1	22	$22/3 = 7.33$
(max) θ	0	1/3	−7/3 ↑	5/3	0	0	0	0	38.33	

Basic	x_1	x_2	x_3	s_1	s_2	s_3	s_4	s_5	Current Value	
x_1	1	3/4	0	1/2	0	−1/4	0	0	27/4	$\dfrac{27/4}{3/4} = 9$
s_2	0	11/4	0	1/2	1	−5/4	0	0	55/4	$\dfrac{55/4}{11/4} = 5 \rightarrow$
x_3	0	−1/4	1	−1/2	0	3/4	0	0	11/4	$\dfrac{11/4}{−1/4} = -$
s_4	0	11/4	0	−1/2	0	−5/4	1	0	55/4	$\dfrac{55/4}{11/4} = 5$
s_5	0	11/4	0	1/2	0	−9/4	0	1	55/4	$\dfrac{55/4}{11/4} = 5$
(max) θ	0	−1/4 ↑	0	1/2	0	7/4	0	0	44.75	

84

Basic	x_1	x_2	x_3	s_1	s_2	s_3	s_4	s_5	Current Value
x_1	1	0	0	4/11	−3/11	1/11	0	0	3
x_2	0	1	0	2/11	4/11	−5/11	0	0	5
x_3	0	0	1	−5/11	1/11	7/11	0	0	4
s_4	0	0	0	−1	−1	0	1	0	0
s_5	0	0	0	0	−1	−1	0	1	0
(max) θ	0	0	0	6/11	1/11	18/11	0	0	46

$x_1 = 3, x_2 = 5, x_3 = 4 \quad s_1 = 0 \quad$ Profit = \$46

15.

Basic	x_1	x_2	s_1	s_2	s_3	s_4	Current Value	
s_1	1	1	1	0	0	0	40	40/1 = 40
s_2	1	0	0	1	0	0	25	25/1 = 25
s_3	1	−1	0	0	1	0	0	0/1 = 0 →
s_4	−1	1	0	0	0	1	8	8/−1 = −
(max) θ	−2.5	−2.5	0	0	0	0	0	
	↑							

Basic	x_1	x_2	s_1	s_2	s_3	s_4	Current Value	
s_1	0	2	1	0	−1	0	40	40/2 = 20 →
s_2	0	1	0	1	−1	0	25	25/1 = 25
x_1	1	−1	0	0	1	0	0	0/−1 = −
s_4	0	0	0	0	1	1	8	8/0 = −
(max) θ	0	−5	0	0	5/2	0	0	
		↑						

Basic	x_1	x_2	s_1	s_2	s_3	s_4	Current Value
x_2	0	1	1/2	0	−1/2	0	20
s_2	0	0	−1/2	1	−1/2	0	5
x_1	1	0	1/2	0	1/2	0	20
s_4	0	0	0	0	1	1	8
(max) θ	0	0	5/2	0	0	0	100

$x_1 = 20, x_2 = 20, s_1 = 0, s_2 = 5, s_3 = 0, s_4 = 8$, max = 100

(16, 24), (17, 23), (18, 22), (19, 21),

17.

Basic	x_1	x_2	s_1	s_2	s_3	c.v.
s_1	2	1	1	0	0	30
s_2	1	2	0	1	0	24
s_3	4	5	0	0	1	72
(max) θ	−9	−7	−2	2	−1	0
$2(s_1 -$ row)	4	2	2	0	0	60
$-2(s_2 -$ row)	−2	−4	0	−2	0	−48
$1(s_2 -$ row)	4	5	0	0	1	72

85

Basic	x_1	x_2	s_1	s_2	s_3	c.v.	
s_1	2	1	1	0	0	30	$30/1 = 30$
s_2	1	2	0	1	0	24	$24/2 = 12$ →
s_3	4	5	0	0	1	72	$72/5 = 14.4$
(max) θ	−3	−4	0	0	0	84	

↑

Basic	x_1	x_2	s_1	s_2	s_3	c.v.	
s_1	3/2	0	1	−1/2	0	18	$\dfrac{18}{3/2} = 12$
x_2	1/2	1	0	1/2	0	12	$\dfrac{12}{1/2} = 24$
s_3	3/2	0	0	−5/2	1	12	$\dfrac{12}{3/2} = 8$ →
(max) θ	−1	0	0	2	0	132	

↑

Basic	x_1	x_2	s_1	s_2	s_3	c.v.
s_1	0	0	1	2	−1	6
x_2	0	1	0	4/3	−1/3	8
x_1	1	0	0	−5/3	2/3	8
(max) θ	0	0	0	1/3	2/3	140

$x_1 = 8$, $x_2 = 8$, $s_1 = 6$, $s_2 = 0$, $s_3 = 0$, max = 140

19. min $\theta = 6x_1 + 24x_2 + 12x_3$

s.t. $x_1 + 2x_2 + \ x_3 \geq 1$

$x_1 + \ \ x_2 + 3x_3 \geq 2$

$x_1 + 3x_2 + \ x_3 \geq 3$

dual: max $\theta = p_1 + 2p_2 + 3p_3$

s.t. $p_1 + \ p_2 + \ p_3 \leq \ 6$

$2p_1 + \ p_2 + 3p_3 \leq 24$

$p_1 + 3p_2 + \ p_3 \leq 12$

b.v.	p_1	p_2	p_3	x_1	x_2	x_3	c.v.	
x_1	1	1	1	1	0	0	6	→
x_2	2	1	3	0	1	0	24	$24/3 = 8$
x_3	1	3	1	0	0	1	12	
(max) θ	−1	−2	−3	0	0	0	0	

↑

b.v.	p_1	p_2	p_3	x_1	x_2	x_3	c.v.
p_3	1	1	1	1	0	0	6
x_2	−1	−2	0	−3	1	0	6
x_3	0	2	0	−1	0	1	+6
(max) θ	+2	+1	0	+3	0	0	+18

86

$\theta_{min} = 18$

$x_1 = 3$

$x_2 = x_3 = 0$

$p_1 = 2$

$p_2 = 1$

$p_3 = 0$

21. $\min \theta = 12x_1 + 6x_2 + 4x_3$

    s.t. $2x_1 + x_2 + 2x_3 \geq 1$

        $x_1 + 2x_2 \qquad \geq 2$

        $3x_1 \qquad + x_3 \geq 1$

dual: $\max \theta = p_1 + 2p_2 + p_3$

    s.t. $2p_1 + p_2 + 3p_3 \leq 12$

        $p_1 + 2p_2 \qquad \leq 6$

        $2p_1 \qquad + p_3 \leq 4$

b.v.	p_1	p_2	p_3	x_1	x_2	x_3	c.v.	
x_1	2	1	3	1	0	0	12	12/1 = 12
x_2	1	2	0	0	1	0	6	6/2 = 3 →
x_3	2	0	1	0	0	1	4	4/0 = ∞
(max) θ	−1	−2	−1	0	0	0	0	
		↑						

b.v.	p_1	p_2	p_3	x_1	x_2	x_3	c.v.	
x_1	3/2	0	3	1	−1/2	0	9	9/3 = 3 →
p_2	1/2	1	0	0	1/2	0	3	3/0 = ∞
x_3	2	0	1	0	0	1	4	4/1 = 4
(max) θ	0	0	−1	0	1	0	6	
			↑					

b.v.	p_1	p_2	p_3	x_1	x_2	x_3	c.v.
p_3	2	0	1	1/3	−1/6	0	3
p_2	1/2	1	0	0	1/2	0	3
x_3	0	0	0	−1/3	1/6	1	1
(max) θ	2	0	0	1/3	5/6	0	9

$\theta_{min} = 9$

$x_1 = 1/3 \qquad p_1 = 2$

$x_2 = 5/6 \qquad p_2 = p_3 = 0$

$x_3 = 0$

23. $\min \theta = 2x_1 + 3x_2 + x_3$

    s.t. $x_1 + x_2 + x_3 \geq 10$

        $2x_1 + 3x_2 + x_3 \geq 15$

        $3x_1 + x_2 + 2x_3 \geq 20$

dual: max $10p_1 + 15p_2 + 20p_3$

s.t. $p_1 + 2p_2 + 3p_3 \leq 2$

$\quad p_1 + 3p_2 + p_3 \leq 3$

$\quad p_1 + p_2 + 2p_3 \leq 1$

b.v.	p_1	p_2	p_3	x_1	x_2	x_3	c.v.	
x_1	1	2	3	1	0	0	2	2/3
x_2	1	3	1	0	1	0	3	3
x_3	1	1	2	0	0	1	1	1/2 →
(max) θ	−10	−15	−20 ↑	0	0	0	0	

b.v.	p_1	p_2	p_3	x_1	x_2	x_3	c.v.	
x_1	−1/2	1/2	0	1	0	−3/2	1/2	$1/2 \cdot 2 = 1$ →
x_2	1/2	5/2	0	0	1	−1/2	5/2	$5/2 \cdot 2/5 = 1$
p_3	1/2	1/2	1	0	0	1/2	1/2	$1/2 \cdot 2 = 1$
(max) θ	0	−5 ↑	0	0	0	10	10	

b.v.	p_1	p_2	p_3	x_1	x_2	x_3	c.v.	
p_2	−1	1	0	2	0	−3	1	$1/-1 = -1$
x_2	3	0	0	−5	1	7	0	$0/3 = 0$ →
p_3	1	0	1	−1	0	2	0	$0/1 = 0$
(max) θ	−5 ↑	0	0	10	0	−5	15	

b.v.	p_1	p_2	p_3	x_1	x_2	x_3	c.v.
p_2	0	1	0	1/3	1/3	−2/3	1
p_1	1	0	0	−5/3	1/3	7/3	0
p_3	0	0	1	2/3	−1/3	−1/3	0
(max) θ	0	0	0	5/3	5/3	20/3	15

$\theta_{min} = 15$

$x_1 = \dfrac{5}{3}$

$x_2 = \dfrac{5}{3}$

$x_3 = \dfrac{20}{3}$

$p_1 = 0$

$p_2 = 0$

$p_3 = 0$

25. a)

$$\text{c.v.} = \begin{bmatrix} 7 + c \\ 1 \\ \dfrac{5}{0} \end{bmatrix}$$

88

c.v. $= (7 + c)s_1 + 1s_2 + 5s_3 + 0 \cdot \theta$

$$= (7 + c)\begin{bmatrix} 1 \\ -1 \\ 0 \\ \overline{1} \end{bmatrix} + 1\begin{bmatrix} 0 \\ 1 \\ 0 \\ \overline{0} \end{bmatrix} + 5\begin{bmatrix} -1 \\ 2 \\ 1 \\ \overline{1} \end{bmatrix} + 0\begin{bmatrix} 0 \\ 0 \\ 0 \\ \overline{1} \end{bmatrix}$$

$$= \begin{bmatrix} 2 + c \\ 4 - c \\ 5 \\ \overline{12 + c} \end{bmatrix}$$

$x_2 = 2 + c > 0; c \geq -2$

$s_2 = 4 - c \geq 0; -c \geq -4; c \leq 4$

$2 \leq c \leq 4$

RHS range for constraint #1 is 5 to 11

$$\text{c.v.} = \begin{bmatrix} 7 \\ 1 + c \\ 5 \\ \overline{0} \end{bmatrix}$$

c.v. $= 7s_1 + (1 + c)s_2 + 5s_3 + 0 \cdot \theta$

$$= 7\begin{bmatrix} 1 \\ -1 \\ 0 \\ \overline{1} \end{bmatrix} + (1 + c)\begin{bmatrix} 0 \\ 1 \\ 0 \\ \overline{0} \end{bmatrix} + 5\begin{bmatrix} -1 \\ 2 \\ 1 \\ \overline{1} \end{bmatrix} + 0\begin{bmatrix} 0 \\ 0 \\ 0 \\ \overline{1} \end{bmatrix}$$

$$= \begin{bmatrix} 2 \\ 4 + c \\ 5 \\ \overline{12} \end{bmatrix}$$

$s_2 = 4 + c \geq 0; c \geq -4$

The RHS range for constraint #2 is -3 to ∞

$$\text{c.v.} = \begin{bmatrix} 7 \\ 1 \\ 5 + c \\ \overline{0} \end{bmatrix}$$

$$= 7\begin{bmatrix} 1 \\ -1 \\ 0 \\ \overline{1} \end{bmatrix} + 1\begin{bmatrix} 0 \\ 1 \\ 0 \\ \overline{0} \end{bmatrix} + (5 + c)\begin{bmatrix} -1 \\ 2 \\ 1 \\ \overline{1} \end{bmatrix} + 0\begin{bmatrix} 0 \\ 0 \\ 0 \\ \overline{1} \end{bmatrix}$$

$$= \begin{bmatrix} 2 - c \\ 10 + 2c \\ 5 + c \\ \overline{124c} \end{bmatrix} \qquad \begin{array}{l} x_2 = 2 - c \geq 0; -c \geq -2; c \leq 2 \\ s_2 = 4 + 2c \geq 0; 2c \geq -4; c \geq -2 \\ x_1 = 5 + c \geq 0; c \geq -5 \\ -2 \leq c \leq 2 \end{array}$$

The RHS range for constraint #3 is 3 to 7

25. b)

$$\text{c.v.} = \begin{bmatrix} x_2 \\ s_2 \\ x_1 \\ \theta \end{bmatrix} = 8s_1 + 6s_2 + 4s_3 + 0 \cdot \theta$$

$$= 8\begin{bmatrix} 1 \\ -1 \\ 0 \\ 1 \end{bmatrix} + 6\begin{bmatrix} 0 \\ 1 \\ 0 \\ 0 \end{bmatrix} + 4\begin{bmatrix} -1 \\ 2 \\ 1 \\ 1 \end{bmatrix} + 0\begin{bmatrix} 0 \\ 0 \\ 0 \\ 1 \end{bmatrix}$$

$$= \begin{bmatrix} 4 \\ 6 \\ 4 \\ 12 \end{bmatrix} \quad \begin{array}{l} x_1 = 4, x_2 = 4, s_1 = 0, s_2 = 6 \\ s_3 = 0, \max = 12 \end{array}$$

27. a) Produce $x_3 = 10$ gloves with a profit of $800

b) Shadow price for the 1st constraint is $60
2nd constraint is $30

c)

$$\text{c.v.} = \begin{bmatrix} 100 + c \\ 40 \\ 50 \\ 0 \end{bmatrix}$$

$$\text{c.v.} = (100 + c)s_1 + 40s_2 + 50s_3 + 0 \cdot \theta$$

$$= (100 + c)\begin{bmatrix} 50 \\ -1 \\ 20 \\ 60 \end{bmatrix} + 40\begin{bmatrix} -40 \\ -1 \\ 50 \\ 30 \end{bmatrix} + 50\begin{bmatrix} 0 \\ 1 \\ 0 \\ 0 \end{bmatrix} + 0\begin{bmatrix} 0 \\ 0 \\ 0 \\ 1 \end{bmatrix}$$

$$= \begin{bmatrix} 3,400 + 50c \\ -190 - c \\ 4,000 + 20c \\ 7,200 + 60c \end{bmatrix} \quad \begin{array}{l} s_1 = 3,400 + 50c \geq 0; 50c \geq -3,400; c \geq -68 \\ x_3 = -90 - c \geq 0; -c \geq 90; c \leq 90 \\ s_2 = 4,000 + 20c \geq 0; 20c \geq -4,000; c \geq -200 \\ -68 \leq c \leq 90 \end{array}$$

The RHS range for constraint #1 is 32 to 190

$$\text{c.v.} = \begin{bmatrix} 100 \\ 40 + c \\ 50 \\ 0 \end{bmatrix}$$

$$\text{c.v.} = 100s_1 + (40 + c)s_2 + 50s_3 + 0 \cdot \theta$$

$$= 100\begin{bmatrix} 50 \\ -1 \\ 20 \\ 60 \end{bmatrix} + (40 + c)\begin{bmatrix} -40 \\ -1 \\ 50 \\ 30 \end{bmatrix} + 50\begin{bmatrix} 0 \\ 1 \\ 0 \\ 0 \end{bmatrix} + 0\begin{bmatrix} 0 \\ 0 \\ 0 \\ 1 \end{bmatrix}$$

$$= \begin{bmatrix} 3,400 - 40c \\ -90 - c \\ 2,000 + 50c \\ 7,200 + 30c \end{bmatrix} \quad \begin{array}{l} s_1 = 3,400 - 40c \geq 0; -40c \geq -3,400; c \leq 85 \\ x_3 = -90 - c \geq 0; -c \geq 90; c \leq 90 \\ s_2 = 2,000 + 50c \geq 0; 50c \geq -2,000; c \geq -40 \\ -40 \leq c \leq 85 \end{array}$$

The RHS range for constraint #2 is 0 to 125

```
$ LINDO
 LINDO (UC 1 APRIL 82)
:MAX 5X1 + 7X2
?ST
?X1 + X2 < 5
?2X1 + 3X2 < 12
?END


:LOOK ALL

MAX      5 X1 + 7 X2
SUBJECT TO
   2)      X1 +  X2 <=    5
   3)     2 X1 + 3 X2 <=    12
END


:TABL

THE TABLEAU
ROW  (BASIS)        X1        X2  SLK    2  SLK    3

  1 ART          -5.000    -7.000    0.000    0.000    0.000

  2 SLK     2     1.000     1.000    1.000    0.000    5.000

  3 SLK     3     2.000     3.000    0.000    1.000   12.000



:PIV
     X2 ENTERS AT VALUE   4.0000    IN ROW    3 OBJ. VALUE=  28.000

:TABL

THE TABLEAU
ROW  (BASIS)        X1        X2  SLK    2  SLK    3

  1 ART          -0.333     0.000    0.000    2.333   28.000

  2 SLK     2     0.333     0.000    1.000   -0.333    1.000

  3        X2     0.667     1.000    0.000    0.333    4.000
```

:PIV
     X1 ENTERS AT VALUE   3.0000   IN ROW   2 OBJ. VALUE= 29.000

:TABL

THE TABLEAU

ROW	(BASIS)	X1	X2	SLK	2	SLK	3
1	ART	0.000	0.000	1.000	2.000	29.000	
2	X1	1.000	0.000	3.000	-1.000	3.000	
3	X2	0.000	1.000	-2.000	1.000	2.000	

:PIV
   LP OPTIMUM FOUND AT STEP   2

        OBJECTIVE FUNCTION VALUE

  1)   29.0000000

VARIABLE	VALUE	REDUCED COST
X1	3.000000	0.000000
X2	2.000000	0.000000

ROW	SLACK OR SURPLUS	DUAL PRICES
2)	0.000000	1.000000
3)	0.000000	2.000000

NO. ITERATIONS=   2

 DC RANGE(SENSITIVITY) ANALYSIS?
?NO
:QUIT
FORTRAN STOP

```
$ RUN LIB:P1P2

PHASE I  -  PHASE II ALGORITHM


Do you want all the tableaus printed (Y/N) ? Y


Enter '1' for MAX, '-1' for MIN ? 1


Enter number of restraints, number of variables ? 2,2
Enter number of <=, number of >=, number of =? 2,0,0


Enter coefficients and constants of <= restraints
Restraint  1    ? 1,1,5

Restraint  2    ? 2,3,12



Enter the objective function coefficients
? 5,7


***************************************************************************
          Decision Variables  1    through  2
            Slack Variables  3    through  4



Simplex Tableau Number   1

      1.00      1.00      1.00      0.00      5.00

      2.00      3.00      0.00      1.00     12.00

     -5.00     -7.00      0.00      0.00      0.00

   Basic           Current
   Variables       Value
   3               5
   4               12
```

93

```
***************************************************************************

Simplex Tableau Number   2

        0.33        0.00       1.00      -0.33       1.00

        0.67        1.00       0.00       0.33       4.00

       -0.33        0.00       0.00       2.33      28.00

Basic             Current
Variables         Value
3                 1
2                 4


***************************************************************************

Simplex Tableau Number   3

        1.00        0.00       3.00      -1.00       3.00

        0.00        1.00      -2.00       1.00       2.00

        0.00        0.00       1.00       2.00      29.00

Basic             Current
Variables         Value
1                 3
2                 2


***************************************************************************

Answers:

Basic             Current
Variables         Value
1                 3
2                 2


Dual
Variables         Value
3                 .999999
4                 2


Optimum Objective Function Value =   29
in 3 Tableaus


***************************************************************************

DO YOU WISH TO RUN THIS PROGRAM AGAIN? NO
```

6-1   #7 using LINDO

```
$ LINDO
 LINDO (UC 1 APRIL 82)
:MAX 6X1 + X2      Subtract 7 from the final answer
?ST
?2X1 + 3X2 < 24
?2X1 - X2 < 8
?-2X1 + 3X2 < 12
?END

:LOOK ALL

MAX       6 X1 +   X2
SUBJECT TO
    2)    2 X1 + 3 X2 <=    24
    3)    2 X1 -   X2 <=     8
    4)  - 2 X1 + 3 X2 <=    12
END
```

:TABL

THE TABLEAU

ROW (BASIS)		X1	X2	SLK 2	SLK 3	SLK 4	
1 ART		-6.000	-1.000	0.000	0.000	0.000	0.000
2 SLK	2	2.000	3.000	1.000	0.000	0.000	24.000
3 SLK	3	2.000	-1.000	0.000	1.000	0.000	8.000
4 SLK	4	-2.000	3.000	0.000	0.000	1.000	12.000

:PIV
    X1 ENTERS AT VALUE   4.0000   IN ROW   3 OBJ. VALUE= 24.000

:TABL

THE TABLEAU

ROW (BASIS)		X1	X2	SLK 2	SLK 3	SLK 4	
1 ART		0.000	-4.000	0.000	3.000	0.000	. 24.000
2 SLK	2	0.000	4.000	1.000	-1.000	0.000	16.000
3	X1	1.000	-0.500	0.000	0.500	0.000	4.000
4 SLK	4	0.000	2.000	0.000	1.000	1.000	20.000

```
:PIV
     X2 ENTERS AT VALUE   4.0000     IN ROW    2 OBJ. VALUE=  40.000

 :TABL

THE TABLEAU
ROW  (BASIS)         X1        X2  SLK    2  SLK    3  SLK    4

  1 ART            0.000     0.000    1.000     2.000     0.000    40.00

  2      X2        0.000     1.000    0.250    -0.250     0.000     4.00

  3      X1        1.000     0.000    0.125     0.375     0.000     6.00

  4 SLK   4        0.000     0.000   -0.500     1.500     1.000    12.00


:PIV
    LP OPTIMUM FOUND  AT STEP      2

          OBJECTIVE FUNCTION VALUE

  1)        *40.0000000   −7 = 33

VARIABLE          VALUE          REDUCED COST
         X1        6.000000          0.000000
         X2        4.000000          0.000000


ROW           SLACK OR SURPLUS      DUAL PRICES
    2)             0.000000          1.000000
    3)             0.000000          2.000000
    4)            12.000000          0.000000

NO. ITERATIONS=          2

  DO RANGE(SENSITIVITY) ANALYSIS?
?NO
:QUIT
FORTRAN STOP
```

6-1   #7 using P1P2

```
$ RUN LIB:P1P2

PHASE I  -   PHASE II ALGORITHM


Do you want all the tableaus printed (Y/N) ? Y


Enter '1' for MAX, '-1' for MIN ? 1
```

```
Enter number of restraints, number of variables ? 3,2
Enter number of <=, number of >=, number of =? 3,0,0


Enter coefficients and constants of <= restraints
Restraint  1    ? 2,3,24

Restraint  2    ? 2,-1,8

Restraint  3    ? -2,3,12



Enter the objective function coefficients
? 6,1     * Subtract 7 from final answer


*************************************************************************


            Decision Variables  1    through  2
                Slack Variables  3    through  5



Simplex Tableau Number   1

      2.00        3.00        1.00        0.00        0.00        24.00

      2.00       -1.00        0.00        1.00        0.00         8.00

     -2.00        3.00        0.00        0.00        1.00        12.00

     -6.00       -1.00        0.00        0.00        0.00         0.00

   Basic            Current
   Variables        Value
   3                24
   4                8
   5                12



*************************************************************************


Simplex Tableau Number   2

      0.00        4.00        1.00       -1.00        0.00        16.00

      1.00       -0.50        0.00        0.50        0.00         4.00

      0.00        2.00        0.00        1.00        1.00        20.00

      0.00       -4.00        0.00        3.00        0.00        24.00
```

```
Basic        Current
Variables    Value
3            16
1            4
5            20
```

```
**********************************************************************
```

Simplex Tableau Number   3

0.00	1.00	0.25	-0.25	0.00	4.00
1.00	0.00	0.13	0.38	0.00	6.00
0.00	0.00	-0.50	1.50	1.00	12.00
0.00	0.00	1.00	2.00	0.00	40.00

```
Basic        Current
Variables    Value
2            4
1            6
5            12
```

```
**********************************************************************
```

Answers:

```
Basic        Current
Variables    Value
2            4
1            6
5            12
```

```
Dual
Variables    Value
3            1
4            2
5            0
```

Optimum Objective Function Value =   *40   −7 = 33
in 3 Tableaus

```
**********************************************************************
```

DO YOU WISH TO RUN THIS PROGRAM AGAIN? NO

```
$ LINDO
 LINDO (UC 1 APRIL 82)
:MAX 2X1 + 5X2 + 8X3      * Subtract 10 from the final answer
?ST
?X1 + X2 + 4X3 <36
?X1 + 2X2 + 3X3 < 42
?END



:LOOK ALL

MAX      2 X1 + 5 X2 + 8 X3
SUBJECT TO
    2)      X1 +  X2 + 4 X3 <=    36
    3)      X1 + 2 X2 + 3 X3 <=    42
END



:TABL

THE TABLEAU
ROW  (BASIS)         X1          X2         X3  SLK    2  SLK     3

  1 ART            -2.000      -5.000     -8.000    0.000     0.000       0.000

  2 SLK     2       1.000       1.000      4.000    1.000     0.000      36.000

  3 SLK     3       1.000       2.000      3.000    0.000     1.000      42.000



:GO
    LP OPTIMUM FOUND  AT STEP      2

           OBJECTIVE FUNCTION VALUE

  1)       108.000000     —      10      = 98

VARIABLE          VALUE          REDUCED COST
      X1        0.000000           0.600000
      X2       12.000000           0.000000
      X3        6.000000           0.000000


ROW          SLACK OR SURPLUS      DUAL PRICES
   2)            0.000000           0.200000
   3)            0.000000           2.400000

NO. ITERATIONS=         2

  DO RANGE(SENSITIVITY) ANALYSIS?
?N
:QUIT
FORTRAN STOP
```

```
$ LINDO
 LINDO (UC 1 APRIL 82)
:MAX 10X1 + 8X2 + 14X3
?ST
?2X1 + 2X2 + 5X3 < 40
?3X1 + X2 + 3X3 < 27
?X1 + 4X2 + 2X3 < 26
?END


:LOOK ALL

MAX      10 X1 + 8 X2 + 14 X3
SUBJECT TO
   2)    2 X1 + 2 X2 + 5 X3 <=    40
   3)    3 X1 +   X2 + 3 X3 <=  27
   4)     X1 + 4 X2 + 2 X3 <=  26
END


:GO
    LP OPTIMUM FOUND  AT STEP      3

         OBJECTIVE FUNCTION VALUE

  1)       128.000000

VARIABLE         VALUE          REDUCED COST
       X1        2.000000          0.000000
       X2        3.000000          0.000000
       X3        6.000000          0.000000


ROW          SLACK OR SURPLUS      DUAL PRICES
   2)             0.000000          1.034483
   3)             0.000000          2.344828
   4)             0.000000          0.896552

NO. ITERATIONS=        3

 DO RANGE(SENSITIVITY) ANALYSIS?
?NO
```

```
:MAX 30X1A + 60X1F + 100X1S + 75X1T + 5X2A + 80X2F + 65X2S + 110X2T
?ST
?X1A + X2A < 5000
?X1F + X2F < 3000
?X1S + X2F < 2000
?X1T + X2T < 1000
?4X1A + 4X1F + 3X1S < 2100
?8X1A + 10X1F + 6X1S + 7X1T < 14000
?X2A + 5X2S + 5X2T < 1500
?3X2A + 8X2F + 6X2T < 2400
?X2A + X2F + 11X2S + 20X2T < 2500
?END


:LOOK ALL

MAX       30 X1A + 60 X1F + 100 X1S + 75 X1T + 5 X2A + 80 X2F
      + 65 X2S + 110 X2T
SUBJECT TO
    2)       X1A +   X2A <=     5000
    3)       X1F +   X2F <=     3000
    4)       X1S +   X2F <=     2000
    5)       X1T +   X2T <=     1000
    6)     4 X1A + 4 X1F + 3 X1S <=     2100
    7)     8 X1A + 10 X1F + 6 X1S + 7 X1T <=     14000
    8)       X2A + 5 X2S + 5 X2T <=     1500
    9)     3 X2A + 8 X2F + 6 X2T <=     2400
   10)       X2A +   X2F + 11 X2S + 20 X2T <=     2500
END


:GO
    LP OPTIMUM FOUND   AT STEP        5

         OBJECTIVE FUNCTION VALUE

  1)          182000.000

VARIABLE           VALUE            REDUCED COST
       X1A         0.000000         103.333328
       X1F         0.000000          73.333328
       X1S       700.000000           0.000000
       X1T      1000.000000           0.000000
       X2A         0.000000          28.693184
       X2F       300.000000           0.000000
       X2S       200.000000           0.000000
       X2T         0.000000         138.750015
```

```
ROW          SLACK OR SURPLUS      DUAL PRICES
   2)          5000.000000           0.000000
   3)          2700.000000           0.000000
   4)          1000.000000           0.000000
   5)             0.000000          75.000000
   6)             0.000000          33.333332
   7)          2800.000000           0.000000
   8)           500.000000           0.000000
   9)             0.000000           9.261364
  10)             0.000000           5.909091

NO. ITERATIONS=        5

 DO RANGE(SENSITIVITY) ANALYSIS?
?N
```

6-2 #1

```
:LOOK ALL

MIN     5 X1 + 7 X2
SUBJECT TO
   2)     2 X1 + 3 X2 >=    12
   3)     5 X1 +   X2 >=    17
END


:GO
   LP OPTIMUM FOUND   AT STEP        3

           OBJECTIVE FUNCTION VALUE

  1)         29.0000000

VARIABLE           VALUE          REDUCED COST
       X1         3.000000           0.000000
       X2         2.000000           0.000000


ROW          SLACK OR SURPLUS      DUAL PRICES
   2)             0.000000          -2.307692
   3)             0.000000          -0.076923

NO. ITERATIONS=        3

 DO RANGE(SENSITIVITY) ANALYSIS?
?N
```

6-2 #5

:<u>LOOK ALL</u>

```
MIN     5 X1 + 2 X2 + 6 X3     * add 8 to the final answer
SUBJECT TO
   2)     2 X1 + 2 X2 + 5 X3 >=   30
   3)     3 X1 +   X2 + 3 X3 >=   27
END
```

:<u>GO</u>

LP OPTIMUM FOUND AT STEP   4

OBJECTIVE FUNCTION VALUE

1)   48.0000000   + 8 = 56

VARIABLE	VALUE	REDUCED COST
X1	6.000000	0.000000
X2	9.000000	0.000000
X3	0.000000	0.250000

ROW	SLACK OR SURPLUS	DUAL PRICES
2)	0.000000	-0.250000
3)	0.000000	-1.500000

NO. ITERATIONS=   4

DO RANGE(SENSITIVITY) ANALYSIS?
?<u>N</u>

6-2 #9

:<u>LOOK ALL</u>

```
MIN     1.4 X1 +   X2 + 1.2 X3
SUBJECT TO
   2)      X1 + 2 X2 + 4 X3 >=   29
   3)    3 X1 + 2 X2 +   X3 >=   23
   4)   10 X1 + 4 X2 + 3 X3 >=   62
END
```

:<u>GO</u>

LP OPTIMUM FOUND AT STEP   3

OBJECTIVE FUNCTION VALUE

1)   14.0000000   thousand

VARIABLE	VALUE	REDUCED COST
X1	3.000000	0.000000
X2	5.000000	0.000000
X3	4.000000	0.000000

```
ROW          SLACK OR SURPLUS      DUAL PRICES
   2)               0.000000        -0.207143
   3)               0.000000        -0.135714
   4)               0.000000        -0.078571

NO. ITERATIONS=          3

 DO RANGE(SENSITIVITY) ANALYSIS?
?NO
```

6-2 #11

```
:LOOK ALL

MIN      X1 +  X2 +  X3 +  X4 +  X5 +  X6
SUBJECT TO
   2)      X1 +  X6  >=     12
   3)      X1 +  X2  >=     14
   4)      X2 +  X3  >=     16
   5)      X3 +  X4  >=     10
   6)      X4 +  X5  >=      6
   7)      X5 +  X6  >=      9
END


:GO
    LP OPTIMUM FOUND   AT STEP       6

         OBJECTIVE FUNCTION VALUE

  1)       34.0000000

VARIABLE          VALUE          REDUCED COST
      X1        9.000000           0.000000
      X2        6.000000           0.000000
      X3       10.000000           0.000000
      X4        0.000000           0.000000
      X5        6.000000           0.000000
      X6        3.000000           0.000000


ROW          SLACK OR SURPLUS      DUAL PRICES
   2)               0.000000        -1.000000
   3)               1.000000         0.000000
   4)               0.000000        -1.000000
   5)               0.000000         0.000000
   6)               0.000000        -1.000000
   7)               0.000000         0.000000

NO. ITERATIONS=          6

 DO RANGE(SENSITIVITY) ANALYSIS?
?NO
```

```
:LOOK ALL

MAX      3 X1 + 5 X2
SUBJECT TO
   2)      X1 +  X2 <=   12
   3)    2 X1 + 4 X2 >=   36
   4)     X1 - 2 X2 >=   0
END


:GO


    NO FEASIBLE SOLUTION AT STEP     2
      SUM OF INFEASIBILITIES=  4.00000
VIOLATED ROWS HAVE NEGATIVE SLACK,
OR(EQUALITY ROWS) NONZERO SLACKS.
ROWS CONTRIBUTING TO INFEASIBILITY HAVE
NONZERO DUAL PRICE.

        OBJECTIVE FUNCTION VALUE

  1)        44.0000000

VARIABLE           VALUE          REDUCED COST
        X1          8.000000          0.000000
        X2          4.000000          0.000000


ROW           SLACK OR SURPLUS      DUAL PRICES
   2)           0.000000             2.666667
   3)          -4.000000            -1.000000
   4)           0.000000            -0.666667

NO. ITERATIONS=        2
:TABL

THE TABLEAU
ROW (BASIS)        X1        X2 SLK   2 SLK   3 SLK   4

  1 ART          0.000     0.000     3.667     0.000     0.667    44.000

  2      X1      1.000     0.000     0.667     0.000    -0.333     8.000

  3 ART          0.000     0.000    -2.667    -1.000    -0.667     4.000

  4      X2      0.000     1.000     0.333     0.000     0.333     4.000
```

:LOOK ALL

```
MIN      6 X1 + 2 X2
SUBJECT TO
    2)      X1 +  X2 <=    10
    3)     3 X1 +  X2 =      18
    4)      X2 =      9
END
```


:GO

        NO FEASIBLE SOLUTION AT STEP   2
           SUM OF INFEASIBILITIES= 6.00000
VIOLATED ROWS HAVE NEGATIVE SLACK,
OR(EQUALITY ROWS) NONZERO SLACKS.
ROWS CONTRIBUTING TO INFEASIBILITY HAVE
NONZERO DUAL PRICE.

            OBJECTIVE FUNCTION VALUE

    1)   24.0000000

VARIABLE	VALUE	REDUCED COST
X1	1.000000	0.000000
X2	9.000000	0.000000

ROW	SLACK OR SURPLUS	DUAL PRICES
2)	0.000000	3.000000
3)	6.000000	-1.000000
4)	0.000000	-2.000000

NO. ITERATIONS=   2

:TABL

THE TABLEAU

ROW	(BASIS)	X1	X2	SLK	2
1	ART	0.000	0.000	-6.000	-24.000
2	X1	1.000	0.000	1.000	1.000
3	ART	0.000	0.000	-3.000	6.000
4	X2	0.000	1.000	0.000	9.000

:LOOK ALL

```
MIN      8 X1 + 10 X2
SUBJECT TO
    2)      X2 <=    8
    3)    4 X1 + 5 X2 >=    30
    4)    3 X1 + 2 X2 >=    19
END
```

:GO
LP OPTIMUM FOUND AT STEP   3

OBJECTIVE FUNCTION VALUE

1)   60.0000000   * also optimal @(15/2, 0), no line segment joining (5, 2) and (15/2, 0)

VARIABLE	VALUE	REDUCED COST
X1	5.000000	0.000000
X2	2.000000	0.000000

ROW	SLACK OR SURPLUS	DUAL PRICES
2)	6.000000	0.000000
3)	0.000000	-2.000000
4)	0.000000	0.000000

NO. ITERATIONS=   3

 DO RANGE(SENSITIVITY) ANALYSIS?
?NO

:LOOK ALL

```
MAX       X1 + 5 X2
SUBJECT TO
    2)      X1 <=    8
    3)      X1 +  X2 >=    12
    4)  -   X1 +  X2 >=    0
END
```

:GO
 UNBOUNDED SOLUTION
 UNBOUNDED VARIABLES ARE:

```
      X2
SLK    4
```

OBJECTIVE FUNCTION VALUE

1)   60.0000000

```
VARIABLE              VALUE           REDUCED COST
       X1           0.000000            4.000000
       X2          12.000000            0.000000


ROW            SLACK OR SURPLUS      DUAL PRICES
    2)             8.000000            0.000000
    3)             0.000000            5.000000
    4)            12.000000            0.000000

NO. ITERATIONS=          1


:LOOK ALL

MIN        X1 + 5 X2
SUBJECT TO
   2)        X1 <=    8
   3)        X1 +  X2 >=     12
   4)  -  X1 +  X2 >=     0
END


:GO
    LP OPTIMUM FOUND  AT STEP        1

        OBJECTIVE FUNCTION VALUE

   1)        36.0000000

VARIABLE              VALUE           REDUCED COST
       X1           6.000000            0.000000
       X2           6.000000            0.000000


ROW            SLACK OR SURPLUS      DUAL PRICES
    2)             2.000000            0.000000
    3)             0.000000           -3.000000
    4)             0.000000           -2.000000

NO. ITERATIONS=          1

 DO RANGE(SENSITIVITY) ANALYSIS?


6-3  #17

:LOOK ALL

MAX        5 X1 + 2 X2
SUBJECT TO
   2)        X1 + 3 X2 <=     24
   3)        X1 +  X2 >=    10
   4)      2 X1 +  X2 =      18
END
```

```
:GO
    LP OPTIMUM FOUND  AT STEP    2

        OBJECTIVE FUNCTION VALUE

  1)       44.0000000

VARIABLE        VALUE          REDUCED COST
     X1       8.000000         0.000000
     X2       2.000000         0.000000


ROW          SLACK OR SURPLUS      DUAL PRICES
   2)           10.000000         0.000000
   3)            0.000000        -1.000000
   4)            0.000000         3.000000

NO. ITERATIONS=        2

 DO RANGE(SENSITIVITY) ANALYSIS?
?NO

:LOOK ALL

MIN      5 X1 + 2 X2
SUBJECT TO
   2)      X1 + 3 X2 <=    24
   3)      X1 +   X2 >=    10
   4)    2 X1 +   X2 =     18
END


:GO
     LP OPTIMUM FOUND  AT STEP    1

        OBJECTIVE FUNCTION VALUE

  1)       42.0000000

VARIABLE        VALUE          REDUCED COST
     X1       6.000000         0.000000
     X2       6.000000         0.000000


ROW          SLACK OR SURPLUS      DUAL PRICES
   2)            0.000000         0.200000
   3)            2.000000         0.000000
   4)            0.000000        -2.600000

NO. ITERATIONS=        1

 DO RANGE(SENSITIVITY) ANALYSIS?
```

a) $24 - \infty$ to $24 + 30$; $-\infty$ to 54

$18 - 5$ to $18 + \infty$; 13 to ∞

$52 - \infty$ to $52 + 20$; $-\infty$ to 72

b)

$$\text{c.v.} = \begin{bmatrix} 18 \\ 20 \\ 48 \\ \hline 0 \end{bmatrix} \qquad \text{c.v.} = 18a_1 + 20a_2 + 48a_3 + 0 \cdot \theta$$

$$\text{c.v.} = 18 \begin{bmatrix} 0 \\ 0 \\ -1 \\ \hline 0 \end{bmatrix} + 20 \begin{bmatrix} 1 \\ 4 \\ 3 \\ \hline 2 \end{bmatrix} + 48 \begin{bmatrix} 0 \\ -1 \\ 0 \\ \hline 0 \end{bmatrix} + 0 \begin{bmatrix} 0 \\ 0 \\ 0 \\ \hline 1 \end{bmatrix}$$

$$\text{c.v.} = \begin{bmatrix} 20 \\ 32 \\ 42 \\ \hline 40 \end{bmatrix} \qquad \min = 40 \qquad x_1 = 0, x_2 = 20 \qquad p_1 = 42, p_2 = 0, p_3 = 32$$

6-4 #1c)

```
:look all

MIN       6 X1 + 2 X2
SUBJECT TO
    2)     X1 + 3 X2 >=    24
    3)    2 X1 +   X2 >=    18
    4)    3 X1 + 4 X2 >=     52
END


:alt
ROW:
?4
VAR:
?x2
NEW COEFFICIENT:
?3
:alt
ROW:
?4
VAR:
?rhs
NEW COEFFICIENT:
?48
:look all


MIN       6 X1 + 2 X2
SUBJECT TO
    2)     X1 + 3 X2 >=    24
    3)    2 X1 +   X2 >=    18
    4)    3 X1 + 3 X2 >=     48
END
```

:go
LP OPTIMUM FOUND AT STEP   3

OBJECTIVE FUNCTION VALUE

1)   36.0000000

VARIABLE	VALUE	REDUCED COST
X1	0.000000	2.000000
X2	18.000000	0.000000

ROW	SLACK OR SURPLUS	DUAL PRICES
2)	30.000000	0.000000
3)	0.000000	-2.000000
4)	6.000000	0.000000

NO. ITERATIONS=   3

DO RANGE(SENSITIVITY) ANALYSIS?
?n

d) $3x_1 + 4x_2 = 52 \rightarrow 3x_1 + 2x_2 = 48$

$x_1 = 0, x_2 = 18$

$3(0) + 2(18) - s_3 = 48 \qquad s_3 = -12$

The surplus variable on constraint #3 is -12.

Thus, the solution is not optimal.

6-4 #5

a) $6 - 3$ to $6 + 6$; 3 to 12

$0 - \infty$ to $0 + 12$; $-\infty$ to 12

$12 - 6$ to $12 + 12$; 6 to 24

b)

$$\text{c.v.} = \begin{bmatrix} 8 \\ 4 \\ 16 \\ \overline{0} \end{bmatrix} \qquad \text{c.v.} = 8s_1 + 4a_2 + 16a_3 + 0 \cdot \theta$$

$$\text{c.v.} = 8\begin{bmatrix} 4 \\ 1 \\ -1 \\ \overline{-3} \end{bmatrix} + 4\begin{bmatrix} -1 \\ 0 \\ 0 \\ \overline{0} \end{bmatrix} + 16\begin{bmatrix} -1 \\ 0 \\ 1 \\ \overline{6} \end{bmatrix} + 0\begin{bmatrix} 0 \\ 0 \\ 0 \\ \overline{1} \end{bmatrix}$$

$$\text{c.v.} = \begin{bmatrix} 12 \\ 8 \\ 8 \\ \overline{72} \end{bmatrix} \qquad \text{min} = 72, x_1 = 8, x_2 = 8$$

$s_1 = 0, p_2 = 12, p_3 = 0$

c) (see next page)

d) $1/2x_1 + x_2 \leq 9 \rightarrow x_1 + 2x_2 \leq 18$ still optimal with 54 @(6, 6) but the column entries are now 1/2 what they were before because of the relationship between the two respective slack variables.

111

```
:LOOK ALL

MIN      6 X1 + 3 X2
SUBJECT TO
   2)      X2 <=    6
   3)  -  X1 + 3 X2 >=    0
   4)      X1 +  X2 =    12
END

:ALT
ROW:
?2
VAR:
?X1
VARIABLE NOT IN THIS ROW.  WANT IT INCLUDED?
?YES
NEW COEFFICIENT:
?.5
:ALT
ROW:
?2
VAR:
?RHS
NEW COEFFICIENT:
?9
:GO
     LP OPTIMUM FOUND   AT STEP        2

            OBJECTIVE FUNCTION VALUE

   1)        54.0000000


VARIABLE          VALUE            REDUCED COST
       X1        6.000000           0.000000
       X2        6.000000           0.000000

ROW           SLACK OR SURPLUS     DUAL PRICES
   2)             0.000000          6.000000
   3)            12.000000          0.000000
   4)             0.000000         -9.000000

NO. ITERATIONS=         2

 DO RANGE(SENSITIVITY) ANALYSIS?
?N
```

6-4 # 9

a) optimal $= -75 + 852 = 777$ @(0, 0, 15)

b) $40 - 4.5$ to $40 + \infty$; 35.5 to ∞

c) $60 - 1.5$ to $60 + \infty$; 58.5 to ∞

d) $35 - \infty$ to $35 + 1$; $-\infty$ to 36

e) $14 - 2.5$ to $14 + \infty$; 11.5 to ∞

```
$ LINDO
 LINDO (UC 1 APRIL 82)
:MAX
?2X1 + X2
?ST
?X1 + X2 < 5
?2X1 + 3X2 < 12
?END


:LOOK ALL

MAX      2 X1 +  X2
SUBJECT TO
    2)     X1 +  X2 <=   5
    3)    2 X1 + 3 X2 <=    12
END


:TABL

THE TABLEAU
ROW  (BASIS)        X1        X2  SLK    2  SLK    3

  1 ART          -2.000    -1.000    0.000    0.000    0.000

  2 SLK     2     1.000     1.000    1.000    0.000    5.000

  3 SLK     3     2.000     3.000    0.000    1.000   12.000



:PIV
      X1 ENTERS AT VALUE   5.0000       IN ROW    2 OBJ. VALUE=   10.000

:TABL

THE TABLEAU
ROW  (BASIS)        X1        X2  SLK    2  SLK    3

  1 ART           0.000     1.000    2.000    0.000   10.000

  2       X1      1.000     1.000    1.000    0.000    5.000

  3 SLK     3     0.000     1.000   -2.000    1.000    2.000


:PIV
      LP OPTIMUM FOUND   AT STEP       1

            OBJECTIVE FUNCTION VALUE

   1)        10.0000000
```

113

```
VARIABLE          VALUE        REDUCED COST
       X1        5.000000        0.000000
       X2        0.000000        1.000000


ROW          SLACK OR SURPLUS     DUAL PRICES
    2)           0.000000         2.000000
    3)           2.000000         0.000000

NO. ITERATIONS=          1
```

Review #1 using P1P2

```
$ RUN LIB:P1P2

PHASE I  -  PHASE II ALGORITHM


Do you want all the tableaus printed (Y/N) ? Y


Enter '1' for MAX, '-1' for MIN ? 1


Enter number of restraints, number of variables ? 2,2
Enter number of <=, number of >=, number of =? 2,0,0


Enter coefficients and constants of <= restraints
Restraint  1    ? 1,1,5

Restraint  2    ? 2,3,12



Enter the objective function coefficients
? 2,1


*********************************************************************************

        Decision Variables  1    through  2
          Slack Variables   3    through  4


Simplex Tableau Number   1

       1.00      1.00      1.00      0.00      5.00

       2.00      3.00      0.00      1.00     12.00

      -2.00     -1.00      0.00      0.00      0.00
```

```
Basic          Current
Variables      Value
3              5
4              12


****************************************************************************

Simplex Tableau Number  2

      1.00          1.00          1.00          0.00          5.00

      0.00          1.00         -2.00          1.00          2.00

      0.00          1.00          2.00          0.00         10.00

Basic          Current
Variables      Value
1              5
4              2


****************************************************************************

Answers:

Basic          Current
Variables      Value
1              5
4              2


Dual
Variables      Value
3              2
4              0


Optimum Objective Function Value =  10
in 2 Tableaus


****************************************************************************

DO YOU WISH TO RUN THIS PROGRAM AGAIN? N
```

Review #3

```
:LOOK ALL

MAX    - 2 X1 + 7 X2
SUBJECT TO
    2)      X1 +  X2 <=   13
    3)      X1 + 2 X2 <=   22
    4)    2 X1 +  X2 <=   20
END


:GO
    LP OPTIMUM FOUND  AT STEP      1

         OBJECTIVE FUNCTION VALUE

  1)       77.0000000

VARIABLE        VALUE          REDUCED COST
    X1        0.000000          5.500000
    X2       11.000000          0.000000


ROW        SLACK OR SURPLUS    DUAL PRICES
  2)             2.000000        0.000000
  3)             0.000000        3.500000
  4)             9.000000        0.000000

NO. ITERATIONS=        1

 DO RANGE(SENSITIVITY) ANALYSIS?
?NO

:QUIT
FORTRAN STOP
```

Review #5

```
:LOOK ALL

MAX    - 3 X1 + 10 X2
SUBJECT TO
    2)    3 X1 + 7 X2 <=   42
    3)      X1 + 5 X2 <=   22
    4)      X2 <=    3
END


:GO
    LP OPTIMUM FOUND  AT STEP      1

         OBJECTIVE FUNCTION VALUE

  1)       30.0000000
```

```
VARIABLE          VALUE              REDUCED COST
        X1        0.000000              3.000000
        X2        3.000000              0.000000


ROW           SLACK OR SURPLUS      DUAL PRICES
    2)            21.000000           0.000000
    3)             7.000000           0.000000
    4)             0.000000          10.000000

NO. ITERATIONS=          1

 DO RANGE(SENSITIVITY) ANALYSIS?
?NO
```

Review #7a)

7(MAX)

:LOOK ALL

```
MAX    - 3 X1 + 7 X2 +10
SUBJECT TO
    2)    2 X1 + 3 X2 <=    24
    3)    2 X1 -   X2 <=     8
    4)  - 2 X1 + 3 X2 <=    12
END
```

:GO
```
    LP OPTIMUM FOUND  AT STEP      2

        OBJECTIVE FUNCTION VALUE

  1)        33.0000000     +      10        =43

VARIABLE          VALUE              REDUCED COST
        X1        3.000000              0.000000
        X2        6.000000              0.000000


ROW           SLACK OR SURPLUS      DUAL PRICES
    2)             0.000000           0.416667
    3)             8.000000           0.000000
    4)             0.000000           1.916667

NO. ITERATIONS=          2

 DO RANGE(SENSITIVITY) ANALYSIS?
?NO
```

Review #7b)

7(MIN)

:<u>LOOK ALL</u>

```
MIN    - 3 X1 + 7 X2 +10
SUBJECT TO
    2)     2 X1 + 3 X2 <=    24
    3)     2 X1 -   X2 <=     8
    4)   - 2 X1 + 3 X2 <=    12
END
```

:<u>GO</u>

```
    LP OPTIMUM FOUND  AT STEP       1

            OBJECTIVE FUNCTION VALUE

  1)          -12.0000000      +      10            = -2

VARIABLE           VALUE           REDUCED COST
        X1       4.000000             0.000000
        X2       0.000000             5.500000


ROW           SLACK OR SURPLUS      DUAL PRICES
    2)           16.000000             0.000000
    3)            0.000000             1.500000
    4)           20.000000             0.000000

NO. ITERATIONS=           1

 DO RANGE(SENSITIVITY) ANALYSIS?
?NO
```

Review #9

:<u>LOOK ALL</u>

```
MAX      4 X1 + 3 X2 + 7 X3
SUBJECT TO
    2)     X1 +   X2 + 4 X3 <=    36
    3)    2 X1 +   X2 + 3 X3 <=    42
END
```

:<u>GO</u>

```
    LP OPTIMUM FOUND  AT STEP       3

            OBJECTIVE FUNCTION VALUE

  1)        114.000000
```

```
VARIABLE            VALUE           REDUCED COST
        X1          6.000000            0.000000
        X2         30.000000            0.000000
        X3          0.000000            4.000000


ROW          SLACK OR SURPLUS      DUAL PRICES
    2)               0.000000         2.000000
    3)               0.000000         1.000000

NO. ITERATIONS=          3

  DO RANGE(SENSITIVITY) ANALYSIS?

?NO
```

Review #11

```
:LOOK ALL

MAX      3 X1 + 5 X2 + 8 X3
SUBJECT TO
    2)      X1 + 2 X2 + 3 X3 <=    36
    3)      X1 + 3 X2 <=    18
END


:GO
    LP OPTIMUM FOUND   AT STEP       2

        OBJECTIVE FUNCTION VALUE

  1)         102.000000

VARIABLE            VALUE           REDUCED COST
        X1         18.000000            0.000000
        X2          0.000000            1.333333
        X3          6.000000            0.000000


ROW          SLACK OR SURPLUS      DUAL PRICES
    2)               0.000000         2.666667
    3)               0.000000         0.333333

NO. ITERATIONS=          2

  DO RANGE(SENSITIVITY) ANALYSIS?
?NO
```

Review #13

```
:LOOK ALL

MAX      3 X1 + 5 X2 - 4 X3
SUBJECT TO
    2)     X1 + 2 X2 + 3 X3 <=    24
    3)    2 X1 + 2 X2 +   X3 <=    18
    4)      X3 <=    3
END


:GO
    LP OPTIMUM FOUND  AT STEP      1

          OBJECTIVE FUNCTION VALUE

    1)         45.0000000

VARIABLE         VALUE          REDUCED COST
        X1      0.000000          2.000000
        X2      9.000000          0.000000
        X3      0.000000          6.500000


ROW           SLACK OR SURPLUS     DUAL PRICES
    2)            6.000000          0.000000
    3)            0.000000          2.500000
    4)            3.000000          0.000000

NO. ITERATIONS=          1

 DO RANGE(SENSITIVITY) ANALYSIS?
?NO
```

Review #15

```
:LOOK ALL

MIN      2 X1 + 5 X2 + 6 X3
SUBJECT TO
    2)    4 X1 + 3 X2 + 2 X3 >=    48
    3)     X1 + 4 X2 + 8 X3 >=    40
    4)    2 X1 + 9 X2 + 7 X3 >=    66
END


:GO
    LP OPTIMUM FOUND  AT STEP      3

          OBJECTIVE FUNCTION VALUE

    1)         48.0000000
```

```
VARIABLE          VALUE              REDUCED COST
       X1       8.000000             0.000000
       X2       4.000000             0.000000
       X3       2.000000             0.000000


ROW         SLACK OR SURPLUS      DUAL PRICES
   2)            0.000000           .261701
   3)            0.000000          -0.448980
   4)            0.000000          -0.272109

NO. ITERATIONS=        3

 DO RANGE(SENSITIVITY) ANALYSIS?
?NO
```

Review #17

```
:LOOK ALL

MAX      10 X1 + 6 X2 + 12 X3
SUBJECT TO
   2)      X1 +   X2 + 4 X3 <=     42
   3)      X1 + 2 X2 + 3 X3 <=     40
   4)    2 X1 +   X2 + 2 X3 <=     30
   5)    3 X1 + 4 X2 +   X3 <=     44
END


:GO
    LP OPTIMUM FOUND   AT STEP        3

        OBJECTIVE FUNCTION VALUE

   1)         172.000000

VARIABLE          VALUE              REDUCED COST
       X1       4.000000             0.000000
       X2       6.000000             0.000000
       X3       8.000000             0.000000


ROW         SLACK OR SURPLUS      DUAL PRICES
   2)            0.000000           0.823529
   3)            0.000000           0.000000
   4)            0.000000           4.235294
   5)            0.000000           0.235294

NO. ITERATIONS=        3

 DO RANGE(SENSITIVITY) ANALYSIS?
?NO
```

:LOOK ALL

```
MIN      5.75 X1 + 4.75 X2 + 3.75 X3
SUBJECT TO
    2)      X1 +  X2 +  X3 <=    10000
    3)      X1 +  X2 +  X3 >=    6000
    4)      X3 <=    2000
    5)      X1 >=    1000
    6)      X2 >=    1000
    7)      X3 >=    1000
    8)     0.25 X1 + 0.25 X2 - 0.75 X3 >=    0
END
```

:GO

LP OPTIMUM FOUND   AT STEP   5

OBJECTIVE FUNCTION VALUE

1)   28000.0000

VARIABLE	VALUE	REDUCED COST
X1	1000.000000	0.000000
X2	3500.000000	0.000000
X3	1500.000000	0.000000

ROW	SLACK OR SURPLUS	DUAL PRICES
2)	4000.000000	0.000000
3)	0.000000	-4.500000
4)	500.000000	0.000000
5)	0.000000	-1.000000
6)	2500.000000	0.000000
7)	500.000000	0.000000
8)	0.000000	-1.000000

NO. ITERATIONS=   5

DO RANGE(SENSITIVITY) ANALYSIS?
?NO

```
:look all

MAX      0.08 S1 + 0.09 S2 + 0.07 S3 + 0.1 B1 + 0.11 B2 + 0.06 N
SUBJECT TO
    2)     S1 +   S2 +   S3 - 0.4 B1 - 0.4 B2 <=    0
    3)     S1 +   S2 +   S3 +  B1 +  B2 +  N <=    0.75
    4)     S1 +   S2 +   S3 <=   0.35
    5)     S1 <=   0.3
    6)     S2 <=   0.3
    7)     S3 <=   0.3
    8)     B1 <=   0.3
    9)     B2 <=   0.3
END



:GO
    LP OPTIMUM FOUND   AT STEP      3

          OBJECTIVE FUNCTION VALUE

    1)       0.764999986E-01

VARIABLE          VALUE            REDUCED COST
        S1      0.000000             0.010000
        S2      0.150000             0.000000
        S3      0.000000             0.020000
        B1      0.300000             0.000000
        B2      0.300000             0.000000
         N      0.000000             0.030000


ROW           SLACK OR SURPLUS     DUAL PRICES
    2)            0.090000            0.000000
    3)            0.000000            0.090000
    4)            0.200000            0.000000
    5)            0.300000            0.000000
    6)            0.150000            0.000000
    7)            0.300000            0.000000
    8)            0.000000            0.010000
    9)            0.000000            0.020000

NO. ITERATIONS=         3

   DO RANGE(SENSITIVITY) ANALYSIS?
?NO
```

```
:LOOK ALL

MIN      5 X1 +  X2
SUBJECT TO
    2)     2 X1 + 3 X2 >=    12
    3)     5 X1 +  X2 >=    17
END


:GO
    LP OPTIMUM FOUND  AT STEP      2

            OBJECTIVE FUNCTION VALUE

    1)          17.0000000

VARIABLE          VALUE           REDUCED COST
      X1          0.000000          0.000000
      X2         17.000000          0.000000


ROW          SLACK OR SURPLUS      DUAL PRICES
    2)          39.000000          0.000000
    3)           0.000000         -1.000000

NO. ITERATIONS=          2

  DO RANGE(SENSITIVITY) ANALYSIS?
?NO
```

Line segment (0, 17) — (3, 2)

Review #25

```
:LOOK ALL

MIN      6 X1 + 8 X2
SUBJECT TO
    2)      X1 + 3 X2 >=    24
    3)     2 X1 +  X2 >=    18
    4)     3 X1 + 4 X2 >=    52
END


:GO
    LP OPTIMUM FOUND  AT STEP      3

            OBJECTIVE FUNCTION VALUE

    1)         104.000000

VARIABLE          VALUE           REDUCED COST
      X1          4.000000          0.000000
      X2         10.000000          0.000000
```

```
ROW          SLACK OR SURPLUS      DUAL PRICES
   2)             10.000000           0.000000
   3)              0.000000           0.000000
   4)              0.000000          -2.000000

NO. ITERATIONS=          3

 DO RANGE(SENSITIVITY) ANALYSIS?
?NO
```

Line segment (4, 10) − (12, 4)

Review #27

```
:LOOK ALL

MIN      3 X1 + 4 X2 + 6 X3 +10
SUBJECT TO
   2)      X1 +   X2 + 4 X3 >=   36
   3)    3 X1 + 2 X2 + 2 X3 >=   48
END
```

```
:GO
    LP OPTIMUM FOUND  AT STEP       2

          OBJECTIVE FUNCTION VALUE

   1)        72.0000000     +      10          =82

VARIABLE          VALUE          REDUCED COST
        X1      12.000000          0.000000
        X2       0.000000          1.600000
        X3       6.000000          0.000000


ROW          SLACK OR SURPLUS      DUAL PRICES
   2)              0.000000         -1.200000
   3)              0.000000         -0.600000

NO. ITERATIONS=          2

 DO RANGE(SENSITIVITY) ANALYSIS?
?NO
```

Review #29a)

```
:LOOK ALL

MAX      4 X1 + 6 X2 + 5 X3
SUBJECT TO
   2)      X1 + 2 X2 + 3 X3 <=   18
   3)      X1 +   X2 +   X3 >=   12
END
```

125

```
:GO
    LP OPTIMUM FOUND  AT STEP      3

              OBJECTIVE FUNCTION VALUE

  1)        72.0000000

VARIABLE            VALUE          REDUCED COST
        X1       18.000000          0.000000
        X2        0.000000          2.000000
        X3        0.000000          7.000000


ROW          SLACK OR SURPLUS     DUAL PRICES
  2)              0.000000          4.000000
  3)              6.000000          0.000000

NO. ITERATIONS=          3

 DO RANGE(SENSITIVITY) ANALYSIS?
?NO
```

Review #29b)

```
:LOOK ALL

MIN      4 X1 + 6 X2 + 5 X3
SUBJECT TO
   2)      X1 + 2 X2 + 3 X3 <=   18
   3)      X1 +  X2 +  X3 >=   12
END


:GO
    LP OPTIMUM FOUND  AT STEP      1

              OBJECTIVE FUNCTION VALUE

  1)        48.0000000

VARIABLE            VALUE          REDUCED COST
        X1       12.000000          0.000000
        X2        0.000000          2.000000
        X3        0.000000          1.000000


ROW          SLACK OR SURPLUS     DUAL PRICES
  2)              6.000000          0.000000
  3)              0.000000         -4.000000

NO. ITERATIONS=          1

 DO RANGE(SENSITIVITY) ANALYSIS?
?NO
```

Review #31

```
:look all

MIN      1400 I + 1000 F + 1200 S
SUBJECT TO
    2)      I + 2 F + 4 S >=    29
    3)    3 I + 2 F +   S >=    23
    4)   10 I + 4 F + 3 S >=    62
    5)    4 I + 3 F + 2 S >=    35
END


:go
    LP OPTIMUM FOUND  AT STEP      5

          OBJECTIVE FUNCTION VALUE

  1)          14000.0000

VARIABLE          VALUE          REDUCED COST
       I         3.000000          0.000000
       F         5.000000          0.000000
       S         4.000000          0.000000


ROW          SLACK OR SURPLUS      DUAL PRICES
    2)          0.000000         -189.743591
    3)          0.000000            0.000000
    4)          0.000000          -82.051277
    5)          0.000000          -97.435898

NO. ITERATIONS=          5

 DO RANGE(SENSITIVITY) ANALYSIS?
?no
```

Review #33

```
:LOOK ALL

MAX      X1 + 7 X2
SUBJECT TO
    2)      X1 + 3 X2 <=    24
    3)      X1 +   X2 >=    10
    4)    2 X1 +   X2 =     18
    5)    5 X1 +   X2 =     20
END
```

:GO

     NO FEASIBLE SOLUTION AT STEP   2
         SUM OF INFEASIBILITIES= 6.00000
VIOLATED ROWS HAVE NEGATIVE SLACK,
OR(EQUALITY ROWS) NONZERO SLACKS.
ROWS CONTRIBUTING TO INFEASIBILITY HAVE
NONZERO DUAL PRICE.

          OBJECTIVE FUNCTION VALUE

   1)   52.5714302

VARIABLE   VALUE   REDUCED COST
       X1   2.571429   0.000000
       X2   7.142857   0.000000

ROW   SLACK OR SURPLUS   DUAL PRICES
   2)   0.000000   0.500000
   3)   -0.285714   -1.000000
   4)   5.714285   -1.000000
   5)   0.000000   0.500000

NO. ITERATIONS=   2

Review #35

:LOOK ALL

MIN   4 X1 + 5 X2
SUBJECT TO
   2)   X1 +   X2 <=   15
   3)   - X1 +   X2 >=   3
   4)   X1 >=   8
END

:GO

     NO FEASIBLE SOLUTION AT STEP   2
         SUM OF INFEASIBILITIES= 2.00000
VIOLATED ROWS HAVE NEGATIVE SLACK,
OR(EQUALITY ROWS) NONZERO SLACKS.
ROWS CONTRIBUTING TO INFEASIBILITY HAVE
NONZERO DUAL PRICE.

          OBJECTIVE FUNCTION VALUE

   1)   69.0000000

VARIABLE   VALUE   REDUCED COST
       X1   6.000000   0.000000
       X2   9.000000   0.000000

```
ROW             SLACK OR SURPLUS        DUAL PRICES
   2)                0.000000             0.500000
   3)                0.000000            -0.500000
   4)               -2.000000            -1.000000

NO. ITERATIONS=          2
```

Review #37

```
:LOOK ALL

MAX     5 X1 + 2 X2
SUBJECT TO
   2)     X1 + 3 X2 <=    24
   3)     X1 +   X2 >=    10
   4)   2 X1 +   X2 =     18
   5)     X2 =     6
END
```

```
:GO
     LP OPTIMUM FOUND   AT STEP      3

          OBJECTIVE FUNCTION VALUE

   1)        42.0000000

VARIABLE            VALUE        REDUCED COST
      X1          6.000000          0.000000
      X2          6.000000          0.000000


ROW             SLACK OR SURPLUS        DUAL PRICES
   2)                0.000000             0.000000
   3)                2.000000             0.000000
   4)                0.000000             2.500000
   5)                0.000000            -0.500000

NO. ITERATIONS=          3

  DO RANGE(SENSITIVITY) ANALYSIS?
?NO
```

Review #39

```
:LOOK ALL

MIN     2 X1 + 8 X2
SUBJECT TO
   2)     X2 <=    8
   3)   4 X1 + 5 X2 >=    30
   4)   3 X1 + 2 X2 >=    19
END
```

```
:GO
     LP OPTIMUM FOUND   AT STEP      2

          OBJECTIVE FUNCTION VALUE

  1)          15.0000000

VARIABLE           VALUE           REDUCED COST
        X1          7.500000           0.000000
        X2          0.000000           5.500000


ROW              SLACK OR SURPLUS      DUAL PRICES
   2)               8.000000            0.000000
   3)               0.000000           -0.500000
   4)               3.500000            0.000000

NO. ITERATIONS=           2

 DO RANGE(SENSITIVITY) ANALYSIS?
?NO
```

Review #41a)

41 MAX

```
:LOOK ALL

MAX      6 X1 + 2 X2
SUBJECT TO
   2)      X1 +  X2 <=   12
   3)     2 X1 + 4 X2 >=    36
END


:GO
     LP OPTIMUM FOUND  AT STEP     2

          OBJECTIVE FUNCTION VALUE

  1)          48.0000000

VARIABLE           VALUE           REDUCED COST
        X1          6.000000           0.000000
        X2          6.000000           0.000000


ROW              SLACK OR SURPLUS      DUAL PRICES
   2)               0.000000           10.000000
   3)               0.000000           -2.000000

NO. ITERATIONS=           2

 DO RANGE(SENSITIVITY) ANALYSIS?
?NO
```

Review #41b)

41 MIN

:<u>LOOK ALL</u>

```
MIN      6 X1 + 2 X2
SUBJECT TO
   2)      X1 +   X2 <=    12
   3)    2 X1 + 4 X2 >=    36
END
```

:<u>GO</u>
     LP OPTIMUM FOUND   AT STEP   1

            OBJECTIVE FUNCTION VALUE

   1)   18.0000000

VARIABLE	VALUE	REDUCED COST
X1	0.000000	5.000000
X2	9.000000	0.000000

ROW	SLACK OR SURPLUS	DUAL PRICES
2)	3.000000	0.000000
3)	0.000000	-0.500000

NO. ITERATIONS=   1

   DO RANGE(SENSITIVITY) ANALYSIS?
?<u>NO</u>

Review #43a)

43 MAX

:<u>LOOK ALL</u>

```
MAX      6 X1 + 2 X2
SUBJECT TO
   2)      X1 +   X2 <=    12
   3)    2 X1 + 4 X2 >=    36
   4)  - 2 X2 <=    0
END
```

:<u>GO</u>
     LP OPTIMUM FOUND   AT STEP   2

            OBJECTIVE FUNCTION VALUE

   1)   48.0000000

VARIABLE	VALUE	REDUCED COST
X1	6.000000	0.000000
X2	6.000000	0.000000

131

```
ROW             SLACK OR SURPLUS      DUAL PRICES
    2)               0.000000          10.000000
    3)               0.000000          -2.000000
    4)              12.000000           0.000000

NO. ITERATIONS=          2

  DO RANGE(SENSITIVITY) ANALYSIS?
?NO
```

Review #43b)

```
43 MIN

:LOOK ALL

MIN      6 X1 + 2 X2
SUBJECT TO
    2)     X1 +  X2 <=    12
    3)    2 X1 + 4 X2 >=    36
    4)  - 2 X2 <=    0
END

:GO
    LP OPTIMUM FOUND   AT STEP       1

         OBJECTIVE FUNCTION VALUE

  1)         18.0000000

VARIABLE          VALUE          REDUCED COST
       X1        0.000000          5.000000
       X2        9.000000          0.000000

ROW             SLACK OR SURPLUS      DUAL PRICES
    2)               3.000000          0.000000
    3)               0.000000         -0.500000
    4)              18.000000          0.000000

NO. ITERATIONS=          1

  DO RANGE(SENSITIVITY) ANALYSIS?
?NO
```

Review #45a)

```
45 MAX

:LOOK ALL

MAX      3 X1 + 4 X2
SUBJECT TO
    2)     X1 +  X2 <=    10
    3)    2 X1 +  X2 >=    12
    4)     X2 >=    4
END
```

```
:GO
     LP OPTIMUM FOUND   AT STEP        3

            OBJECTIVE FUNCTION VALUE

   1)          38.0000000

 VARIABLE             VALUE          REDUCED COST
        X1          2.000000           0.000000
        X2          8.000000           0.000000


 ROW            SLACK OR SURPLUS      DUAL PRICES
    2)             0.000000             5.000000
    3)             0.000000            -1.000000
    4)             4.000000             0.000000

 NO. ITERATIONS=          3

  DO RANGE(SENSITIVITY) ANALYSIS?
?NO
```

Review #45b)

45 MIN

```
:LOOK ALL

MIN      3 X1 + 4 X2
SUBJECT TO
    2)      X1 +  X2 <=    10
    3)     2 X1 +  X2 >=    12
    4)      X2 >=   4
END


:GO
     LP OPTIMUM FOUND   AT STEP        1

            OBJECTIVE FUNCTION VALUE

   1)          28.0000000

 VARIABLE             VALUE          REDUCED COST
        X1          4.000000           0.000000
        X2          4.000000           0.000000


 ROW            SLACK OR SURPLUS      DUAL PRICES
    2)             2.000000             0.000000
    3)             0.000000            -1.500000
    4)             0.000000            -2.500000

 NO. ITERATIONS=          1

  DO RANGE(SENSITIVITY) ANALYSIS?
?NO
```

47 MAX

:<u>LOOK ALL</u>

```
MAX       X1 + 2 X2
SUBJECT TO
   2)      X1 +  X2 <=    10
   3)     3 X1 +  X2 =     18
END
```

:<u>GO</u>

 LP OPTIMUM FOUND   AT STEP   2

          OBJECTIVE FUNCTION VALUE

  1)   15.9999990

VARIABLE	VALUE	REDUCED COST
X1	4.000000	0.000000
X2	6.000000	0.000000

ROW	SLACK OR SURPLUS	DUAL PRICES
2)	0.000000	2.500000
3)	0.000000	-0.500000

NO. ITERATIONS=   2

 DO RANGE(SENSITIVITY) ANALYSIS?
?<u>NO</u>

Review #47b)

47 MIN

:<u>LOOK ALL</u>

```
MIN       X1 + 2 X2
SUBJECT TO
   2)      X1 +  X2 <=    10
   3)     3 X1 +  X2 =     18
END
```

:<u>GO</u>

 LP OPTIMUM FOUND   AT STEP   1

          OBJECTIVE FUNCTION VALUE

  1)   6.00000000

VARIABLE	VALUE	REDUCED COST
X1	6.000000	0.000000
X2	0.000000	1.666667

```
ROW             SLACK OR SURPLUS      DUAL PRICES
   2)                 4.000000           0.000000
   3)                 0.000000          -0.333333

NO. ITERATIONS=              1

 DO RANGE(SENSITIVITY) ANALYSIS?
?NO
```

Review #49a)

```
49 MAX

:LOOK ALL.

MAX       5 X1 +   X2
SUBJECT TO
   2)      X2 <=    6
   3)  -  X1 + 3 X2 >=    0
   4)      X1 +  X2 =     12
END


:GO
    LP OPTIMUM FOUND   AT STEP        2

          OBJECTIVE FUNCTION VALUE

   1)         48.0000000

VARIABLE           VALUE        REDUCED COST
      X1          9.000000          0.000000
      X2          3.000000          0.000000


ROW             SLACK OR SURPLUS      DUAL PRICES
   2)                 3.000000           0.000000
   3)                 0.000000          -1.000000
   4)                 0.000000           4.000000

NO. ITERATIONS=              2

 DO RANGE(SENSITIVITY) ANALYSIS?
?NO
```

Review #49b)

```
49 MIN

:LOOK ALL

MIN       5 X1 +   X2
SUBJECT TO
   2)      X2 <=    6
   3)  -  X1 + 3 X2 >=    0
   4)      X1 +  X2 =     12
END
```

```
:GO
    LP OPTIMUM FOUND   AT STEP        1

            OBJECTIVE FUNCTION VALUE

    1)          36.0000000

VARIABLE            VALUE           REDUCED COST
        X1          6.000000           0.000000
        X2          6.000000           0.000000


ROW             SLACK OR SURPLUS     DUAL PRICES
    2)              0.000000          4.000000
    3)             12.000000          0.000000
    4)              0.000000         -5.000000

NO. ITERATIONS=          1

 DO RANGE(SENSITIVITY) ANALYSIS?
?NO
```

Review #51

max $\quad 4x_1 + 6x_2 + 5x_3 + 3s_1 - 2p_2$

$s_1 = 18 - x_1 - 2x_2 - 3x_3$

$p_2 = x_1 + x_2 + x_3 - 12$

$4x_1 + 6x_2 + 5x_3 + 3(18 - x_1 - 2x_2 - 3x_3) - 2(x_1 + x_2 + x_3 - 12)$

$-x_1 - 2x_2 - 7x_3 + 78$

```
:LOOK ALL

MAX    -  X1 - 2 X2 - 7 X3        + 78
SUBJECT TO
    2)      X1 + 2 X2 + 3 X3 <=    18
    3)      X1 +  X2 +  X3 >=    12
END


:GO
    LP OPTIMUM FOUND   AT STEP        1

            OBJECTIVE FUNCTION VALUE

    1)         -12.0000000      +      78       = 66

VARIABLE            VALUE           REDUCED COST
        X1         12.000000           0.000000
        X2          0.000000           1.000000
        X3          0.000000           6.000000
```

136

```
ROW            SLACK OR SURPLUS       DUAL PRICES
   2)              6.000000            0.000000
   3)              0.000000           -1.000000

NO. ITERATIONS=        1

 DO RANGE(SENSITIVITY) ANALYSIS?
?NO
```

Review #53

a)   24 − 7.5 to 24 + 15; 16.5 to 39

    18 − 7.5 to 18 + 15; 10.5 to 33

    3 − 3 to 3 + 3; 0 to 6

b)

$$\text{c.v.} = \begin{bmatrix} 27 \\ 15 \\ 6 \\ \hline 0 \end{bmatrix} \qquad \text{c.v.} = 27s_1 + 15s_2 + 6a_3 + 0 \cdot \theta$$

$$\text{c.v.} = 27\begin{bmatrix} \dfrac{2}{3} \\ \dfrac{-1}{3} \\ 0 \\ \dfrac{7}{3} \end{bmatrix} + 15\begin{bmatrix} \dfrac{-1}{3} \\ \dfrac{2}{3} \\ 0 \\ \dfrac{1}{3} \end{bmatrix} + 6\begin{bmatrix} \dfrac{-5}{3} \\ \dfrac{1}{3} \\ \dfrac{1}{-34} \\ \dfrac{}{3} \end{bmatrix} + 0\begin{bmatrix} 0 \\ 0 \\ 0 \\ 1 \end{bmatrix}$$

$$\text{c.v.} = \begin{bmatrix} 3 \\ 3 \\ 6 \\ \hline 0 \end{bmatrix} \qquad \begin{array}{l} \max = 0 \quad x_1 = 3, x_2 = 3, x_3 = 6 \\ s_1 = 0, s_2 = 0, p_3 = 0 \end{array}$$

Review #53c)

```
:LOOK ALL

MAX      3 X1 + 5 X2 − 4 X3
SUBJECT TO
   2)      X1 + 2 X2 + 3 X3 <=    24
   3)     2 X1 +  X2 +  X3 <=    18
   4)       X3 >=    3
END
```

```
:ALT
ROW:
?2
VAR:
?X3
NEW COEFFICIENT:
?4
:GO
      LP OPTIMUM FOUND  AT STEP      3

            OBJECTIVE FUNCTION VALUE

  1)        21.0000000

VARIABLE          VALUE          REDUCED COST
      X1          6.000000          0.000000
      X2          3.000000          0.000000
      X3          3.000000          0.000000


ROW          SLACK OR SURPLUS      DUAL PRICES
  2)              0.000000          2.333333
  3)              0.000000          0.333333
  4)              0.000000        -13.666666

NO. ITERATIONS=          3

 DO RANGE(SENSITIVITY) ANALYSIS?
?NO
```

d) $x_3 \geq 3 \;\rightarrow\; x_2$ to $x_3 \geq 3$

A negative number now exists in the objective function row.

Review #55

a) $5 - 1.67$ to $5 + 15$; 3.33 to 20

b) $6 - \infty$ to $6 + 1$; $-\infty$ to 7

c) $10 - 1.67$ to $10 + 5$; 8.33 to 15

d) $-\infty$ to 3; -3 to ∞

e) $-\infty$ to 1; -1 to ∞

CHAPTER 7
Problem Set 7-1

1. $4(4^3) = 4^{(1+3)} = 4^4 = 256$

4. $(8^{1/2})(2^{1/2}) = (4^{1/2})(2^{1/2})(2^{1/2}) = (2)(2^1) = 4$

7. $[(3^{-1})(3^{2/3})]^3 = (3^{-1/3})^3 = 3^{-1} = \frac{1}{3}$

10. $\left(\frac{1}{e}\right)^{-4} = e^4 = 54.59815$

13. $f(x) = 4^{-x}$

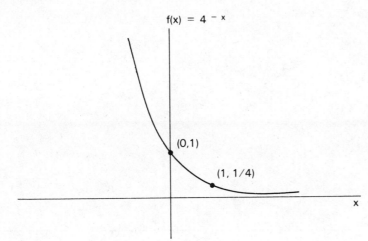

$4^0 = 1$

$4^{-1} = \frac{1}{4}$

$4^{-2} = \frac{1}{16}$

$4^{-(-1)} = 4$

17. $f(x) = 3^{-x^2}$

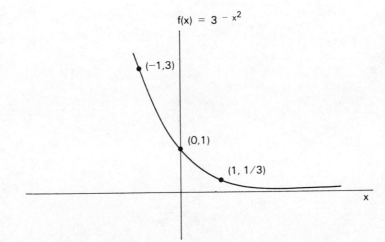

$3^{(0^2)} = 1$

$3^{(-1^2)} = 3^{-1} = \frac{1}{3}$

$3^{(-2^2)} = 3^{-4} = \frac{1}{81}$

$3^{(-[(-1)^2])} = 3^1 = 3$

Problem Set 7-2

1. $2^x = 3$

$\log 2^x = \log 3$

$x \log 2 = \log 3$

$x = \frac{\log 3}{\log 2} = 1.584963$

4. $10^x = 6$

     $\log 10^x = \log 6$

     $x \log 10 = \log 6$

         $x = \log 6 = 0.778151$

7. $1.06^x = 3$

     $\log 1.06^x = \log 3$

     $x \log 1.06 = \log 3$

         $x = \dfrac{\log 3}{\log 1.06} = 18.85418$

10. $10^x = 3$

     $\log 10^x = \log 3$

     $x \log 10 = \log 3$

         $x = \log 3 = 0.477121$

11. $\log 125 = \log 5^3 = 3 \log 5 = 2.09691$

17. $(0.5)^x = 8$

     $\log(0.5)^x = \log 8$

     $x \log(0.5) = \log 8$

         $x = \dfrac{\log 8}{\log(0.5)} = -3$

Problem Set 7-3

1. $\log_3 9 = 2$

4. $2^y = N$

7. $16^{1/2} = 4$

10. $\log_3\left(\dfrac{1}{9}\right) = -2$

13. $10^2 = 100$

17. $10^{(-0.3010)} = 0.5$

21. $\log_2 4 = x;\ 2^x = 4;\ x = 2$

25. $\log_4 2 = x;\ 4^x = 2;\ x = 0.5$

29. $10^{\log 5} = x;\ \log x = \log 5;\ x = 5$

33. $\ln\left(\dfrac{x^2 z^3}{y^2}\right)$

37. $\log_a(x/z) = \log_a x - \log_a z = 4.2 - (-1.2) = 5.4$

41. $\log_a \sqrt{xy} = \dfrac{1}{2}[\log_a x + \log_a y] = \dfrac{1}{2}(4.2 + 1.4) = \dfrac{5.6}{2} = 2.8$

45. $2 \ln x + 3 \ln y = \ln x^2 + \ln y^3 = \ln(x^2 y^3)$

49. $(\ln y)/x = \dfrac{1}{x} \ln y = \ln y^{1/x}$

53. $\ln x = -1.1$

$e^{\ln x} = e^{-1.1}$

$x = e^{-1.1} = 0.332871$

57. $\ln(0.5x - 2) = -0.5$

$e^{\ln(0.5x-2)} = e^{-0.5}$

$0.5x - 2 = e^{-0.5}$

$x = \dfrac{e^{-0.5} + 2}{0.5} = 5.213061$

59. $F = P(1 + i)^n$

$5{,}000 = 2{,}000(1 + 0.085)^n$

divide both sides by 1,000 and take logarithms

$2.5 = (1 + 0.085)^n$

$\ln 2.5 = n \ln 1.085$

$\dfrac{\ln 2.5}{\ln 1.085} = n$

$11.231808 = n$

61. $4{,}000 = 1{,}000(1 + i)^{10}$

$4 = (1 + i)^{10}$

$\ln 4 = 10 \ln (1 + i)$

$\dfrac{\ln 4}{10} = \ln (1 + i)$

$0.138629 = \ln(1 + i)$

$e^{0.138629} = e^{\ln(1+i)}$

$e^{0.138629} = 1 + i$

$e^{0.138629} - 1 = i$

$0.1486984 = i$

1. 2.718282

3. ln 8.46 = 2.13535

5. ln 0.08 = −2.52573

7. ln 2.27 = 0.81978

9. ln 58 = 4.06044

11. ln 425 = 6.05209

13. ln e = 1

15. $\log_b N$ means the power to which b must be raised to obtain N. Since $b > 0$ is required, N must be positive because a positive number raised to any power is a positive number.

17. $e^{0.25} = 1.2840$

19. $e^{-0.25} = 0.7788$

21. $e^{1.6} = 4.9530$

23. $e^{-2} = 0.1353$

25. antiln(0.17) = $e^{0.17} = 1.1853$

27. antiln(−1.3) = $e^{-1.3} = 0.2725$

29. antiln(−0.01) = $e^{-0.01} = 0.9900$

31. $\log_5 25 = 2$

33. $7^2 = 49$

35. $\log_{27} 3 = \dfrac{1}{3}$

37. $8^{1/3} = 2$

39. $e^1 = e$

41. $\log_7 1 = 0$

43. $2^x = 32, x = 5$

45. $\left(\dfrac{1}{5}\right)^x = 5, x = -1$

47. $3^3 = x, x = 27$

49. $\log_e x = 1, e^1 = x = 2.7183$

51. $e^{\ln e} = x, e = x = 2.7183$

53. $3^{\log_3 5} = x, 5 = x$

55. $2\log_a x - \left[\dfrac{1}{3}(\log_a y + \log_a z)\right]$

$2(0.6) - \left[\dfrac{1}{3}(1.8 + 1.2)\right]$

$1.2 - 1 = 0.2$

57. $2 \ln x - \dfrac{1}{2} \ln(y^2) + \ln z = \ln x^2 - \ln y + \ln z = \ln\left(\dfrac{x^2 z}{y}\right)$

59. $\ln x = 0.84; \; x = e^{0.84} = 2.3164.$

61. $\ln x = -2.3; \; x = e^{-2.3} = 0.1003.$

63. $\ln(1 + x) = 1.2; \; 1 + x = e^{1.2}; \; x = e^{1.2} - 1 = 3.3201 - 1 = 2.3201.$

65. $(6.75)^x = 4:$ $\quad \ln(6.75)^x = \ln 4$

$$x \ln(6.75) = \ln 4$$

$$x = \frac{\ln 4}{\ln 6.75}$$

$$= \frac{1.38629}{1.90954}$$

$$= 0.72598.$$

67. $(0.23)^x = 0.15:$ $\quad \ln(0.23)^x = \ln(0.15)$

$$x \ln(0.23) = \ln(0.15)$$

$$x = \frac{\ln(0.15)}{\ln(0.23)}$$

$$= \frac{-1.89712}{-1.46968}$$

$$= 1.29084.$$

69. $3^{-x} = 2:$ $\quad \ln(3^{-x}) = \ln 2$

$$-x \ln 3 = \ln 2$$

$$x = -\frac{\ln 2}{\ln 3}$$

$$= -\frac{0.69315}{1.09861}$$

$$= -0.63093.$$

71. $(0.2)^{-x} = 0.7:$ $\quad \ln(0.2)^{-x} = \ln(0.7)$

$$-x \ln(0.2) = \ln(0.7)$$

$$x = -\frac{\ln(0.7)}{\ln(0.2)}$$

$$= -\frac{-0.35667}{-1.60944}$$

$$= -0.22161.$$

73. $\left(\dfrac{4}{x}\right)^{-5} = 0.26:$ $\qquad \left(\dfrac{x}{4}\right)^{5} = 0.26$

$$\ln\left(\dfrac{x}{4}\right)^{5} = \ln(0.26)$$

$$5 \ln\left(\dfrac{x}{4}\right) = \ln(0.26)$$

$$\ln\left(\frac{x}{4}\right) = \frac{\ln(0.26)}{5}$$

$$\text{antiln}\left[\ln\left(\frac{x}{4}\right)\right] = \text{antiln}\left[\frac{\ln(0.26)}{5}\right]$$

$$\frac{x}{4} = \text{antiln}\left(\frac{-1.34707}{5}\right)$$

$$\frac{x}{4} = \text{antiln}(-0.26941)$$

$$\frac{x}{4} = e^{-0.26941}$$

If Table I is used,

$$\frac{x}{4} = e^{-0.27}$$

$$\frac{x}{4} = 0.7634$$

$$x = 3.1 \text{ rounded.}$$

If a calculator is used, the result is $x = 3.05531$.

75. $e^x = 25$: $\ln(e^x) = \ln 25$

$$x \ln e = \ln 25$$

$$x(1) = 3.21888.$$

77. $x^{10} - 1 = 0$: $\qquad x^{10} = 1$

$$\ln(x^{10}) = \ln 1$$

$$10 \ln x = 0$$

$$\ln x = 0$$

$$\text{antiln}(\ln x) = \text{antiln}(0)$$

$$x = e^0$$

$$x = 1.$$

79. $(1 + x)^{15} = 2.5$: $\qquad \ln(1 + x)^{15} = \ln 2.5$

$$15 \ln(1 + x) = \ln 2.5$$

$$\ln(1 + x) = \frac{\ln 2.5}{15}$$

$$= \frac{0.91629}{15}$$

$$\ln(1 + x) = 0.06109$$

$$\text{antiln}[\ln(1 + x)] = \text{antiln}(0.06109)$$

$$1 + x = e^{0.06109}.$$

If Table I is used,

$$1 + x = e^{0.06}$$

$$1 + x = 1.0618$$

$$x = 0.0618, \text{ or } 0.062 \text{ rounded.}$$

More accurately, by calculator, $x = 0.06299$.

144

81. $(1 + x) = \text{antiln}(0.14)$: $1 + x = e^{0.14} = 1.1503$

$$x = 0.1503$$

83. $x[1 + (1.01)^{50}] = 5$.

First compute $(1.01)^{50}$ using Tables I and II. Thus,

$$
\begin{aligned}
(1.01)^{50} &= \text{antiln}[\ln(1.01)^{50}] \\
&= \text{antiln}[50 \ln(1.01)] \\
&= \text{antiln}[50(0.00995)] \\
&= \text{antiln}(0.4975) \\
&= e^{0.4975} \\
&= e^{0.50} \\
&= 1.6487 \text{ or } 1.65, \text{ rounded.}
\end{aligned}
$$

Then,

$$
\begin{aligned}
x[1 + 1.65] &= 5 \\
x(2.65) &= 5
\end{aligned}
$$

$$x = \frac{5}{2.65} = 1.89, \text{ rounded.}$$

More accurately, by calculator, $x = 1.89062$.

1. a) Interest = (Principal)(Rate)(Time in years)

   $\quad\quad = \quad$ (500) $\quad$ (0.07) $\quad\quad$ (1)

   $\quad\quad = \boxed{\$35.00}$

   b) Amount = Principal + Interest

   $\quad\quad = \$500.00 + \$35.00$

   $\quad\quad = \boxed{\$535.00}$

5. a) Interest = (Principal)(Rate)(Time in years)

   $\quad\quad = \quad$ (100) $\quad$ (0.36) $\quad\quad$ (4/12)

   $\quad\quad = \boxed{\$12.00}$

   b) Amount = Principal + Interest

   $\quad\quad = \$100.00 + \$12.00$

   $\quad\quad = \boxed{\$112.00}$

9. a) Interest = (Principal)(Rate)(Time in years)

   $\quad\quad = \quad$ (5,000) $\quad$ (0.24) $\quad\quad$ (3)

   $\quad\quad = \boxed{\$3,600.00}$

   b) Amount = Principal + Interest

   $\quad\quad = \quad$ (5,000) $\quad + \quad$ (3,600)

   $\quad\quad = \boxed{\$8,600.00}$

13. $\text{Yield} = \dfrac{\text{Annual Dividend}}{\text{Price per Share of Stock}} = \dfrac{1.92}{24} = 0.08$

    $\quad\quad = \boxed{8\%}$

17. $i = \dfrac{\left(\dfrac{F}{P} - 1\right)}{n} = \dfrac{\dfrac{520}{500} - 1}{\left(\dfrac{3}{12}\right)} = \dfrac{.04}{\left(\dfrac{3}{12}\right)} = 0.16 = \boxed{16\%}$

21. $P = \dfrac{F}{1 + in} = \dfrac{1,000}{1 + (0.07)\left(\dfrac{18}{12}\right)} = \boxed{\$904.98}$

25. $F = \dfrac{P}{(1 - dn)} = \dfrac{2,000}{\left(1 - (0.15)\left(\dfrac{18}{12}\right)\right)} = \boxed{\$2,580.65}$

29. interest for 1 year $= \left(\dfrac{2}{3}\right)(580.65) = 387.10$

    $i_e = \dfrac{\text{Interest amount for 1 year}}{\text{Amount borrower receives}} = \dfrac{389.10}{2,000} = 19.355\%$

    $\quad\quad = \boxed{19.355\%}$

Problem Set 8-2

1. $F = P(1 + i)^n$

   $= 200(1 + 0.05)^{20}$

   $= 200(1.05)^{20}$

   $= 200(2.65330)$

   $= \boxed{\$530.66}$

5. $F = P(1 + i)^n$

   $= 150\left(1 + \dfrac{0.08}{4}\right)^{8(4)}$

   $= 150(1.02)^{32}$

   $= 150(1.88454)$

   $= \boxed{\$282.68}$

9. $F = P(1 + i)^n$

   $20,000 = 5,000(1 + 0.07)^n$

   $\dfrac{20,000}{5,000} = (1.07)^n$

   $4 = (1.07)^n$

   $\ln 4 = \ln(1.07)^n = n(\ln 1.07)$

   $\dfrac{\ln 4}{\ln 1.07} = n$

   $\dfrac{1.38629}{.06766} = \boxed{20.49 \text{ years}}$

13. $F = P(1 + i)^n$

    $= 5,000\left(1 + \dfrac{0.0525}{365}\right)^{6(365)}$

    $= 5,000(1.0001438)^{2190}$

    $= 5,000(1.37023)$

    $= \boxed{\$6,851.14}$

Problem Set 8-3

1. $P = F(1 + i)^{-n}$

   $= 1,000(1 + 0.08)^{-20}$

   $= 1,000(1.08)^{-20}$

   $= 1,000(.21455)$

   $= \boxed{\$214.55}$

5. $P = F(1 + i)^{-n}$

   $= 1,000\left(1 + \dfrac{0.08}{4}\right)^{-7(4)}$

   $= 1,000(1.02)^{-28}$

   $= 1,000(.57437)$

   $= \boxed{\$574.37}$

9. $P = F(1 + i)^{-n}$

   $= 1,000\left(1 + \dfrac{0.08}{365}\right)^{-2(365)}$

   $= 1,000(1.0002192)^{-730}$

   $= 1,000(.85216)$

   $= \boxed{\$852.16}$

Problem Set 8-4

1. $r_e = (1 + i)^m - 1; \quad i = \dfrac{j}{m}$

   $= \left(1 + \dfrac{.08}{4}\right)^4 - 1; \quad i = \dfrac{.08}{4}$

   $= (1.02)^4 - 1$

   $= \boxed{8.243\%}$

5. $r_e = (1 + i)^m - 1; \quad i = \dfrac{j}{m}$

   $= \left(1 + \dfrac{.10}{12}\right)^{12} - 1; \quad i = \dfrac{.10}{12}$

   $= (1.0083)^{12} - 1$

   $= \boxed{10.471\%}$

147

9. $r_e = (1 + i)^m - 1; \quad i = \dfrac{j}{m}$

$\quad = \left(1 + \dfrac{.09}{12}\right)^{12} - 1; \quad i = \dfrac{.09}{12}$

$\quad = (1.0075)^{12} - 1$

$\quad = \boxed{9.381\%}$

Problem Set 8-5

1. $F = Pe^{jt}$

$\quad = 1{,}000e^{0.06(5)}$

$\quad = 1{,}000e^{0.30}$

$\quad = \boxed{\$1{,}349.86}$

9. $r_e = e^j - 1$

$\quad = e^{0.05} - 1$

$\quad = 1.0513 - 1$

$\quad = \boxed{5.13\%} \text{ or } \boxed{.0513}$

17. $S = Pe^{ni}$

$\quad = 5{,}000e^{(20)(.068)}$

$\quad = \boxed{\$19{,}480.97}$

5. $P = Fe^{-jt}$

$\quad = 800e^{-0.085(10)}$

$\quad = 800e^{-0.85}$

$\quad = \boxed{\$341.93}$

13. $j = \ln(1 + r_e)$

$\quad = \ln(1 + 0.12)$

$\quad = \ln(1.12)$

$\quad = .1133$

$\quad = \boxed{11.33\%}$

21. $S = Pe^{ni}$

$\quad = 24e^{360(.05)}$

$\quad = 24e^{18}$

$\quad = \boxed{\$1{,}575{,}839{,}260}$

Problem Set 8-6

1. $F = R\left[\dfrac{(1 + i)^n - 1}{i}\right]$

$n = (3 \text{ yrs})(12 \text{ mths}) = 36 \text{ periods}$

$i = \dfrac{.12}{12} = .01$

$R = 500$

$F = 500\left[\dfrac{\left(1 + \dfrac{.12}{12}\right)^{36} - 1}{\dfrac{.12}{12}}\right]$

$\quad = 500\left[\dfrac{(1.01)^{36} - 1}{.01}\right]$

$\quad = 500(43.077)$

$\quad = \boxed{\$21{,}538.50}$

More accurately by calculator, \$21,538.44

5. $F = R\left[\dfrac{(1 + i)^n - 1}{i}\right]$

$R = 500$

$n = (2 \text{ yrs})(15) = 30 \text{ periods}$

$i = \dfrac{.06}{2}$

$F = 500\left[\dfrac{\left(1 + \dfrac{.06}{2}\right)^{30} - 1}{\dfrac{.06}{2}}\right]$

$\quad = 500\left[\dfrac{(1.03)^{30} - 1}{.03}\right]$

$\quad = 500(47.575)$

$\quad = \boxed{\$23{,}787.50}$

More accurately by calculator, \$23,787.71

9. $R = F\left[\dfrac{i}{(1+i)^n - 1}\right]$

$= 100{,}000\left[\dfrac{.08}{(1+.08)^{10} - 1}\right]$

$= 100{,}000\left[\dfrac{.08}{1.158925}\right]$

$= \boxed{\$6{,}902.95}$

11. $F = R\left[\dfrac{(1+i)^n - 1}{i}\right]$

$R = 1{,}000$

$n = (4)(25) = 100$

$i = \dfrac{.08}{4}$

$F = 1{,}000\left[\dfrac{\left(1 + \dfrac{.08}{4}\right)^{100} - 1}{\dfrac{.08}{4}}\right]$

$= 1{,}000\left[\dfrac{(1.02)^{100} - 1}{.02}\right]$

$= 1{,}000(312.2325)$

$= \boxed{\$312{,}232.50}$

More accurately by calculator, $312,232.31

Problem Set 8-7

1. $P_n = R\left[\dfrac{1 - (1+i)^{-n}}{i}\right]$

$= 400\left[\dfrac{1 - \left(1 + \dfrac{0.08}{4}\right)^{-5(4)}}{\left(\dfrac{0.08}{4}\right)}\right]$

$= 400\left[\dfrac{.3270287}{.02}\right]$

$= \boxed{\$6{,}540.57}$

5. a) $\$500(4)(3) = \boxed{\$6{,}000}$

b) $P_n = R\left[\dfrac{1 - (1+i)^{-n}}{i}\right]$

$= 500\left[\dfrac{1 - \left(1 + \dfrac{0.08}{4}\right)^{-3(4)}}{\left(\dfrac{0.08}{4}\right)}\right]$

$= 500\left[\dfrac{.2115068}{.02}\right]$

$= \boxed{\$5{,}287.67}$

9. a) $R = P\left[\dfrac{i}{1 - (1+i)^{-n}}\right]$

$= 100{,}000\left[\dfrac{\left(\dfrac{0.12}{2}\right)}{1 - \left(1 + \dfrac{0.12}{2}\right)^{-7(2)}}\right]$

$= 100{,}000\left[\dfrac{0.06}{.557699}\right]$

$= \boxed{\$10{,}758.49}$

149

b) $\dfrac{\text{1st Payment}}{\text{Interest}} = 100{,}000(0.12)\left(\dfrac{6}{12}\right) = \boxed{\$6{,}000}$

Amount Applied to reduce balance $=$ $\begin{array}{r} 10{,}758.49 \\ -6{,}000.00 \\ \hline \boxed{\$4{,}758.49} \end{array}$

New Balance $=$ $\begin{array}{r} 100{,}000.00 \\ -4{,}758.49 \\ \hline \boxed{\$95{,}241.51} \end{array}$

c) $\dfrac{\text{2nd Payment}}{\text{Interest}} = 95{,}241.51(0.12)\left(\dfrac{6}{12}\right) = \boxed{\$5{,}714.49}$

Amount Applied to reduce balance $=$ $\begin{array}{r} 10{,}758.49 \\ -5{,}714.49 \\ \hline \boxed{\$5{,}044.00} \end{array}$

New Balance $\$95{,}241.51 - \$5{,}044.00 = \boxed{\$90{,}197.51}$

13. $P = R\left[\dfrac{1 - (1 + i)^{-n}}{i}\right]$

$= 1{,}000\left[\dfrac{1 - \left(1 + \dfrac{0.07}{12}\right)^{-10(12)}}{\left(\dfrac{0.07}{12}\right)}\right]$

$= 1{,}000\left[\dfrac{.5024037}{.0058333}\right]$

$= \boxed{\$86{,}126.85}$

More accurately by calculator, $86,126.35

Problem Set 8-8

1. $F = R\left[\dfrac{(1 + i)^n - 1}{i}\right]$

$R = 100$

$i = \dfrac{.06}{2}$

$n = (2)(5) = 10$

$F = 100\left[\dfrac{\left(1 + \dfrac{.06}{2}\right)^{10} - 1}{\dfrac{.06}{2}}\right]$

$= 100\left[\dfrac{(1.03)^{10} - 1}{.03}\right]$

$= 100(11.4639)$

$= \boxed{\$1{,}146.39}$

5. $F = R\left[\dfrac{(1 + i)^n - 1}{i}\right]$

$R = \dfrac{F}{\left[\dfrac{(1 + i)^n - 1}{i}\right]}$

$F = 10{,}000$

$i = \dfrac{.08}{1}$

$n = 1(20) = 20$

$P = \dfrac{F}{(1 + i)^n}$

$= \dfrac{10{,}000}{(1 + .08)^{20}}$

$= \dfrac{10{,}000}{4.66096}$

$= \boxed{\$2{,}145.48}$

150

9. $F = R\left[\dfrac{(1 + i)^n - 1}{i}\right]$

$R = 250$

$i = \dfrac{.08}{4}$

$n = (5)(4) = 20$

$F = 250\left[\dfrac{\left(1 + \dfrac{.08}{4}\right)^{20} - 1}{\dfrac{.08}{4}}\right]$

$= 250\left[\dfrac{(1.02)^{20} - 1}{.02}\right]$

$= 250(24.29736)$

$= \boxed{\$6,074.34}$

17. *Step 1*

$P = R\left[\dfrac{1 - (1 + i)^{-n}}{i}\right]$

$= 10,000\left[\dfrac{1 - (1 + .06)^{-5}}{.06}\right]$

$= 10,000\left[\dfrac{1 - .7472557}{.06}\right]$

$= \$42,124.05$

Step 2

$R = F\left[\dfrac{i}{(1 + i)^n - 1}\right]$

$= 42,124.05\left[\dfrac{\dfrac{.08}{2}}{\left(1 + \dfrac{.08}{2}\right)^{20} - 1}\right]$

$= 42,124.05\left[\dfrac{.04}{2.19112 - 1}\right]$

$= 42,124.05[.0335818]$

$= \boxed{\$1,414.60}$

13. *Step 1*

$F = 3,000\left(1 + \dfrac{.12}{12}\right)^{40}$

$= 3,000(1.01)^{40}$

$= 3,000(1.48886)$

$= 4,466.58$

Step 2

$P = 4,466.58\left(1 + \dfrac{.08}{4}\right)^{-21/3}$

$= 4,466.58(1.02)^{-7}$

$= 4,466.58(.8705569)$

$= \boxed{\$3,888.41}$

1. Using the table or a calculator one gets $\boxed{6.3\%}$

5. $$5{,}800 = 500 \left[\frac{\left(1 + \frac{.12}{2}\right)^n - 1}{\frac{.12}{2}} \right]$$

$$11.6 = \frac{1.06^n - 1}{.06}$$

$$.696 = 1.06^n - 1$$

$$1.696 = 1.06^n$$

$$\ln 1.696 = n \ln 1.06$$

$$\frac{\ln 1.696}{\ln 1.06} = n$$

$$\frac{.52827}{.05827} = n$$

$$\boxed{9.06 = n}$$

So 10 deposits are made. After a payment, amount is 5745.66, so last payment is $5800 - 5745.66 = \$54.34$

9. $$F = R \left[\frac{e^{it} - 1}{e^{i/m} - 1} \right]$$

$$= 500 \left[\frac{e^{(.06)(10)} - 1}{e^{(.06)/2} - 1} \right]$$

$$= 500 \left[\frac{1.8221188 - 1}{1.0304545 - 1} \right]$$

$$= 500[26.994986] = \boxed{\$13{,}497.49}$$

13. $$P = R \left[\frac{1 - e^{-jt}}{e^{j/m} - 1} \right]$$

$$= 2{,}000 \left[\frac{1 - e^{-(.10)(5)}}{e^{(.10)/2} - 1} \right]$$

$$= 2{,}000 \left[\frac{1 - .6065306}{1.0512711 - 1} \right]$$

$$= 2{,}000[7.6742922] = \$15{,}348.58$$

1. $I = Pin$

$$I = 500(.09)\left(\frac{15}{12}\right)$$

$$= 500(.1125)$$

$$\boxed{I = 56.25}$$

3. $I = Pin$

$$175 = 2,000(.07)(n)$$

$$175 = 140(n)$$

$$1.25 = n$$

$$\boxed{n = 15 \text{ mths}}$$

5. Det E 1.52 15.5

$$\frac{1.52}{15.5} = .098$$

$$\boxed{9.8\%}$$

7. $I = Pin$

$$60 = 500(i)\left(\frac{9}{12}\right)$$

$$60 = 375i$$

$$i = .16$$

$$\boxed{i = 16\%}$$

9. $P = \dfrac{F}{1 + in}$

$$P = \frac{1,500}{1 + (.10)(2)}$$

$$= \frac{1,500}{1.2}$$

$$\boxed{P = \$1,250}$$

11. $P = F(1 - dn)$

$$P = 1,000(1 - (.18)(2))$$

$$= .640(1,000)$$

$$\boxed{P = \$640}$$

13.
$$P = F(1 - dn)$$

$$2,400 = 3,000(1 - (d)(2))$$

$$2,400 = 3,000 - 3,000(2)d$$

$$2,400 - 3,000 = -6,000d$$

$$\frac{-600}{6,000} = -d$$

$$-.1 = -d$$

$$d = .1$$

$$\boxed{d = 10\%}$$

15. $F = P(1 + i)^n$

$$F = 4,000\left(1 + \frac{.08}{4}\right)^{(7)(4)}$$

$$= 4,000(1 + .02)^{28}$$

$$= 4,000(1.74102)$$

$$\boxed{F = \$6,964.08}$$

17. $F = P(1 + i)^n$

$$F = 2,500\left(1 + \frac{.12}{12}\right)^{(3)(12)}$$

$$= 2,500(1 + .01)^{36}$$

$$= 2,500(1.43077)$$

$$\boxed{F = \$3,576.93}$$

19.
$$F = P(1 + i)^n$$

$$2 = 1(1 + .09)^n$$

$$\ln 2 = n \ln(1 + .09)$$

$$.693 = n(\ln 1.09)$$

$$\frac{.69315}{.08618} = n$$

$$\boxed{n = 8.043 \text{ yrs}}$$

21.
$$F = P(1 + i)^n$$
$$350{,}000 = 125{,}000(1 + i)^5$$
$$2.8 = (1 + i)^5$$
$$\ln 2.8 = 5 \ln(1 + i)$$
$$\frac{\ln 2.8}{5} = \ln(1 + i)$$
$$.20592 = \ln(1 + i)$$
$$e^{.20592} = 1 + i$$
$$1.2287 = 1 + i$$
$$\boxed{22.87\% = i}$$

23.
$$F = P(1 + i)^n$$
$$500{,}000 = P\left(1 + \frac{.07}{2}\right)^{40}$$
$$500{,}000 = P(1.035)^{40}$$
$$500{,}000 = P(3.95926)$$
$$P = \frac{500{,}000}{3.95926}$$
$$\boxed{P = 126{,}286}$$

25.
$$F = R\left[\frac{(1 + i)^n - 1}{i}\right]$$
$$F = 500\left[\frac{\left(1 + \frac{.08}{4}\right)^{40} - 1}{\frac{.08}{4}}\right]$$
$$= 500\left[\frac{(1.02)^{40} - 1}{.02}\right]$$
$$= 500(60.4)$$
$$\boxed{F = \$30{,}200}$$

More accurately by calculator, $30,200.99

27.
$$R = F\left[\frac{i}{(1 + i)^n - 1}\right]$$
$$R = 8{,}000\left[\frac{\frac{.08}{4}}{\left(1 + \frac{.08}{4}\right)^{(5)(4)} - 1}\right]$$
$$= 8{,}000\left[\frac{.02}{(1.02)^{20} - 1}\right]$$
$$= 8{,}000(.0412)$$
$$\boxed{R = \$329.60}$$

More accurately by calculator, $329.25

29.
$$R = P\left[\frac{i}{1 - (1 + i)^{-n}}\right]$$
$$R = 12{,}000\left[\frac{\frac{.12}{12}}{1 - \left(1 + \frac{.12}{12}\right)^{-30}}\right]$$
$$= 12{,}000\left[\frac{.01}{1 - (1.01)^{-30}}\right]$$
$$= 12{,}000\left[\frac{.01}{.258}\right]$$
$$= 12{,}000(.039)$$
$$\boxed{R = \$468}$$

More accurately by calculator, $464.98

31. a)
$$R = P\left[\frac{i}{1 - (1 + i)^{-n}}\right]$$
$$R = 50{,}000\left[\frac{\frac{.08}{12}}{1 - \left(1 + \frac{.08}{12}\right)^{-20(12)}}\right]$$

154

$$R = 50,000 \left[\frac{.0067}{1 - (1 + .0067)^{-240}} \right]$$

$$= 50,000 \left[\frac{.0067}{1 - (.2014)} \right]$$

$$= 50,000(.0084)$$

$$\boxed{R = \$420}$$

More accurately by calculator, $418.22

b) $\text{Interest} = (50,000)(.08)\left(\frac{1}{12}\right)$

$$\boxed{I = \$333.33}$$

Beginning Balance		50,000
Payment	420	
Interest	333.30	
Reduction of bal.	86.70	86.70
New balance		49,913.30

c) $\text{Interest} = (49,913.30)(.08)\left(\frac{1}{12}\right)$

$$\boxed{I = \$332.75}$$

Beginning Balance		49,913.30
Payment	420	
Interest	332.75	
Reduction of bal.	87.25	87.25
New balance		49,826.05

33. $R = P \left[\dfrac{i}{1 - (1 + i)^{-n}} \right]$

$$R = 10,000 \left[\frac{.07}{1 - (1 + .07)^{-10}} \right]$$

$$R = 10,000 \left[\frac{.07}{1 - (.508)} \right]$$

$$R = 10,000(.142)$$

$$\boxed{R = \$1,420.00}$$

More accurately by calculator, $1,423.78

35. $F = P(1 + i)^n$

$$F = 25,000(1 + .07)^{15}$$

$$= 25,000(2.76)$$

$$\boxed{F = 69,000 \text{ barrels a year}}$$

More accurately by calculator,
68,996 barrels per year

37. Bring both amounts back to the present

$8,000, 7%, 4 periods	8,000(.762895) =	$6,103.16
$12,000, 7%, 9 periods	12,000(.543934) =	$6,527.21
		$12,630.37

Now find the payment for the Future Value of an annuity:

$$R = 12,630.37 \left[\frac{.07}{1 - (1 + .07)^{-9}} \right]$$

$$R = 12,630.37 [.1534865]$$

$$\boxed{R = \$1,938.59}$$

155

39. $P = 1{,}500\left[\dfrac{1 - (1 + .01)^{-36}}{.01}\right]$

$P = 1{,}500[43.077] = 64{,}616$ barrels

41. *Step 1*

$F = 20{,}000(1 + .05)^{-10}$

$F = 20{,}000(1.62889) = 32{,}577.80$

Step 2

$P = 32{,}577.80(1 + .06)^{-10}$

$P = 32{,}577.80(.558395) = 18{,}191.28$

Step 3

$F = 18{,}191.28(1 + .08)^{10}$

$F = 18{,}191.28(2.15892) = 39{,}273.52$

More accurately by calculator, \$39,273.71

43. Using a calculator or the tables, the interest rate to make payments of \$2,500 to grow to \$41,000 in 12 years is $\boxed{5.5\%}$

45. $150{,}000 = 1{,}800\left[\dfrac{1 - \left(1 + \dfrac{.14}{12}\right)^{-n}}{\dfrac{.14}{12}}\right]$

$83.333 = \dfrac{1 - (1.011667)^{-n}}{.011667}$

$.97222 = 1 - (1.011667)^{-n}$

$-n\,\ln(1.011667) = \ln(.027778)$

$-n = \dfrac{-3.5835}{.0116}$

$n = 308.95$

Total payments $= (308)(1800) + (.95)(1800)$

$= \$556{,}110$

47. $r = (1 + i)^n - 1$

$r = \left(1 + \dfrac{.12}{4}\right)^4 - 1$

$r = 1.12551 - 1 = \boxed{12.551\%}$

49. $r = \left(1 + \dfrac{.06}{365}\right)^{365} - 1$

$r = 1.06183 - 1 = \boxed{6.183\%}$

51. $P = Fe^{-jt}$

$P = 10{,}000e^{-.08(7)}$

$P = 10{,}000e^{-.56}$

$P = 10{,}000(.571209) = \boxed{\$5{,}712.09}$

53. $j = \ln(1 + r)$

$j = \ln(1 + .12) = \boxed{11.33\%}$

55. $R = 20{,}000\left[\dfrac{e^{.14/2} - 1}{1 - e^{-(.14)(10)}}\right]$

$R = 20{,}000\left[\dfrac{e^{.07} - 1}{1 - e^{-1.4}}\right]$

$20{,}000\left[\dfrac{1.0725 - 1}{1 - .2466}\right] = \boxed{\$1{,}920}$

More accurately by calculator, \$1,924.82

57. $R = 1,000 \left[\dfrac{1 - e^{-.12(8)}}{e^{.12/12} - 1} \right]$

    $R = 1,000 \left[\dfrac{1 - e^{-.96}}{e^{.01} - 1} \right]$

    $R = 1,000 \left[\dfrac{1 - .3829}{1.0101 - 1} \right] = \$61,100$

More accurately by calculator, \$61,402.67

59. $F = 400 \left[\dfrac{e^{.08(12)} - 1}{e^{.08/2} - 1} \right]$

    $F = 400 \left[\dfrac{e^{.96} - 1}{e^{.04} - 1} \right]$

    $F = 400 \left[\dfrac{2.6117 - 1}{1.0408 - 1} \right]$

    $= \$15,800$

More accurately by calculator, \$15,796.77

1. a) $P(M) = \dfrac{300}{1,000} = 0.3$

    b) $P(B) = \dfrac{-550}{1,000} = 0.55$

    c) $P(M \cap S) = 0$

    d) $P(B \cap M) = \dfrac{125}{1,000} = 0.125$

    e) $P(A \cap C) = 0$

    f) $P(A \cap L) = \dfrac{30}{1,000} = 0.03$

    g) $P(L \cap A) = \dfrac{30}{1,000} = 0.03$

    h) $P(A|L) = \dfrac{30}{200} = 0.15$

    i) $P(L|A) = \dfrac{30}{150} = 0.2$

    j) $P(A|M) = \dfrac{45}{300} = 0.15$

    k) $P(S|B) = \dfrac{275}{550} = 0.5$

    l) $P(L \cup M) = \dfrac{200 + 300}{1,000} = 0.5$

    m) $P(B \cup S) = \dfrac{550 + 500 - 275}{1,000} = 0.775$

    n) $P(M \cup C) = \dfrac{300 + 300 - 130}{1,000} = 0.47$

    o) $P(B \cup C) = \dfrac{550 + 300}{1,000} = 0.85$

    p) $P(A') = 1 - P(A) = 1 - \dfrac{150}{1,000} = 0.85$

    q) $P(M') = 1 - P(M) = 1 - \dfrac{300}{1,000} = 0.7$

    r) $P(L' \cap M') = 1 - P(L \cup M) = 1 - \dfrac{200 + 300}{1,000}$

    $$= 1 - 0.5 = 0.5$$

    s) $M \cup S$

    t) $B \cup C$

    u) B or $A' \cap C'$

    v) $A' \cap M'$

    w) $B \cup M$

    x) $L \cup C$

5.

	Y	G	T	totals
R	40	0	160	200
W	10	20	50	80
B	50	30	40	120
totals	100	50	250	400

   a) $P(R) = \dfrac{200}{400} = 0.5$

   b) $P(G) = \dfrac{50}{400} = 0.125$

   c) $P(W \cup G) = \dfrac{80 + 50 - 20}{400} = 0.275$

   d) $P(R \cap B) = 0$

   e) $P(R \cap G) = \dfrac{0}{400} = 0$

   f) $P(R \cap R) = 0$

   g) $P(Y) = \dfrac{100}{400} = 0.25$

   h) $P(R \cup G) = \dfrac{200 + 50 - 0}{400} = 0.625$

   i) $P(B \cap T) = \dfrac{40}{400} = 0.1$

   j) $P(G|B) = \dfrac{30}{120} = 0.25$

   k) $P(R|Y) = \dfrac{40}{100} = 0.4$

   l) $P(R|G) = \dfrac{0}{50} = 0$

m) no

$P(W \cap Y) \neq 0$

n) no

$P(W|Y) \neq P(W)$
$0.1 \quad \neq \quad 0.2$

o) no

$P(W \cap T) \neq 0$

p) yes

$P(W|T) = P(W)$
$0.2 \quad = \quad 0.2$

q) Yes, $P(R \cap G) = 0$

r) No

$P(R|G) \neq P(R)$
$0 \quad \neq \quad 0.5$

7.

	H	M	L	totals
M	10	80	10	100
F	20	160	20	200
totals	30	240	30	300

Problem Set 9-2

1.

	L	M	S	totals
A	0.03	0.045	0.075	0.15
B	0.15	0.125	0.275	0.55
C	0.02	0.13	0.15	0.30
	0.20	0.30	0.50	1.00

5. $P(H \cap J) = 0.09$

$P(H) = 0.1$

$$P(J|H) = \frac{P(H \cap J)}{P(H)} = \frac{0.09}{0.1} = 0.9$$

9. $P(X) = 0.6$

$P(Y) = 0.4$

$P(XY) = 0.1$

$$P(X|Y) = \frac{P(XY)}{P(Y)} = \frac{0.1}{0.4} = 0.25$$

$$P(Y|X) = \frac{P(XY)}{P(X)} = \frac{0.1}{0.6} = 0.167$$

13. $P(S) = 0.4$

$P(C) = 0.5$

$P(S|C) = 0.7$

a) $P(C \cap S) = P(C) \cdot P(S|C) = 0.5 \times 0.7 = 0.35$

b) $P(S') = 1 - 0.4 = 0.6$

c) $P(C \cup S) = P(C) + P(S) = 0.5 + 0.4 = 0.9$

d) $P(C' \cup S') = 1 - P(C \cap S) = 1 - 0.35 = 0.65$

17.

$P(F) = 0.01 + 0.001 = 0.011$

21. a) $P(H \cap 7) = P(H) \cdot P(7) = \dfrac{1}{2} \times \dfrac{1}{6} = \dfrac{1}{12}$

b) $P(H \cup 7) = P(H) + P(7) - P(H \cap 7) = \dfrac{1}{2} + \dfrac{1}{6} - \dfrac{1}{12} = \dfrac{7}{12}$

c) $P(H \cap E) = P(H) \cdot P(E) = \dfrac{1}{2} \times \dfrac{1}{2} = \dfrac{1}{4}$

d) $P(H \cap 8^+) = P(H) \cdot P(8^+) = \dfrac{1}{2} \times \dfrac{10}{36} = \dfrac{5}{36}$

25. $P(T \cap F) = 1 - P(T' \cup F')$

$P(T') = \dfrac{2}{5} \times \dfrac{1}{4} = 0.1$

$P(F') = 0$

$P(T \cap F) = 1 - (0.1 + 0) = 0.9$

Problem Set 9-3

1. $P(G|P) = ?$

$P(G) = 0.875$

$P(G') = 0.125$

$P(P|G) = 0.64$

$P(P|G') = 0.24$

$P(PG) = P(G)P(P|G) = (0.875)(0.64) = 0.56$

$P(PG') = P(G')P(P|G') = (0.125)(0.24) = 0.03$

$P(G|P) = \dfrac{P(PG)}{P(PG) + P(PG')} = \dfrac{0.56}{0.56 + 0.03} = \dfrac{0.56}{0.59} \approx 0.95$

5. $P(R) = 0.95 \qquad P(R') = 0.05$

$P(A|R) = 0.9$

$P(A|R') = 0.04$

a) $P(R|A) = ?$

$P(AR) = P(R)P(A|R) = (0.95)(0.9) = 0.855$

$P(AR') = P(R')P(A|R') = (0.05)(0.04) = 0.002$

$P(R|A) = \dfrac{P(AR)}{P(AR) + P(AR')} = \dfrac{0.855}{0.855 + 0.002} = \dfrac{0.855}{0.857} \approx 0.998$

b) $P(R|A') = \dfrac{P(A'|R)P(R)}{P(A'|R)P(R) + P(A'|R')P(R')}$

$= \dfrac{(0.1)(0.9)}{(0.1)(0.9) + (0.96)(0.05)} = \dfrac{0.09}{0.09 + 0.048} = 0.652$

9. $P(J|M) = \dfrac{P(M|J)P(J)}{P(M|J)P(J) + P(M|J')P(J')}$

$= \dfrac{(0.001)(0.5)}{(0.001)(0.5) + (0.0015)(0.5)} = \dfrac{0.0005}{0.00125} = 0.4$

$P(A|M) = \dfrac{(0.002)(0.25)}{(0.002)(0.25) + (0.001)(0.75)} = \dfrac{0.0005}{0.00125} = 0.4$

$P(S|M) = \dfrac{(0.001)(0.25)}{(0.001)(0.25) + (0.0015)(0.75)} = \dfrac{0.00025}{0.00125} = 0.2$

Problem Set 9-4

1. a) $\left(\dfrac{7}{10}\right)\left(\dfrac{6}{9}\right) = \dfrac{42}{90} = 0.467$

b) $\left(\dfrac{3}{10}\right)\left(\dfrac{2}{9}\right) = \dfrac{6}{90} = 0.067$

c) $\left(\dfrac{3}{10}\right)\left(\dfrac{7}{9}\right) + \left(\dfrac{7}{10}\right)\left(\dfrac{3}{9}\right) = \dfrac{21}{90} + \dfrac{21}{90} = 0.467$

d) $P(>1) = 1 - P(0) = 1 - \left(\dfrac{7}{10}\right)\left(\dfrac{6}{9}\right)\left(\dfrac{5}{8}\right) = 1 - \dfrac{210}{720} = 0.708$

5. a) WM

b) $P(WM) = P(W)P(M|W) = \left(\dfrac{2}{3}\right)\left(\dfrac{1}{2}\right) = \dfrac{1}{3}$

c) WW

d) $P(WW) = P(W)P(W|W) = \left(\dfrac{2}{3}\right)\left(\dfrac{1}{2}\right) = \dfrac{1}{3}$

Problem Set 9-6

1. a) $P(1) = \dfrac{3!}{1!2!}(0.3)^1(0.7)^2 = 3(0.3)(0.49) = 0.441$

b) $P(>1) = 1 - P(0) = 1 - 0.343 = 0.657$

$P(0) = \dfrac{3!}{0!3!}(0.3)^0(0.7)^3 = 1(1)(0.343) = 0.343$

c) $P(2) = \dfrac{5!}{2!3!}(0.3)^2(0.7)^3 = 10(0.09)(0.343) = 0.3087$

d) $P(>2) = P(3) + P(4)$

$P(3) = \dfrac{4!}{3!1!}(0.3)^3(0.7)^1 = 4(0.027)(0.7) = 0.0756$

$P(4) = \dfrac{4!}{4!0!}(0.3)^4(0.7)^0 = 1(0.0081)(1) = 0.0081$

$P(>2) = 0.0756 + 0.0081 = 0.0837$

5. a) $P(>1 \text{ free}) = 1 - P(0 \text{ free})$

$$P(0) = \frac{4!}{0!4!}(0.3^0)(0.7)^4 = 1(1)(0.2401) = 0.2401$$

$P(>1) = 1 - 0.2401 = 0.7599$

b) $P(>3 \text{ free}) = P(3) + P(4)$

$$P(3) = \frac{4!}{3!1!}(0.3)^3(0.7)^1 = 4(0.027)(0.7) = 0.0756$$

$$P(4) = \frac{4!}{4!0!}(0.3)^4(0.7)^0 = 1(0.0081)(1) = 0.0081$$

$P(>3) = 0.0756 + 0.0081 = 0.0837$

9. a) $\sum\limits_{Z=0}^{15} C_X^{100}(0.05)^X(0.95)^{200-X}$

b) $\sum\limits_{X=11}^{200} C_X^{200}(0.05)^X(0.95)^{200-X}$

Problem Set 9-7

1.

1 Roll	2 Prob. (X)	3 Payout	$(2 \cdot 3)$
2	1/36	2	2/36
3	2/36	−3	−6/36
4	3/36	4	12/36
5	4/36	−5	−20/36
6	5/36	6	30/36
7	6/36	−7	−42/36
8	5/36	8	40/36
9	4/36	−9	−36/36
10	3/36	10	30/36
11	2/36	−11	−22/36
12	1/36	12	12/36
			EMV $= \Sigma = 0$

5. EMV (1) $= -2(0.1) + 5(0.2) + 5(0.25) + 5(0.4) + 5(0.05) = 6.825$

EMV (2) $= -4(0.1) + 3(0.2) + 10(0.25) + 10(0.4) + 10(0.05) = 7.20$

EMV (3) $= -6(0.1) + 1(0.2) + 8(0.25) + 15(0.4) + 15(0.05) = 8.35$

EMV (4) $= -8(0.1) + -1(0.2) + 6(0.25) + 13(0.4) + 20(0.05) = 6.70$

1. a) $P(Y) = \dfrac{120}{400} = 0.30.$

   b) $P(E) = \dfrac{52}{400} = 0.13.$

   c) $P(C) = \dfrac{200}{400} = 0.50.$

   d) $P(X \cap G) = \dfrac{60}{400} = 0.15.$

   e) $P(G \cap X) = \dfrac{60}{400} = 0.15.$

   f) The assumption underlying the table is that each car has one of the noted malfunctions at a time, so E and G are mutually exclusive and $P(E \cap G) = 0$.

   g) Z and X are different makes of cars. Hence, Z and X are mutually exclusive and $P(Z \cap X) = 0$.

   h) $P(Y \cap C) = \dfrac{60}{400} = 0.15$

   i) $P(X|C) = \dfrac{23}{200} = 0.115.$

   j) $P(C|X) = \dfrac{23}{100} = 0.23.$

   k) $P(E|Z) = \dfrac{15}{180} = 0.0833.$

   l) $P(Z|G) = \dfrac{48}{148} = 0.324.$

   m) $P(X \cup Y) = \dfrac{100 + 120}{400} = 0.55.$

   n) $P(X \cup C) = \dfrac{100 + 200 - 23}{400} = \dfrac{277}{400} = 0.6925.$

   o) $P(G \cup C) = \dfrac{148 + 200}{400} = \dfrac{348}{400} = 0.87.$

   p) $P(Y \cup G) = \dfrac{120 + 148 - 40}{400} = \dfrac{228}{400} = 0.57$

3. a) The situation described indicates that the weather pattern persists for periods of days, so tomorrow's weather is related to (not independent of) today's weather.

   b) If the card is black, it cannot be a diamond, so B and D are mutually exclusive. However, $P(B|D) = 0$, whereas $P(B)$ is $1/2$, so $P(B|D) \neq P(B)$, so B and D are not independent.

   c) A person can have brown eyes and dark hair, so B and D are not mutually exclusive. The author ventures the guess (with a high subjective probability) that a person with brown eyes is more likely to have dark than light hair, so his response is that B and D are not independent.

5. a) Marking a given entry by *, we have:

	B	B'	
A	0.48	0.22	0.70*
A'	0.18	0.12*	0.30
	0.66	0.34*	1.00

b) $P(A)P(B) = (0.70)(0.66) = 0.462$, whereas $P(AB) = 0.48$. A and B are not independent because $P(AB) \neq P(A)P(B)$.

c) $P(B'|A') = 0.12/0.30 = 0.40$.

d) $P(A \cup B') = P(A) + P(B') - P(AB') = 0.70 + 0.34 - 0.22 = 0.82$.

7. Let A and B mean winning offices A and B, respectively. The probability of winning A if he wins B is $P(A|B)$. We have:

$$P(A|B) = \frac{P(AB)}{P(B)} = \frac{0.10}{0.25} = 0.40.$$

9. The box contains $GGGGGGDD$.

a) $P(GG) = \dfrac{6}{8} \cdot \dfrac{5}{7} = 0.536.$

b) $P(DD) = \dfrac{2}{8} \cdot \dfrac{1}{7} = 0.0357.$

c) This is the probability of GD or DG, which are mutually exclusive. Hence,

$$P(GD \cup DG) = P(GD) + P(DG) - 0$$

$$= \frac{6}{8} \cdot \frac{2}{7} + \frac{2}{8} \cdot \frac{6}{7} = \frac{24}{56} = 0.429.$$

d) At least one defective means 1 or 2 or 3 defectives. The complement of the foregoing is 0 defective. Hence,

$$P(1 \text{ or } 2 \text{ or } 3 \text{ defective}) = 1 - P(0 \text{ defective}) = 1 - P(GGG)$$

$$= 1 - \frac{6}{8} \cdot \frac{5}{7} \cdot \frac{4}{6} = \frac{9}{14} = 0.643.$$

11. The exercises will be held outdoors if either it does not rain on Friday, F', or it does rain on Friday and does not rain on Saturday, FS'.

$$
\begin{aligned}
P(\text{outdoors}) &= P(F') &&+ P(FS') - 0 \\
&= P(F') &&+ P(F)P(S'|F) \\
&= (1 - 0.3) &&+ (0.3)(0.4) \\
&= 0.70 &&+ 0.12 &&= 0.82.
\end{aligned}
$$

13.

	B	B'	
A	0.12	0.28	0.40
A'	0.18	0.42	0.60
	0.30	0.70	

Probability of being offered a job at at least one company is
$P(A \text{ or } B) = 0.40 + 0.30 - 0.12 = 0.58$.

Probability of being offered a job at exactly one of the companies is
$P(A B') + P(B A') = 0.28 + 0.18 = 0.46$.

15.

	II	II'	
I	0.15	0.45	0.60
I'	0.15	0.25	0.40
	0.30	0.70	

a) $P(I\ II) = 0.15$ does not equal $P(I)\ P(II) = (0.6)(0.3) = 0.18$.

b) If outcomes are to be independent, then $P(I\ II)$ must $= P(I)\ P(II)$, so that $P(I\ II) = (0.6)(0.3) = 0.18$. We are lead to the following:

	II	II'	
I	0.18	0.42	0.60
I'	0.12	0.28	0.40
	0.30	0.70	

The table shows the desired probability, $P(I'\ II') = 0.28$.

17. Assuming independence, $P(A\ B) = P(A)P(B) = (0.01)(0.005) = 0.00005$. We are now able to complete the table:

	B	B'	
A	0.00005	0.00995	0.0100
A'	0.00495	0.98505	0.99000
	0.00500	0.99500	

a) From the table, $P(A\ B) = 0.00005$.

b) From the table, $P(A'\ B') = 0.98505$.

c) $P(A\ or\ B) = P(A) + P(B) - P(A\ B) = 0.01000 + 0.00500 - 0.00005 = 0.01495$.

d) $P(A\ B') + P(A'\ B) = 0.00995 + 0.00495 = 0.01490$.

19. $(1/2)^5 = 1/32$.

21. $P(Y\,|\,X) = \dfrac{P(X\ Y)}{P(X)}$. Hence, $0.80 = \dfrac{0.60}{P(X)}$ and $P(X) = 0.75$.

$P(X\,|\,Y) = \dfrac{P(X\ Y)}{P(Y)}$. Hence, $0.75 = \dfrac{0.60}{P(Y)}$ and $P(Y) = 0.80$.

23. a) $P(P\,|\,G) = \dfrac{P(P\ G)}{P(G)}$. Substituting the given data, $0.90 = \dfrac{P(P\ G)}{0.60}$ from which we find $P(P\ G) = 0.54$.

b) Similarly, substituting in $P(P\,|\,G') = \dfrac{P(P\ G')}{P(G')}$, we have $0.40 = \dfrac{P(P\ G')}{0.40}$ so that $P(P\ G') = P(G'\ P) = 0.16$. The completed table for the problem follows:

	P	P'	
G	0.54	0.06	0.60
G'	0.16	0.24	0.40
	0.70	0.30	

25. Letting M mean Mr. M wins and W mean Ms. W runs, the events possible are shown in the table, where * indicates the desired probability, $P(M)$.

	W	W'	
M	.12	.54*	.66
M'	.28	.06	.34
	.4	.6	1.0

We have

$$P(M) = P(MW) + P(MW').$$
$$= P(W)P(M\,|\,W) + P(W')P(M\,|\,W')$$
$$= (0.4)(0.3) + (0.6)(0.9)$$
$$= 0.12 + 0.54$$
$$= 0.66.$$

27. We have given $P(B) = 0.01$; $P(L|B) = 0.10$; $P(L|B') = 0.50$. It follows that $P(B') = 0.99$. Applying Bayes' rule,

$$P(B|L) = \frac{P(L|B)P(B)}{P(L|B)P(B) + P(L|B')P(B')}$$

$$= \frac{(0.10)(0.01)}{(0.10)(0.01) + (0.50)(0.99)} = \frac{0.001}{0.496} = \frac{1}{496} = 0.002.$$

29. We are given $P(X) = 0.008$; $P(I|X) = 0.75$; $P(I|X') = 0.01$. It follows that $P(X') = 1 - P(X) = 1 - 0.008 = 0.992$. Applying Bayes' rule,

$$P(X|I) = \frac{P(I|X)P(X)}{P(I|X)P(X) + P(I|X')P(X')}$$

$$= \frac{(0.75)(0.008)}{(0.75)(0.008) + (0.01)(0.992)} = \frac{0.00600}{0.01592} = 0.377.$$

31. a) $E(x) = 0(.55) + 1(.35) + 2(.05) + 3(.05) = \boxed{.600}$

 b) $(0 - .6)^2(.55) + (1 - .6)^2(.35) + (2 - .6)^2(.05) + (3 - .6)^2(.05) = .198 + .056 + .098 + .288 = \boxed{.640}$

 c) $\sigma = \sqrt{.64} = \boxed{.8}$

33. a)

 b) $\dfrac{20 + 18 + 12 + 10}{25 + 15 + 20 + 18 + 12 + 10} = \dfrac{60}{100} = \boxed{.60}$

 c) 0

 d) $E(x) = 0\left(\dfrac{25}{100}\right) + 1\left(\dfrac{15}{100}\right) + 2\left(\dfrac{20}{100}\right) + 3\left(\dfrac{18}{100}\right) + 4\left(\dfrac{12}{100}\right) + 5\left(\dfrac{10}{100}\right) = \boxed{2.07}$

 e) $u = 2.07$

 $\sigma^2 = (0 - 2.07)^2(.25) + (1 - 2.07)^2(.15) + (2 - 2.07)^2(.2) + (3 - 2.07)^2(.18) + (4 - 2.07)^2(.12)$
 $\qquad + (5 - 2.07)^2(.1) = 1.07 + .17 + .00 + .16 + .45 + .86 = 2.71$

 $\sigma = \sqrt{2.71} = 1.65$

 $n = 4, p = 0.001, q = 0.999.$

37. a) $P(1) = C_1^4(0.001)^1(0.999)^3 = 4(0.001)(0.997003) = 0.003988.$

 b) The probability of more than 1 is $P(2) + P(3) + P(4)$ or $1 - P(0) - P(1)$. The latter is simpler. We have

$$1 - P(0) - P(1) = 1 - C_0^4(0.001)^0(0.999)^4 - P(1)$$

$$= 1 - 1(1)(0.996006) - 0.003988$$

$$= 0.000006.$$

166

39. a) $(0.2)^5 = 0.00032$.

b) Probability for four correct or five correct is:

$$C_4^5(0.2)^4(0.8) + C_5^5(0.2)^5 = 5(0.0016)(0.8) + 0.00032 = 0.00672.$$

c) $C_3^5(0.2)^3(0.8)^2 = 10(0.00512) = 0.05120$.

d) $C_3^5(0.2)^3(0.8)^2 + C_4^5(0.2)^4(0.8) + C_5^5(0.2)^5 = 10(0.00512) + 5(0.00128) + 0.00032 = 0.05792$.

41. a) Probability of at least one success is $1 -$ probability of all 100 being failures $= 1 - (0.7)^{100}$.

b) The probability of at most one success is the probability of zero or one success $= (0.3)^0(0.7)^{100} + 100(0.3)(0.7)^{99} = (0.7)^{100} + 30(0.7)^{99}$.

c) $C_5^{100}(0.3)^5(0.7)^{95}$.

d) The probability of at most three successes is the probability of zero, one, two, or three successes:

$$(0.7)^{100} + 100(0.3)(0.7)^{99} + C_2^{100}(0.3)^2(0.7)^{98} + C_3^{100}(0.3)^3(0.7)^{97}.$$

43. a) Probability of 0 or 1 defective $= (0.9)^{10} + 10(0.9)^9(0.1)$
$$= 0.348678 + 0.387420 = 0.7361.$$

b) If we select n items, the probability of at least one good is $1 -$ probability of all defective $= 1 - (0.1)^n$. We want this probability to be 0.99. Hence,

$$1 - (0.1)^n = 0.99$$
$$(0.1)^n = 0.01$$
$$n = 2.$$

$n = 3$, $p = 0.80$, $q = 0.20$, where p is the probability of busy and q is the probability of free.

45. a) The probability that at least one operator will be free is $1 - P(0 \text{ free}) = 1 - C_0^3(0.2)^0(0.8)^3 = 1 - (1)(1)(0.512) = 0.488$.

b) This is

$$P(2 \text{ free}) + P(3 \text{ free}) = C_2^3(0.2)^2(0.8) + C_3^3(0.2)^3(0.8)^0$$
$$= 3(0.04)(0.8) + 1(0.008)(1)$$
$$= 0.104.$$

47. a) 0.778

b) 0.072

c) 0.004

49. a) $\sum_{0}^{10} = 0.034$.

b) $\sum_{10}^{25} = 1 - \sum_{0}^{9} = 1 - 0.013 = 0.987$.

c) $\sum_{16}^{25} = 1 - \sum_{0}^{15} = 1 - 0.575 = 0.425$.

d) $\sum_{15}^{20} = \sum_{0}^{20} - \sum_{0}^{14} = 0.991 - 0.414 = 0.577$.

e) $P(10) = \sum_{0}^{10} - \sum_{0}^{9} = 0.034 - 0.013 = 0.021$.

51. $100P(2 \text{ or } 7 \text{ or } 11) - 16P(3 \text{ or } 4 \text{ or } 5 \text{ or } 6 \text{ or } 8 \text{ or } 9 \text{ or } 10 \text{ or } 12)$

$$= 100\left(\frac{1 + 6 + 2}{36}\right) - 16\left(\frac{2 + 3 + 4 + 5 + 5 + 4 + 3 + 1}{36}\right) = \$13.$$

53. The conditions of the problem lead to the following payoff table:

Probability	Demand	A_0 Make 0	A_1 Make 1	A_2 Make 2	A_3 Make 3
0.1	0	0	−5	−10	−15
0.2	1	0	10	5	0
0.4	2	0	10	20	15
0.3	3	0	10	20	30

Multiplying payoffs by probabilities, we have:

	A_0	A_1	A_2	A_3
	0	−0.5	−1.0	−1.5
	0	2.0	1.0	0.0
	0	4.0	8.0	6.0
	0	3.0	6.0	9.0
EMV	0	8.5	14.0	13.5

The choice should be the act with the largest EMV, which is to make 2 units.

55. ($40,000)(0.0010) + ($80,000)(0.0008) + ($120,000)(0.0006) + ($160,000)(0.0004) + ($200,000)(0.0002) = $280.

1. a) $f(x) = 3x - 2$

    $f(3) = 3(3) - 2$

    $\quad = 9 - 2$

    $\quad = 7$

    b) $f(-2) = 3(-2) - 2$

    $\quad\quad = -6 - 2$

    $\quad\quad = -8$

    c) $f(a) = 3a - 2$

    d) $[f(a)]^2 = (3a - 2)^2$

    $\quad\quad\quad = (3a - 2)(3a - 2)$

    $\quad\quad\quad = 9a^2 - 6a - 6a + 4$

    $\quad\quad\quad = 9a^2 - 12a + 4$

    e) $f(ab) = 3ab - 2$

    f) $f(3y + 4) = 3(3y + 4) - 2$

    $\quad\quad\quad\quad = 9y + 12 - 2$

    $\quad\quad\quad\quad = 9y + 10$

    g) $f(x + 1) = 3(x + 1) - 2$

    $\quad\quad\quad\quad = 3x + 3 - 2$

    $\quad\quad\quad\quad = 3x + 1$

    h) $f(x + 1) - f(x) = [3(x + 1) - 2] - [3x - 2]$

    $\quad\quad\quad\quad\quad\quad = 3x + 3 - 2 - [3x - 2]$

    $\quad\quad\quad\quad\quad\quad = 3x + 1 - 3x + 2$

    $\quad\quad\quad\quad\quad\quad = 3$

5. $p(x) = 2x^{-1} - 3x^{-2}$

    a) $p(2) = 2(2^{-1}) - 3(2^{-2})$

    $\quad\quad = \dfrac{2}{2} - \dfrac{3}{4}$

    $\quad\quad = \dfrac{4}{4} - \dfrac{3}{4} = \dfrac{1}{4}$

    b) $p(3) = 2(3^{-1}) - 3(3^{-2})$

    $\quad\quad = \dfrac{2}{3} - \dfrac{3}{9}$

    $\quad\quad = \dfrac{6}{9} - \dfrac{3}{9} = \dfrac{3}{9} = \dfrac{1}{3}$

    c) $p(a) = \dfrac{2}{a} - \dfrac{3}{a^2}$

    $\quad\quad = \dfrac{2a}{a^2} - \dfrac{3}{a^2} = \dfrac{2a - 3}{a^2}$

d) $p(x + 1) = \dfrac{2}{x + 1} - \dfrac{3}{(x + 1)^2}$

$$= \dfrac{2x + 2}{(x + 1)^2} - \dfrac{3}{(x + 1)^2} = \dfrac{2x - 1}{(x + 1)^2}$$

9. $f(x) = 2x^2 - 10x + 8$ find $f(x + \Delta x) - f(x)$ if x changes from zero by the amount $\Delta x = 0.1$

$$f(0.1) - f(0) = [2(0.1)^2 - 10(0.1) + 8] - [2(0)^2 - 10(0) + 8]$$
$$= 0.02 - 1 + 8 - 8$$
$$= -0.98$$

13. $f(x) = 2x^2$

a) $f(x + \Delta x) - f(x) = [2(x + \Delta x)^2] - [2x^2]$
$$= 2(x^2 + 2x(\Delta x) + (\Delta x)^2) - 2x^2$$
$$= 2x^2 + 4x(\Delta x) + 2(\Delta x)^2 - 2x^2$$
$$= 4x(\Delta x) + 2(\Delta x)^2$$

b) $g(x) = x^2 + 2x - 10$

$$g(x + \Delta x) - g(x) = [(x^2 + 2x(\Delta x) + (\Delta x)^2) + (2x + 20x - 10)] - [x^2 + 2x - 10]$$
$$= x^2 + 2x(\Delta x) + (\Delta x)^2 + 2x + 20x - 10 - x^2 - 2x + 10$$
$$= 2x(\Delta x) + (\Delta x)^2 + 2(\Delta x)$$

15. $C(g) = 50 + g + 0.1g^2$

a) $C(g) - C(g - 1) = [50 + g + 0.1g^2] - [50 + (g - 1) + 0.1(g - 1)^2]$
$$= 50 + g + 0.1g^2 - 50 - (g - 1) - 0.1(g^2 - 2g + 1)$$
$$= 50 + g + 0.1g^2 - 50 - g + 1 - 0.1g^2 + 0.2g - 0.1$$
$$= 0.2g + .9$$

b) marginal cost of the 10th gallon is

$$0.2(10) + 0.90 = \$2.90$$

c) marginal cost of the 50th gallon is

$$0.2(50) + .90 = \$10.90$$

Problem Set 10-2

1. $\lim\limits_{x \to 1}(x^2 + 2x - 2) = \lim\limits_{x \to 1} x^2 + \lim\limits_{x \to 1} 2x - \lim\limits_{x \to 1}(2)$

$$= 1 + 2 \lim\limits_{x \to 1} x - 2$$

$$= 1 + 2 - 2 = 1$$

5. $\lim\limits_{x \to 1} \dfrac{x^2 - 1}{x + 1} = \lim\limits_{x \to 1} \dfrac{(x - 1)(x + 1)}{x + 1}$

$$= \lim\limits_{x \to 1} x - 1$$

$$= 0$$

9. $\lim\limits_{x \to a}(x - 1)^{1/3} = (a - 1)^{1/3}$

13. $\displaystyle\lim_{x\to 3/2}\frac{4x^2 - 9}{2x - 3} = \lim_{x\to 3/2}\frac{(2x - 3)(2x + 3)}{2x - 3}$

$\displaystyle\qquad\qquad\qquad = \lim_{x\to 3/2} 2x + 3$

$\displaystyle\qquad\qquad\qquad = 6$

17. $\left.\begin{array}{l}\displaystyle\lim_{x\to 1/2^+}\frac{2x + 1}{2x - 1} = +\infty \\[3mm] \displaystyle\lim_{x\to 1/2^-}\frac{2x + 1}{2x - 1} = -\infty\end{array}\right\}$ thus $\displaystyle\lim_{x\to 1/2}\frac{2x + 1}{2x - 1}$ does not exist

21. $\displaystyle\lim_{a\to 0}\frac{\dfrac{1}{2 + a} - \dfrac{1}{2}}{a}\left(\frac{2(2 + a)}{2(2 + a)}\right)$

$\displaystyle\lim_{a\to 0}\frac{2 - 2 - a}{2a(2 + a)}$

$\displaystyle\lim_{a\to 0}\frac{-a}{2a(2 + a)}$

$\displaystyle\lim_{a\to 0}\frac{-1}{4 + a} = \frac{-1}{4}$

25. $\displaystyle\lim_{x\to 2}\left(\frac{x}{x - 2} - \frac{2}{x - 2}\right) = \lim_{x\to 2^+}\left(\frac{x - 2}{x - 2}\right) = 1$

29. $\displaystyle\lim_{x\to 2}\frac{x^2 + x - 6}{x^2 - 4} = \lim_{x\to 2}\frac{(x + 3)(x - 2)}{(x + 2)(x - 2)}$

$\displaystyle\qquad\qquad\qquad = \lim_{x\to 2}\frac{x + 3}{x + 2} = \frac{5}{4}$

Problem Set 10-3

1. $f(x) = x^3 + 2x - 4$ is continuous

5. $f(x) = \dfrac{x^2 - 4}{x - 2}$ is discontinuous at $x = 2$

9. $f(x) = \begin{cases}x^2 + 1 & x \geq 2 \\ x + 3 & x < 2\end{cases}$ is continuous

Problem Set 10-4

1. $f(x) = 3x + 2$ at $x = 1$

   1) $f(x + \Delta x) = 3(x + \Delta x) + 2$
   $\qquad\qquad = 3x + 3\Delta x + 2$

   2) $\dfrac{\Delta f(x)}{\Delta x} = \dfrac{f(x + \Delta x) - f(x)}{\Delta x}$

   $\qquad = \dfrac{3x + 3\Delta x + 2 - (3x + 2)}{\Delta x}$

   $\qquad = \dfrac{3\Delta x}{\Delta x} = 3$

171

3) $\lim_{\Delta x \to 0} 3 = 3$

at $x = 1$ slope $= 3$

5. $f(x) = 1/x$ at $x = 2$

   1) $f(x + \Delta x) = \dfrac{1}{x + \Delta x}$

   2) $\dfrac{\Delta f(x)}{\Delta x} = \dfrac{\dfrac{1}{x + \Delta x} - \dfrac{1}{x}}{\Delta x}\left(\dfrac{x(x + \Delta x)}{x(x + \Delta x)}\right)$

   $= \dfrac{x - x - \Delta x}{x \Delta x (x + \Delta x)}$

   $= \dfrac{-\Delta x}{x \Delta x (x + \Delta x)}$

   $= \dfrac{-1}{x(x + \Delta x)}$

   $= \dfrac{-1}{x^2 + x \Delta x}$

   3) $\lim_{\Delta x \to 0} \dfrac{-1}{x^2 + x \Delta x} = \dfrac{-1}{x^2}$

   slope at $x = 2$ is $-\dfrac{1}{4}$

9. $f(x) = x^4$ at $x = -1$

   1) $f(x + \Delta x) = (x + \Delta x)^4$

   $= x^4 + 4x^3 \Delta x + 6x^2 \Delta x^2 + 4x \Delta x^3 + \Delta x^4$

   2) $\dfrac{\Delta f(x)}{\Delta x} = 4x^3 + 6x^2 \Delta x + 4x \Delta x^2 + \Delta x^3$

   3) $\lim_{\Delta x \to 0} = 4x^3$

   slope at $x = -1$ is -4

13. $f'(x) = \lim_{\Delta x \to 0} \dfrac{(x + \Delta x)^{1/3} - x^{1/3}}{\Delta x}$

Problem Set 10-5

1. $f(x) = 2 + k$
   $f'(x) = 0$

5. $f(x) = \dfrac{x}{3} + 4$

   $f'(x) = \dfrac{1}{3}$

9. $f(x) = .01x^2 + 2x + 100$
   $= (2)(.01)x' + 2$
   $= .02x + 2$

172

13. $f(x) = \dfrac{2}{x} - \dfrac{1}{x^2}$

$$= 2x^{-1} - x^{-2}$$
$$= (-1)(2)x^{-1-1} - (-2)x^{-2-1}$$
$$= -2x^{-2} + 2x^{-3}$$

$$= \dfrac{-2}{x^2} + \dfrac{2}{x^3}$$

17. $f(x) = \dfrac{1}{3x} + \dfrac{2}{x^{1/2}}$

$$= \dfrac{1}{3}x^{-1} + 2(x^{-1/2})$$

$$= (-1)\left(\dfrac{1}{3}\right)x^{-2} + (2)\left(\dfrac{-1}{2}\right)(x^{-3/2})$$

$$= \dfrac{-1}{3}x^{-2} + x^{-3/2}$$

$$= \dfrac{-1}{3x^2} - \dfrac{1}{x^{3/2}}$$

21. $\dfrac{d}{dz}(a^z + b) = \dfrac{d}{dz}az + \dfrac{d}{dz}b$

$$= a$$

25. $f(x) = 3;\ x = 1$

$f'(x) = 0$

$f'(1) = 0$

29. $f(x) = 3x^2 - 2x + 5;\ x = 0.5$

$f'(x) = 6x - 2$

$f'(0.5) = 6(0.5) - 2 = 1$

33. $f(x) = 8x^{1/3} + x;\ x = 8$

$f'(x) = \dfrac{1}{3}8x^{-2/3} + 1$

$f'(x) = \dfrac{8}{3x^{2/3}} + 1$

$f'(8) = \dfrac{8}{3(8^{2/3})} + 1 = \dfrac{8}{12} + 1 = \dfrac{5}{3}$

37. $f(x) = 3x^{1/3} - 4x;\ x > 0$

$f'(x) = \dfrac{1}{3}3x^{-2/3} - 4$

$f'(x) = \dfrac{1}{x^{2/3}} - 4 = 0$

$\dfrac{1}{x^{2/3}} = 4 \qquad 4x^{2/3} = 1 \qquad \boxed{x = \dfrac{1}{8}}$

41. $c(y) = .001y^2 + 2y + 500$

   $c'(y) = .002y + 2$

   a) $c'(1,000) = .002(1,000) + 2 = \$4/\text{yard}$

   b) $c'(2,000) = .002(2,000) + 2 = \$6/\text{yard}$

Problem Set 10-6

1. $f'(x) = 5(6x - 5)^4(6)$

   $= 30(6x - 5)^4$

5. $f'(x) = \dfrac{1}{2}(4x)^{-1/2}(4)$

   $= \dfrac{2}{(4x)^{1/2}}$

   $= \dfrac{1}{x^{1/2}}$

9. $f'(x) = \dfrac{5}{2}(3x^2 - 6x + 2)^{3/2}(6x - 6)$

   $= 15(3x^2 - 6x + 2)^{3/2}(x - 1)$

13. $f'(x) = (-1)4(2x - 3)^{-2}(2)$

   $= \dfrac{-8}{(2x - 3)^2}$

17. $f'(x) = (-2)(9)(3x - 5)^{-3}(3)$

   $= \dfrac{-54}{(3x - 5)^3}$

21. $f'(x) = 3 + \dfrac{-1}{2}(5 + 2x)^{-3/2}(2)$

   $= 3 - \dfrac{1}{(5 + 2x)^{3/2}}$

Problem Set 10-7

1. $f'(x) = (3x - 2)(2) + (2x + 5)(3)$

   $= 6x - 4 + 6x + 15$

   $= 12x + 11$

5. $f'(x) = x(4)(x - 1)^3(1) + (x - 1)^4(1)$

   $= 4x(x - 1)^3 + (x - 1)^4$

   $= (x - 1)^3(5x - 1)$

9. $f'(x) = 2x\left(\dfrac{1}{3}\right)(3x^2 + 7)^{-2/3}(6x) + (3x^2 + 7)^{1/3}(2)$

   $= 4x^2(3x^2 + 7)^{-2/3} + 2(3x^2 + 7)^{1/3}$

   $= \dfrac{4x^2 + 6x^2 + 14}{(3x^2 + 7)^{2/3}} = \dfrac{2(5x^2 + 7)}{(3x^2 + 7)^{2/3}}$

13. $f'(x) = \dfrac{(2x + 3)(2x) - (x^2)(2)}{(2x + 3)^2}$

$ = \dfrac{4x^2 + 6x - 2x^2}{(2x + 3)^2} = \dfrac{2x(x + 3)}{(2x + 3)^2}$

17. $f'(x) = \dfrac{(3x + 2)^{1/2}(1) - x(1/2)(3x + 2)^{-1/2}(3)}{((3x + 2)^{1/2})^2}$

$ = \dfrac{(3x + 2)^{1/2} - \dfrac{3}{2}x(3x + 2)^{-1/2}}{(3x + 2)}$

$ = \dfrac{3x + 4}{2(3x + 2)^{3/2}}$

1. $f(x) = 3x^2 + 2x + 5$.

   a) $f(0) = 5$.

   b) $f(1) = 10$.

   c) $f(-1) = 6$.

   d) $f(5) = 90$.

   e) $f(2a) = 3(2a)^2 + 2(2a) + 5 = 12a^2 + 4a + 5$.

   f) $f\left(\dfrac{1}{x+1}\right) = 3\left[\dfrac{1}{(x+1)^2}\right] + 2\left(\dfrac{1}{x+1}\right) + 5 = \dfrac{3 + 2(x+1) + 5(x+1)^2}{(x+1)^2}$

   $$= \dfrac{3 + 2x + 2 + 5x^2 + 10x + 5}{(x+1)^2}$$

   $$= \dfrac{5x^2 + 12x + 10}{(x+1)^2}.$$

   g) $f(x+1) - f(x) = [3(x+1)^2 + 2(x+1) + 5] - (3x^2 + 2x + 5)$

   $$= 3x^2 + 6x + 3 + 2x + 2 + 5 - 3x^2 - 2x - 5$$

   $$= 6x + 5.$$

   h) $f(x) - f(x-a) = (3x^2 + 2x + 5) - [3(x-a)^2 + 2(x-a) + 5]$

   $$= 3x^2 + 2x + 5 - 3x^2 + 6ax - 3a^2 - 2x + 2a - 5$$

   $$= 6ax - 3a^2 + 2a.$$

3. $f(x) = 32x^{-1} - 2x^{-2/3} + 24x^{-1/2}$

   $$f(64) = \dfrac{32}{64} - \dfrac{2}{(64)^{2/3}} + \dfrac{24}{(64)^{1/2}}$$

   $$= \dfrac{1}{2} - \dfrac{2}{16} + \dfrac{24}{8}$$

   $$= \dfrac{8 - 2 + 48}{16} = \dfrac{54}{16} = \dfrac{27}{8}.$$

5. a) $f(x) = 3x^2 - 2x + 4$:

   $$\Delta f(x) = f(x + \Delta x) - f(x)$$

   $$= 3(x + \Delta x)^2 - 2(x + \Delta x) + 4 - (3x^2 - 2x + 4)$$

   $$= 3[x^2 + 2x(\Delta x) + (\Delta x)^2] - 2x - 2(\Delta x) + 4 - 3x^2 + 2x - 4$$

   $$= 3x^2 + 6x(\Delta x) + 3(\Delta x)^2 - 2x - 2(\Delta x) + 4 - 3x^2 + 2x - 4$$

   $$= \Delta x[6x + 3(\Delta x) - 2].$$

   b) If $x = 2$, $\Delta x = 0.1$:

   $$\Delta f(x) = 0.1[6(2) + 3(0.1) - 2]$$

   $$= 0.1(10.3)$$

   $$= 1.03.$$

7. $(3(0^2) - 2(0) + 5) = 5$

9. Numerator approaches 2, denominator approaches 0. No limit exists.

11. $2\left(\dfrac{1}{8^{2/3}}\right) = \dfrac{1}{2}$

13. $[b^2 + 2(b)b + b^2] = 4b^2$

15. $\lim\limits_{x \to 0} x^{2/3} = 0$

17. $\lim\limits_{x \to 0}(8 + x)^{1/3} = 8^{1/3} = 2$

19. $f'(x) = \lim\limits_{\Delta x \to 0} \dfrac{f(x + \Delta x) - f(x)}{\Delta x}$

21. $f(x + \Delta x) - f(x) = (x + \Delta x)^2 + 3(x + \Delta x) - 2 - x^2 - 3x + 2$

$\qquad\qquad\qquad\quad = x^2 + 2x(\Delta x) + (\Delta x)^2 + 3x + 3(\Delta x) - 2 - x^2 - 3x + 2$

$\qquad\qquad\qquad\quad = \Delta x[2x + (\Delta x) + 3].$

$\quad f'(x) = \lim\limits_{\Delta x \to 0} \dfrac{\Delta x[2x + \Delta x + 3]}{\Delta x}$

$\qquad\quad = \lim\limits_{\Delta x \to 0}(2x + \Delta x + 3)$

$\qquad\quad = 2x + 3.$

23. $f(x + \Delta x) - f(x) = \dfrac{2}{3(x + \Delta x) - 5} - \dfrac{2}{3x - 5}$

$\qquad\qquad\qquad\quad = \dfrac{2(3x - 5) - 2[3(x + \Delta x) - 5]}{[3(x + \Delta x) - 5](3x - 5)} = \dfrac{-6\Delta x}{[3(x + \Delta x) - 5](3x - 5)}.$

$\quad f'(x) = \lim\limits_{\Delta x \to 0} \dfrac{\dfrac{-6\Delta x}{[3(x + \Delta x) - 5](3x - 5)}}{\Delta x}$

$\qquad\quad = \lim\limits_{\Delta x \to 0} \dfrac{-6}{[3(x + \Delta x) - 5](3x - 5)}$

$\qquad\quad = -\dfrac{6}{(3x - 5)^2}.$

25. $f(x + \Delta x) - f(x) = (x + \Delta x)^{3/2} - x^{3/2}.$

$\quad f'(x) = \lim\limits_{\Delta x \to 0} \dfrac{(x + \Delta x)^{3/2} - x^{3/2}}{\Delta x}$

$\qquad\quad = \lim\limits_{\Delta x \to 0}\left[\dfrac{(x + \Delta x)^{3/2} - x^{3/2}}{\Delta x}\right]\left[\dfrac{(x + \Delta x)^{3/2} + x^{3/2}}{(x + \Delta x)^{3/2} + x^{3/2}}\right].$

$\quad f'(x) = \lim\limits_{\Delta x \to 0} \dfrac{(x + \Delta x)^3 - x^3}{\Delta x[(x + \Delta x)^{3/2} + x^{3/2}]}$

$\qquad\quad = \lim\limits_{\Delta x \to 0} \dfrac{x^3 + 3x^2(\Delta x) + 3x(\Delta x)^2 + (\Delta x)^3 - x^3}{\Delta x[(x + \Delta x)^{3/2} + x^{3/2}]}$

$\qquad\quad = \lim\limits_{\Delta x \to 0} \dfrac{\Delta x[3x^2 + 3x(\Delta x) + (\Delta x)^2]}{\Delta x[(x + \Delta x)^{3/2} + x^{3/2}]}$

$\qquad\quad = \dfrac{3x^2}{2x^{3/2}} = \dfrac{3x^{1/2}}{2}.$

27. $f'(x) = \lim\limits_{\Delta x \to 0} \dfrac{\dfrac{12}{x + \Delta x} - \dfrac{12}{x}}{\Delta x}$

$\quad = \lim\limits_{\Delta x \to 0} \dfrac{12x - 12x - 12\Delta x}{\Delta x(x + \Delta x)(x)}$

$\quad = \lim\limits_{\Delta x \to 0} \dfrac{-12}{(x + \Delta x)(x)} = -\dfrac{12}{x^2};$

then the slope at $x = 2$ is $\quad f'(2) = -\dfrac{12}{2^2} = -3.$

29. $f'(x) = -4$

31. $f'(x) = x^3 - 5x + 1$

33. $f'(x) = y - 2ax$

35. $f(x) = \dfrac{1}{3}x^{-2} - \dfrac{1}{x}$

$\quad f'(x) = \dfrac{-2}{3}x^{-3} + \dfrac{1}{x^2}$

$\quad f'(x) = -\dfrac{2}{3x^3} + \dfrac{1}{x^2}$

37. $f'(x) = \dfrac{4}{3}(6)x^{1/3} - \dfrac{2}{3}(3)x^{-1/3} - 2$

$\quad = 8x^{1/3} - \dfrac{2}{x^{1/3}} - 2$

39. $f'(x) = -\dfrac{1}{2}x^{-3/2} + \dfrac{1}{3}x^{-4/3} + 4 = -\dfrac{1}{2x^{3/2}} + \dfrac{1}{3x^{4/3}} +$

41. $f(x) = 2xy - 2 + 3x^2$

43. $f'(x) = \dfrac{x^2}{2} + \dfrac{18}{x^2} + 2; \; f'(2) = 2 + \dfrac{18}{4} + 2 = 8.5.$

45. $f'(x) = 1 - \dfrac{6}{x^{3/2}}; \; f'(4) = 1 - \dfrac{6}{4^{3/2}} = 1 - \dfrac{6}{8} = 0.25.$

47. $f'(x) = 2 - \dfrac{72}{x^2}; \; 2 - \dfrac{72}{x^2} = 0.$

$\quad\quad\quad\quad 2x^2 - 72 = 0$

$\quad\quad\quad\quad\quad\quad x^2 = 36.$

$\quad\quad\quad\quad x = 6 \text{ and } -6.$

49. $f'(x) = 3x^2 - 12;$ $3x^2 - 12 = 0$
$$x^2 = 4$$
$$x = 2 \text{ and } -2.$$

51. $f'(x) = 0.1 - \dfrac{6.4}{x^{3/2}};$ $0.1 - \dfrac{6.4}{x^{3/2}} = 0$
$$0.1x^{3/2} = 6.4$$
$$x^{3/2} = 64$$
$$(x^{3/2})^{2/3} = (64)^{2/3}$$
$$x = (4)^2 = 16.$$

53. $f(x) = (2x^3 + 3x^2 + 4x - 50)^{3/2}:$
$$f'(x) = \frac{3}{2}(2x^3 + 3x^2 + 4x - 50)^{1/2}(6x^2 + 6x + 4)$$
$$= 3(2x^3 + 3x^2 + 4x - 50)^{1/2}(3x^2 + 3x + 2).$$

55. $f'(x) = \dfrac{1}{2}(10x)^{-1/2}(10) = \dfrac{5}{(10x)^{1/2}}$

57. $f(x) = \left(5 - \dfrac{2}{x}\right)^3 = (5 - 2x^{-1})^3.$
$$f'(x) = 3(5 - 2x^{-1})^2[-2(-1)x^{-2}]$$
$$= 6\left(5 - \frac{2}{x}\right)^2\left(\frac{1}{x^2}\right).$$

59. $f(x) = x - \dfrac{1}{(5 - 0.3x)^{1/3}} = x - (5 - 0.3)^{-1/3}.$
$$f'(x) = 1 - \left(-\frac{1}{3}\right)(5 - 0.3x)^{-4/3}(-0.3)$$
$$= 1 - \frac{0.1}{(5 - 0.3x)^{4/3}}.$$

61. $f(x) = x + \dfrac{50}{(2 + 0.5x)} = x + 50(2 + 0.5x)^{-1}.$
$$f'(x) = 1 - 50(2 + 0.5x)^{-2}(0.5)$$
$$= 1 - \frac{25}{(2 + 0.5x)^2}.$$

Setting $f'(x) = 0$, we have

$$1 - \frac{25}{(2 + 0.5x)^2} = 0$$
$$(2 + 0.5x)^2 = 25$$
$$2 + 0.5x = 5 \text{ or } -5.$$
$$x = 6 \text{ and } x = -14.$$

63. $f(x) = 2x(x^3 - 5x)^{1/2}$.

$$f'(x) = 2x\left(\frac{1}{2}\right)(x^3 - 5x)^{-1/2}(3x^2 - 5) + (x^3 - 5x)^{1/2}(2)$$

$$= \frac{x(3x^2 - 5)}{(x^3 - 5x)^{1/2}} + 2(x^3 - 5x)^{1/2}.$$

65. $f(x) = (2x + 1)(4x - 5)^{1/2}$.

$$f'(x) = (2x + 1)\left(\frac{1}{2}\right)(4x - 5)^{-1/2}(4) + (4x - 5)^{1/2}(2)$$

$$= \frac{2(2x + 1)}{(4x - 5)^{1/2}} + 2(4x - 5)^{1/2}.$$

67. $f(x) = \dfrac{x}{1 - 0.5x^2}$.

$$f'(x) = \frac{(1 - 0.5x^2)(1) - x(-x)}{(1 - 0.5x^2)^2} = \frac{1 + 0.5x^2}{(1 - 0.5x^2)^2}.$$

69. $f(x) = \dfrac{2x - 1}{(2x + 3)^{1/2}}$.

$$f'(x) = \frac{(2x + 3)^{1/2}(2) - (2x - 1)\left(\frac{1}{2}\right)(2x + 3)^{-1/2}(2)}{2x + 3}$$

$$= \frac{2(2x + 3)^{1/2} - \dfrac{2x - 1}{(2x + 3)^{1/2}}}{2x + 3}$$

$$= \frac{2(2x + 3)^1 - (2x - 1)}{(2x + 3)^{3/2}}$$

$$= \frac{2x + 7}{(2x + 3)^{3/2}}.$$

1. $A(x) = \dfrac{100}{x} + 0.4x + 1$

a) find the derivative

$A'(x) = 100x^{-1} + .04x + 1$

$= -100x^{-2} + .04$

$= -\dfrac{100}{x^2} + .04$

factor and set equal to 0

$$.04\left(-\dfrac{2,500}{x^2} + 1\right) = 0$$

$.04 \neq 0 \qquad -\dfrac{2,500}{x^2} + 1 = 0$

$$-\dfrac{2,500}{x^2} = -1$$

$$-2,500 = -x^2$$

$$-50 = -x$$

$$x = 50$$

In order to obtain the minimum cost per gallon 50 gallons should be produced.

b) Plug 50 into the original equation

$A(50) = \dfrac{100}{50} + .04(50) + 1$

$= 2 + 2 + 1$

$= 5$

The minimum average cost per gallon is $5.00

c) Second derivative test

$A''(x) = -100x^{-2} + .04$

$= 200x^{-3}$

$= \dfrac{200}{x^3}$

$A''(50) = \dfrac{200}{(50)^3}$

$= \dfrac{200}{12,500}$

$= .0016$

The test is positive which indicates a minimum.

5. $f(x) = 5x - x^2$

   derivative

   $f'(x) = 5 - 2x$

   set it equal to 0

   $5 - 2x = 0$

   $5 = 2x$

   $x = \dfrac{2}{5}$

   $x = 2.5$

   $f(2.5) = 5(2.5) - (2.5)^2$

   $= 12.5 - 6.25$

   $= 6.25$

   local optimum points (2.5, 6.25)

   Second derivative test

   $f''(x) = -2$

   $f''(2.5) = -2$

   test is negative proving a maximum point.

9. $f(x) = 30x - 3x^2 + 10$

   derivative

   $f'(x) = 30 - 6x$

   Set equal to 0

   $30 - 6x = 0$

   $30 = 6x$

   $x = 5$

   $f(5) = 30(5) - 3(5)^2 + 10$

   $= 150 - 75 + 10$

   $= 85$

   local optimum points (5, 85)

   Second derivative test

   $f''(x) = -6$

   $f''(5) = -6$

   test is negative proving a maximum point.

13. $f(x) = 3x^3 + 27$

   derivative

   $f'(x) = 9x^2$

   Set equal to 0

   $9x^2 = 0$

   $x^2 = 0$

   There are no local extremes

17. $f(x) = x^3 - 9x^2 + 27x$ on $[-1, 1]$

find the derivative

$f'(x) = 3x^2 - 18x + 27$

factor and set equal to 0

$3(x^2 - 6x + 9)$

$3(x - 3)(x - 3)$

$3 \neq 0 \quad x - 3 = 0$

$\qquad\qquad x = 3$

$f(3) = 3^3 - 9(3)^2 + 27(3)$

$\quad = 27 - 81 + 81$

$\quad = 27$

(3, 27)

$f''(x) = 6x - 18$ $f''(3) = 6(3) - 18$

$\qquad = 6(x - 3)$ $= 18 - 18$

$6 \neq 0 \quad x - 3 = 0$ $= 0$

$\qquad\qquad x = 3$ (3, 0) is an inflection point

$f(-1) = (-1)^3 - 9(-1)^2 + 27(-1)$ $f(1) = 1^3 - 9(1)^2 + 27(1)$

$\qquad = -1 - 9 - 27$ $= 1 - 9 + 27$

$\qquad = -37$ $= 19$

$(-1, -37)$ (1, 19)

$f'(-1) = 3 + 18 + 27 = 48$ $f'(1) = 3 - 18 + 27 = 12$

The point is a minimum   The point is a maximum

21. $f(x) = 4x^3 - 3x^4 + 4$ on $[-1, 2]$

derivative

$f'(x) = 12x^2 - 12x^3$

factor and set equal to 0

$12x^2(1 - x) = 0$

$12x^2 = 0 \qquad 1 - x = 0$

$\quad x = 0 \qquad\qquad x = 1$

$f(0) = 4(0)^3 - 3(0)^4 + 4$

$\quad = 4$

(0, 4) inflection pt.

$f(1) = 4(1)^3 - 3(1)^4 + 4$

$\quad = 4 - 3 + 4$

$\quad = 5$

(1, 5) maximum

$f''(x) = 24x - 36x^2$

$f''(0) = 24(0) - 36(0)^2$

$\quad\quad = 0$

$f''(1) = 24(1) - 36(1)^2$

$\quad\quad\quad 24 - 36 = -12$

negative proves maximum

$f(-1) = 4(-1)^3 - 3(-1)^4 + 4$

$\quad\quad = -4 - 3 + 4$

$\quad\quad = -3$

$(-1, -3)$

$f'(-_1^+) > 0$ so end point minimum at $(-1, -3)$

25. $f(x) = x^{3/2} - 12x^{1/2}$

derivative

$f'(x) = \dfrac{3}{2}x^{1/2} - 6x^{-1/2}$

factor and set equal to 0

$\dfrac{3}{2}x^{-1/2}(x - 4)$

$\dfrac{3}{2}x^{1/2} = 0 \quad\quad x - 4 = 0$

$\quad x = 0 \quad\quad\quad\quad x = 4$

$f(0) = 0^{3/2} - 12(0)^{1/2}$

$\quad\quad = 0$

$(0, 0)$ inflection pt.

$f(4) = 4^{3/2} - 12(4)^{1/2}$

$\quad\quad = 8 - 24$

$\quad\quad = -16$

$(4, -16)$ minimum

Second derivative test

$f''(x) = \dfrac{3}{4}x^{-1/2} + 3x^{-3/2}$

$f''(4) = \dfrac{3}{4}(4)^{-1/2} + 3(4)^{-3/2}$

$\quad\quad = \dfrac{3}{4}(.5) + 3(.125)$

$\quad\quad = .375 + .375$

$\quad\quad = .75$

positive indicates minimum

Problem Set 11-2

1. $f(x) = x^5 - 2x^4 + x^3 + 3$

   first derivative

   $f'(x) = 5x^4 - 8x^3 + 3x^2$

   second derivative

   $f''(x) = 20x^3 - 24x^2 + 6x$

5. $f(x) = 3x^4 - 5x^3 + 2x^2$

   first derivative

   $f'(x) = 12x^3 - 15x^2 + 4x$

   second derivative

   $f''(x) = 36x^2 - 30x + 4$

9. $f(x) = \dfrac{3x + 4}{x - 3}$

   first derivative

   $$f'(x) = \frac{3(x - 3) - (3x + 4)(1)}{(x - 3)^2} = \frac{-13}{(x - 3)^2}$$

   second derivative

   $$f''(x) = \frac{26}{(x - 3)^3}$$

13. $f(x) = x^3 - 6x^2 + 9x + 1$

    derivative

    $f'(x) = 3x^2 - 12x + 9$

    factor and set equal to 0

    $3(x^2 - 4x + 3) = 0$

    $3 \neq 0 \qquad x^2 - 4x + 3 = 0$

    $\qquad\qquad (x - 3)(x - 1) = 0$

    $\qquad\qquad x = 3 \qquad x = 1$

    so

    $f(3) = (3)^3 - 6(3)^2 + 9(3) + 1$ To find inflection points set $f''(x) = 0$

    $\quad = 27 - 54 + 27 + 1$ $f''(x) = 6x - 12$

    $\quad = 1$ $6(x - 2) = 0$

    $(3, 1)$ $6 \neq 0 \qquad x = 2$

    $f(1) = (1)^3 - 6(1)^2 + 9(1) + 1$ $f''(2) = 6(2) - 12$

    $\quad = 1 - 6 + 9 + 1 = 5$ $= 0$

    $(1, 5)$ $(2, 0)$ is a point of inflection

Second derivative test

$f''(x) = 6x - 12$

$f(3) = 6(3) - 12$

$\quad = 18 - 12$

$\quad = +6$

Positive indicates minimum

$f(1) = 6(1) - 12$

$\quad = 6 - 12$

$\quad = -6$

negative indicates maximum

17. $f(x) = -x^3 - 12x^2 - 45x + 2$

derivative

$f'(x) = -3x^2 - 24x - 45$

factor and set equal to 0

$-3(x^2 + 8x + 15)$

$-3(x + 3)(x + 5)$

$-3 \neq 0 \quad x + 3 = 0 \qquad x + 5 = 0$

$\qquad\qquad x = -3 \qquad\quad x = -5$

find local optimum points

$f(-3) = -(-3)^3 - 12(-3)^2 - 45(-3) + 2$

$\quad = 27 - 108 + 135 + 2$

$\quad = 56$

$(-3, 56)$

$f(-5) = -(-5)^3 - 12(-5)^2 - 45(-5) + 2$

$\quad = 125 - 300 + 225 + 2$

$\quad = 52$

$(-5, 52)$

Second derivative test

$f''(x) = -6x - 24$

$f''(-3) = -6(-3) - 24$

$\qquad = 18 - 24$

$\qquad = -6$

$f''(-5) = -6(-5) - 24$

$\qquad = 30 - 24$

$\qquad = 6$

Test proves maximum point

Now $f''(x) = -6x - 24 = 0$

if $\qquad -6(x + 4) = 0 \quad$ so

Test proves minimum

pt of inflection at $(-4, 54)$

$-6 \neq 0$

$x = -4$

Problem Set 11-3

1.

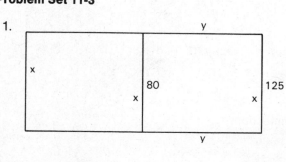

$xy = 3,300$

$y = \dfrac{3,300}{x}$

186

$$2(125x) + 2(125y) + 80x = w$$

$$2(125x) + 2(125)\left(\frac{3,300}{x}\right) + 80x = w$$

$$250 + 250\left(\frac{3,300}{x}\right) + 80x = w$$

$$330x + 825,000x^{-1} = w$$

derivative

$$f'(x) = 330 - 825,000x^{-2}$$

$$330 - 825,000x^{-2} = 0$$

$$825,000x^{-2} = 330$$

$$\frac{825,000}{x^2} = 330$$

$$825,000 = 330x^2$$

$$\frac{825,000}{330} = x^2$$

$$x^2 = 2,500$$

$$x = 50$$

$$xy = 3,300$$

$$50y = 3,300$$

$$y = \frac{3,300}{50} \qquad y = 66$$

50×66 dimensions will minimize the total wall cost.

$$f(x, y) = 2(125)(50) + 2(125)(66) + 80(50)$$

$$= 12,500 + 16,500 + 4,000 = \$33,000.00$$

minimum wall cost is $33,000.00

5.

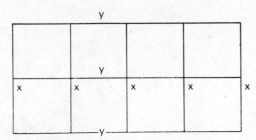

$$xy = 13,500$$

$$y = \frac{13,500}{x}$$

$$5x(100) + 3y(100) = w$$

substitute y value into the equation

$$5x(100) + 300\left(\frac{13,500}{x}\right)$$

$$500x + 4,050,000x^{-1} = w$$

$$f'(x) = 500 - 4,050,000x^{-2}$$

187

factor and set equal to 0

$500(1 - 8,100x^{-2})$

$500 \neq 0 \qquad 1 - \dfrac{8,100}{x^2} = 0$

$$\dfrac{8,100}{x^2} = 1$$

$$8,100 = x^2$$

$$x = 90$$

substitute x into original equation to find y

$$y = \dfrac{13,500}{90}$$

$$y = 150$$

Dimensions for minimum total wall cost is
90×150

Substitute (x, y) into cost equation

$5x(100) + 3y(100)$

$5(90)(100) + 3(150)(100)$

$45,000 + 45,000 = 90,000$

minimum cost is $90,000

9.

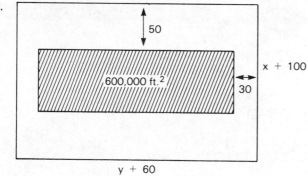

$A = (x + 100)(y + 60)$

$xy = 600,000$

$$y = \dfrac{600,000}{x}$$

$$A = (x + 100)\left(\dfrac{600,000}{x} + 60\right)$$

$$= 600,000 + 60x + \dfrac{60,000,000}{x} + 6,000$$

$$= 606,000 + 60x + 60,000,000x^{-1}$$

find the derivative

$f'(x) = 60 - 60,000,000x^{-2}$

188

factor and set equal to 0

$60(1 - 1,000,000x^{-2})$

$60 \neq 0 \qquad 1 - 1,000,000x^{-2} = 0$

$$1 = \frac{1,000,000}{x^2}$$

$$x^2 = 1,000,000$$

$$x = 1,000$$

substitute x into original equation to find y

$$y = \frac{600,000}{1,000}$$

$$= 600$$

$x = 1,000$, $y = 600$ are the dimensions to the plant now we need to find the dimensions to the buffer strip.

$A = (x + 100)(y + 60)$

$(1,000 + 100)(600 + 60)$

$(1,100)(660)$

$1,100 \times 660$ are the dimensions to the buffer strip, increase would be 10,000 square feet.

13.

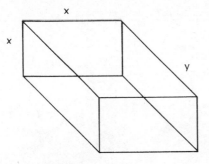

$x^2y = 500$

$$y = \frac{500}{x^2}$$

$$4xy + x^2 = A$$

$$4x\left(\frac{500}{x^2}\right) + x^2 = A$$

$$\frac{2,000}{x} + x^2 = A$$

derivative

$f'(x) = 2,000x^{-1} + x^2$

$\qquad = -2,000x^{-2} + 2x$

factor and set equal to 0

$2x(1 - 1,000x^{-3})$

$$2x = 0 \qquad 1 - \frac{1,000}{x^3} = 0$$
$$x = 0$$

$$1 = \frac{1,000}{x^3}$$

$$x^3 = 1,000$$

$$x = 10$$

substitute both x's to find the y's

$$y = \frac{500}{0} \qquad \text{undefined}$$

$$y = \frac{500}{(10)^2}$$

$$y = \frac{500}{100}$$

$$y = 5$$

dimensions are

$10'' \times 10'' \times 5''$

minimum surface area is:

$$4(10)(5) + (10)^2 = A$$
$$200 + 100 = \underline{300\ in^2}$$
$$\text{Area} = 300 \text{ sq in.}$$

17.

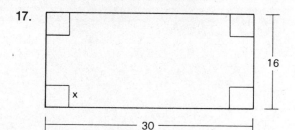

dimensions of finished box

$(30 - 2x) \times (16 - 2x) \times (x)$

$v = (30 - 2x)(16 - 2x)(x)$

$\qquad (480 - 60x - 32x + 4x^2)(x)$

$\qquad (480 - 92x + 4x^2)(x)$

$\qquad 480x - 92x^2 + 4x^3$

$\qquad 4x^3 - 92x^2 + 480x$

$f'(x) = 12x^2 - 184x + 480$

$\qquad 4(3x^2 - 46x + 120)$

$\qquad 4(3x - 10)(x - 12)$

$4 \neq 0 \qquad 3x - 10 = 0 \qquad x - 12 = 0$

$\qquad\qquad\qquad 3x = 10 \qquad\qquad x = 12$

$$x = \frac{10}{3}$$

second derivative test

$$f''(x) = 24x - 184$$

$$f''\left(\frac{10}{3}\right) = 24\left(\frac{10}{3}\right) - 184$$

$$\frac{240}{3} - 184 = 80 - 184 = -104$$

negative indicates a maximum

$$f''(12) = 24(12) - 184$$
$$= 288 - 184$$
$$= 104$$

positive indicates a minimum

the squares (that is x) will be $\dfrac{10''}{3} \times \dfrac{10''}{3}$

21.

a) $\dfrac{80}{\pi}$ (sq mi)

circumference = πr^2

number of calls/mth = $\left(\dfrac{80}{\pi}\right)(\pi r^2)$

$$= 80r^2$$

b) $2.00 per mile
    r = traveled miles
    $24.00 is fixed
    fixed cost − mileage cost
    $24.00 − 2r$ = net travel income per call

c) as computed in 21A the number of calls per month is $80r^2$
    net travel income was found in 21b ($24.00 − 2r$)
    Therefore the total net monthly travel income is:
    $80r^2($24.00 − 2r$)$

d) $f(r) = 1,920r^2 - 160r^3$
    $f'(r) = 3,840r - 480r^2$
    $\quad\ = 480r(8 - r)$

    $480r = 0 \qquad 8 - r = 0$
    $\quad r = 0 \qquad\quad r = 8$

e) $80(8)^2(24 - 2(8))$
    $5,120(8)$
    $40,960.

25.

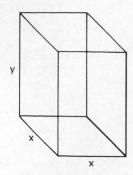

$$4x + y = 108$$
$$y = 108 - 4x$$
$$x^2y = \text{volume}$$

substitute the y value into the equation

$$x^2(108 - 4x) = \text{volume}$$

find the derivative

$$f(x) = 108x^2 - 4x^3$$
$$f'(x) = 216x - 12x^2$$

factor and set equal to 0

$$12x(18 - x)$$

$$12x = 0 \qquad 18 - x = 0$$
$$x = 0 \qquad\qquad x = 18$$

impossible to have a side be 0 inches.

plug 18 into the original equation

$$y = 108 - 4(18)$$
$$y = 36$$

dimensions are $18'' \times 18'' \times 36''$

maximum volume is $(18)^2 36 = 11,664 \text{ in}^3$

29. max $C(p) = p(1 - p)^9$

$$C'(p) = p9(1 - p)^8(-1) + (1 - p)^9(1)$$
$$= -9p(1 - p)^8 + (1 - p)^9$$

set $C'(p) = 0$

$$9p(1 - p)^8 = (1 - p)^9$$
$$9p = 1 - p$$

$$p = \frac{1}{10} \text{ or } .10$$

$$C''(p) = -9p(8)(1 - p)^7(-1) + 9(1 - p)^8(-1)$$
$$= 72p(1 - p)^7 - 9(1 - p)^8$$
$$C''(.1) = 72(.1)(1 - .1)^7 - 9(1 - .1)^8$$
$$= 3.444 - 3.874$$
$$= -.43$$

Problem Set 11-4

1. $A(y) = 2{,}500(.04y + 9)^{-1} + .16y$

   a) $A(y) = 2{,}500(-1)(.04y + 9)^{-2}(.04) + .16$

      set $A'(y) = 0$

      $$\frac{-100}{(.04y + 9)^2} = -.16$$

      $(.04y + 9)^2 = 625$

      $.04y + 9 = 25$

      $y = 400$ barrels

   b) $A(400) = \dfrac{2{,}500}{(.04(400) + 9)} + .16(400)$

      $= \dfrac{2{,}500}{25} + 64$

      $= \$164/\text{barrel}$

5. $f'(x) = \dfrac{1}{2}(10{,}000 - x^2)^{-1/2}(-2x)$

   $= \dfrac{-x}{(10{,}000 - x^2)^{1/2}}$

   $f'(60) = \dfrac{-60}{(10{,}000 - 60^2)^{1/2}} = -.75$

   using $y = mx + b$

   $y = -.75x + b$

   $80 = -.75(60) + b$

   $125 = b$ so $Q = Q(0, 125)$

9. $f(x) = a(bx + c)^{-1} + kx$

   a) $f'(x) = a(-1)(bx + c)^{-2}(b) + k$

      $= \dfrac{-ab}{(bx + c)^2} + k$

      set $f'(x) = 0$

      $(bx + c)^2 = \dfrac{ab}{k}$

      $bx + c = \left(\dfrac{ab}{k}\right)^{1/2}$

      $x = \dfrac{\left(\dfrac{ab}{k}\right)^{1/2} - c}{b}$

   b) $f''(x) = -ab(-2)(bx + c)^{-3}(b)$

      $= \dfrac{2ab^2}{(bx + c)^3}$ is $+$

      so it is a minimum

193

Problem Set 11-5

1. a) $\dfrac{N}{Q}$

   b) $\dfrac{cN}{Q}$

   c) uQ

   d) $\dfrac{p(uQ)}{2}$

   e) $S(Q) = \dfrac{cN}{Q} + uN + \dfrac{p(uQ)}{2}$

   f) $S(Q) = CNQ^{-1} + \dfrac{pu}{2}Q$

   $S'(Q) = (-1)CNQ^{-2} + \dfrac{pu}{2}$

   set $S'(Q) = 0$

   $\dfrac{-CN}{Q^2} = \dfrac{-pu}{2}$

   $Q^2 = \dfrac{2CN}{pu}$

   $Q = \sqrt{\dfrac{2CN}{pu}}$

   g) $Q = \sqrt{\dfrac{2(12)(2400)}{(.25)(4)}} = 240$ units

Problem Set 11-6

1. $f(x) = x^3 - 18x^2 + 96x - 100$

   $f'(x) = 3x^2 - 36x + 96$

   $f''(x) = 6x - 36$

   $3x^2 - 36x + 96 = 0$

   $3(x^2 - 12x + 32) = 0$

   $3(x - 8)(x - 4) = 0$

   $3 \neq 0 \qquad x - 8 = 0 \qquad x - 4 = 0$

   $\qquad\qquad\qquad x = 8 \qquad\qquad x = 4$

   $f(8) = (8)^3 - 18(8)^2 + 96(8) - 100$

   $\quad = 512 - 1,152 + 768 - 100 \qquad (8, 28)$

   $\quad = 28$

   $f(4) = (4)^3 - 18(4)^2 + 96(4) - 100$

   $\quad = 64 - 288 + 384 - 100 \qquad (4, 60)$

   $\quad = 60$

   $f''(8) = 6(8) - 36 = 12$ positive $=$ minimum

   $f''(4) = 6(4) - 36 = -12$ negative $=$ maximum

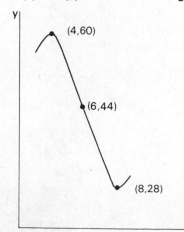

194

1. $f(x) = .5x^2 - 50x + 2{,}500$

    derivative

    $f'(x) = x - 50$

    factor and set equal to 0

    $x - 50 = 0$

    $\quad\quad x = 50$

    $f(50) = .5(50^2) - 50(50) + 2{,}500 = 1{,}250$

    second derivative test

    $\quad f''(x) = 1$

    $f''(50) = 1$

    positive indicates minimum

3. $c(y) = .002y^2 + 5y + 100$

    $c'(y) = .004y + 5$

    marginal cost at output of 2,000 yds.

    $.004(2{,}000) + 5$

    $8 + 5 = \$13.00/\text{yd}$

    marginal cost @ output of 2,500 yds.

    $.004(2{,}500) + 5$

    $10 + 5 = \$15.00/\text{yd}$

5. $f(x) = .1x^2 - 4x + 50$

    derivative

    $f'(x) = .2x - 4$

    factor and set equal to 0

    $.2(x - 20) = 0$

    $.2 \neq 0 \quad x - 20 = 0$

    $\quad\quad\quad\quad\quad x = 20$

    $f(20) = .1(20)^2 - 4(20) + 50$

    $\quad\quad = 40 - 80 + 50$

    $\quad\quad = 10$

    (20, 10)

    second derivative test

    $f''(x) = .2$

    $f(20) = .2$

    positive test indicates a minimum @ (20, 10)

7. $f(x) = 2x^3 - 3x^2 - 12x$

    derivative

    $f'(x) = 6x^2 - 6x - 12$

factor and set equal to 0

$6(x^2 - x - 2)$

$6(x + 1)(x - 2)$

$6 \neq 0 \qquad x + 1 = 0 \qquad x - 2 = 0$

$\qquad\qquad\qquad x = -1 \qquad\quad x = 2$

$$f(-1) = 2(-1)^3 - 3(-1)^2 - 12(-1)$$
$$= -2 - 3 + 12$$
$$= 7$$

$(-1, 7)$

$$f(2) = 2(2)^3 - 3(2)^2 - 12(2)$$
$$= 16 - 12 - 24$$
$$= -20$$

$(2, -20)$

second derivative test

$$f''(x) = 12x - 6$$
$$f(-1) = 12(-1) - 6$$
$$= -12 - 6$$
$$= -18$$

negative test proves maximum @ $(-1, 7)$

$$f(2) = 12(2) - 6$$
$$= 24 - 6$$
$$= 18$$

positive test indicates minimum @ $(2, -20)$

9. $f(x) = x^3 + x^2 + x - 4;\ f'(x) = 3x^2 + 2x + 1$ is zero where

$$3x^2 + 2x + 1 = 0.$$

By the quadratic formula

$$x = \frac{-2 \pm \sqrt{4 - 4(3)(1)}}{6} = \frac{-2 \pm \sqrt{-8}}{6},$$

so no real values for x make $f'(x) = 0$. The function $f(x)$ has no local extreme points.

11. $f(x) = 3x^4 - 16x^3 + 24x^2 + 10.$

$f'(x) = 12x^3 - 48x^2 + 48x$ is zero where

$$12x^3 - 48x^2 + 48x = 0$$
$$12x(x^2 - 4x + 4) = 0$$
$$12x(x - 2)(x - 2) = 0$$
$$x^* = 0 \text{ and } x^* = 2.$$

$f''(x) = 36x^2 - 96x + 48$

$f''(0) = 48$, so we have a local minimum at $x = 0$.

$f''(2) = 0$, and the test fails.

196

At the left of $x = 2$, say $x = 1$, $f(1) = 21$. At $x = 2$, $f(2) = 26$. At the right of $x = 2$, say $x = 3$, $f(3) = 37$. Summarizing,

$$f(1) = 21, f(2) = 26, f(3) = 37$$

so the curve is neither higher nor lower on both sides of $x = 2$, and we do not have an extreme point.

Answer:　(0, 10) is a local minimum.

13.　$f(x) = 2x + \dfrac{98}{x}$; $f'(x) = 2 - \dfrac{98}{x^2}$ is zero where

$$2 - \frac{98}{x^2} = 0$$

$$2x^2 = 98$$

$$x^2 = 49$$

$$x = 7 \text{ and } x = -7.$$

$f(7) = 14 + 14 = 28$ and $f(-7) = -14 - 14 = -28$.

$$f''(x) = \frac{196}{x^3}$$

$f''(7)$ is positive, so (7, 28) is a local minimum.

$f''(-7)$ is negative, so (-7, -28) is a local maximum.

15.

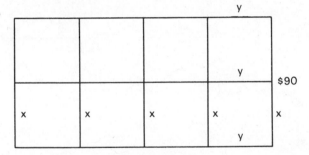

$$xy = 80,000 \qquad y = \frac{80,000}{x}$$

$$6x(90) + 3y(90) = \text{wall cost}$$

$$540x + 270y =$$

$$540x + 270\left(\frac{80,000}{x}\right) =$$

$$540x + \frac{21,600,000}{x} =$$

Derivative

$$f'(x) = 540x + 21,600,000x^{-1}$$

$$= 540 - 21,600,000x^{-2}$$

factor and set equal to 0

$$540 - \frac{21,600,000}{x^2}$$

$$540\left(1 - \frac{40,000}{x^2}\right) = 0$$

197

$540 \neq 0 \qquad 1 - \dfrac{40{,}000}{x^2} = 0$

$$\dfrac{40{,}000}{x^2} = 1$$

$$40{,}000 = x^2$$

$$200 = x$$

plug x into original equation

$$y = \dfrac{80{,}000}{200}$$

$y = 400$ feet $(200, 400)$

Second Derivative Test

$f''(x) = 43{,}200{,}000x^{-3}$

$f''(200) = 43{,}200{,}000(200)^{-3}$

$\qquad\quad = 5.4$

positive indicates a minimum.

17.

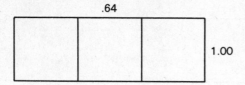

$$xy = 1{,}250$$

$$y = \dfrac{1{,}250}{x}$$

$4x(1.00) + 2y(.64) =$ dimensions for minimum cost

$$4x + 1.28y =$$

$$4x + 1.28\left(\dfrac{1{,}250}{x}\right) =$$

$$4x + \dfrac{1{,}600}{x} =$$

$f'(x) = 4x + 1{,}600y^{-1}$

$\qquad = 4 - 1{,}600x^{-2}$

factor and set equal to 0

$$4\left(1 - \dfrac{400}{x^2}\right) = 0$$

$4 \neq 0 \qquad 1 - \dfrac{400}{x^2} = 0$

$$1 = \dfrac{400}{x^2}$$

$$x^2 = 400$$

$$x = 20$$

198

plug x into original equation

$$y = \frac{1,250}{20}$$

$$= 62.5 \qquad (20, 62.5)$$

Second Derivative Test

$$f''(x) = 3,200x^{-3}$$

$$f''(20) = 3,200(20)^{-3}$$

$$= .4 \qquad \text{positive indicates minimum}$$

minimum cost $= 4(20)(1.00) + 2(62.5)(.64)$

$$= 80 + 80$$

$$= \$160.00$$

19.

The plant area, xy, is to be 5400 square feet. Hence, $xy = 5400$, and $y = 5400/x$. The total area for the plot, T, is

$$T = (x + 40)(y + 60) = xy + 40y + 60x + 2,400.$$

$$= 5,400 + 40\left(\frac{5,400}{x}\right) + 60x + 2,400.$$

$$T' = -\frac{40(5,400)}{x^2} + 60.$$

Setting $T' = 0$, we have:

$$-\frac{40(5,400)}{x^2} + 60 = 0$$

$$-40(5,400) + 60x^2 = 0$$

$$x^2 = \frac{40(5,400)}{60}$$

$$= 3,600$$

$$x = 60.$$

By substitution, $y = 5,400/60 = 90$. The plant dimensions $x = 60$ feet, $y = 90$ feet lead to a plot area of $(60 + 40)(90 + 60) = 15,000$ square feet. The area is minimal because T' is (always) positive.

21. The volume condition remains $V = x^2y = 32$, so that $y = 32/x^2$. The *cost* expression is

$$C = x^2(8) + 4xy(1) = 8x^2 + 4x\left(\frac{32}{x^2}\right)$$

$$C = 8x^2 + 128x^{-1}$$
$$C' = 16x - 128x^{-2}.$$

Setting $C' = 0$: $16x - 128x^{-2} = 0$.

Multiplying both sides of the last equation by x^2 yields

$$16x^3 - 128 = 0$$

$$x^3 = \frac{128}{16} = 8$$

$$x = 2.$$

Substitution shows $y = 32/x^2 = 8$. The dimensions are 2″ by 2″ by 8″. The cost is $C = 8(2^2) + 4(2)(8) = 96$ cents $= \$0.96$. This is minimal because C'' is (always) positive.

23. $L + 2\pi r = 120$, so $L = 120 - 2\pi r$.

Area = Two circular ends plus cylindrical surface
$$= 2\pi r^2 + 2\pi rL.$$
$$A(r) = 2\pi r^2 + 2\pi r(120 - 2\pi r)$$
$$= 2\pi r^2 + 240\pi r - 4\pi^2 r^2.$$
$$A'(r) = 4\pi r + 240\pi - 8\pi^2 r.$$

Setting $A'(r) = 0$ and factoring,

$$4\pi(r + 60 - 2\pi r) = 0.$$

Hence,

$$r + 60 - 2\pi r = 0$$

$$r = \frac{60}{2\pi - 1}$$

$$= \frac{60}{2(3.1416) - 1}$$

$$r = 11.357$$

$$L = 120 - 2\pi r = 120 - 2(3.1416)(11.357)$$
$$= 48.642.$$

Summary: Base radius 11.357 inches, length 48.642 inches.

25. Let L be number of units per lot. The

Number of setups in a year $= \dfrac{9{,}600}{L}$.

Annual setup cost at \$250 each $= 250\left(\dfrac{9{,}600}{L}\right)$.

Cost of 9,600 units at \$2 $= 2(9{,}600)$.

Annual cost of inventory of $\dfrac{L}{2}$ units at \$1.20 per unit $= \dfrac{L}{2}(1.20) = 0.60L$.

a) $C(L) = \dfrac{250(9,600)}{L} + 2(9,600) + 0.60L.$

b) $C'(L) = -\dfrac{250(9,600)}{L^2} + 0.6$

   $C'(L) = 0$ when $0.6 = \dfrac{250(9,600)}{L^2}$ or $L^2 = \dfrac{250(9,600)}{0.6} = 4,000,000.$

   $L = \sqrt{4,000,000} = 2,000$ units

27. $f(x) = 25(x^2 + 9)^{1/2} + 20(10 - x).$

a) $f'(x) = \dfrac{25}{2}(x^2 + 9)^{-1/2}(2x) - 20 = \dfrac{25x}{(x^2 + 9)^{1/2}} - 20$

   Setting $f'(x) = 0$, we have

   $$\dfrac{25x}{(x^2 + 9)^{1/2}} - 20 = 0$$

   $$25x - 20(x^2 + 9)^{1/2} = 0$$
   $$25x = 20(x^2 + 9)^{1/2}$$
   $$625x^2 = 400(x^2 + 9)$$
   $$225x^2 = 3,600$$
   $$x^2 = 16$$
   $$x = 4 \text{ and } -4,$$

   but the problem stipulates $x \geq 0$, so we have $x = 4$ as the candidate point.

b)   To the left of $x = 4$, say $x = 0$,

   $$f(0) = 25(0 + 9)^{1/2} + 20(10 - 0) - 275.$$

   To the right of $x = 4$, say $x = 5$,

   $$f(5) = 25(25 + 9)^{1/2} + 20(10 - 5) = 25(34)^{1/2} + 100 = 25(5.83) + 100 = 245.8$$

   At $x = 4$

   $$f(4) = 25(16 + 9)^{1/2} + 20(10 - 4) = 245.$$

   In summary,

   $$f(0) = 275, f(4) = 245, f(5) = 245.8$$

   and the curve is higher than $f(4)$ on both sides, so we have a local minimum at $x = 4$.

29. $p(h) = (10 + 2h)^{1/2} - 0.1h.$

a) $p'(h) = \dfrac{1}{2}(10 + 2h)^{-1/2}(2) - 0.1 = \dfrac{1}{(10 + 2h)^{1/2}} - 0.1$

   Setting $p'(h) = 0$, we have

   $$\dfrac{1}{(10 + 2h)^{1/2}} - 0.1 = 0$$

   $$1 - 0.1(10 + 2h)^{1/2} = 0$$
   $$(10 + 2h)^{1/2} = 10$$
   $$10 + 2h = (10)^2 = 100$$
   $$h = 45 \text{ inches.}$$

201

$$p''(h) = -\frac{1}{(10 + 2h)^{3/2}}$$

and $p''(45)$ is negative, so we have a maximum.

b) $p_{max} = p(45) = [10 + 2(45)]^{1/2} - 0.1(45) = \$5.50$ per tree.

31. a) Writing Σx_i rather than $\sum\limits_{i=1}^{n}$

$$\bar{x} = \text{average} = \frac{\Sigma x_i}{n}.$$

b)
$$\frac{dS(a)}{da} = \frac{d}{da}\Sigma(x_i - a)^2$$

$$= \Sigma\frac{d}{da}(x_i - a)^2$$

$$= \Sigma 2(x_i - a)(-1)$$
$$= \Sigma[-2x_i + 2a]$$
$$= -2\Sigma x_i + 2\Sigma a.$$

In the last, Σa is the sum of a constant, which is na, so we have

$$\frac{dS(a)}{da} = -2\Sigma x_i + 2na.$$

Setting the derivative equal to zero, we find

$$-2\Sigma x_i + 2na = 0$$
$$2na = 2\Sigma x_i$$

$$a = \frac{\Sigma x_i}{n} = \bar{x}.$$

$S''(a) = 2$, which is positive, so we have a minimum.

33. $f(x) = h(a^2 + x^2)^{1/2} + g(b - x)$.

$$f'(x) = h\left(\frac{1}{2}\right)(a^2 + x^2)^{-1/2}(2x) - g.$$

Setting $f'(x) = 0$, we have

$$\frac{hx}{(a^2 + x^2)^{1/2}} - g = 0$$

$$hx = g(a^2 + x^2)^{1/2}$$
$$h^2x^2 = g^2(a^2 + x^2)$$
$$h^2x^2 - g^2x^2 = a^2g^2$$

$$x^2 = \frac{a^2g^2}{h^2 - g^2}$$

$$x = \frac{ag}{(h^2 - g^2)^{1/2}}.$$

35. $f(x) = x(1 - x)^{1/2}$.

$$f'(x) = x\left(\frac{1}{2}\right)(1 - x)^{-1/2}(-1) + (1 - x)^{1/2}$$

$$= \frac{-x}{2(1 - x)^{1/2}} + (1 - x)^{1/2}.$$

202

Setting $f'(x) = 0$, we have

$$\frac{-x}{2(1-x)^{1/2}} + (1-x)^{1/2} = 0$$

$$-x + 2(1-x) = 0$$

$$-x + 2 - 2x = 0$$

$$x = \frac{2}{3}.$$

$$f''(x) = \frac{2(1-x)^{1/2}(-1) - (-x)(2)\left(\frac{1}{2}\right)(1-x)^{-1/2}(-1)}{4(1-x)} + \frac{1}{2}(1-x)^{-1/2}(-1)$$

$$= \frac{-2(1-x)^{1/2} - \dfrac{x}{(1-x)^{1/2}}}{4(1-x)} - \frac{1}{2(1-x)^{1/2}}.$$

Because both terms of the foregoing are negative at $x = 2/3$, we have a maximum at $x = 2/3$.

37. $f(x) = 8x - 0.5x^2 - 20$.

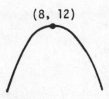

$f'(x) = 8 - x$ is zero at $x = 8$; $f(8) = 12$.

$f''(x) = -1$ is negative.

The graph is a vertical parabola opening downward with vertex (maximum) at (8, 12).

39. $f(x) = x^3 - 6x^2 + 15x - 4$.

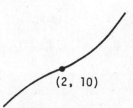

$f'(x) = 3x^2 - 12x + 15$ is zero where

$$3x^2 - 12x + 15 = 0$$

$$x^2 - 4x + 5 = 0.$$

By the quadratic formula,

$$x = \frac{4 \pm \sqrt{16 - 4(1)(5)}}{2} = \frac{4 \pm \sqrt{-4}}{2},$$

so there are no extreme points.

$$f''(x) = 6x - 12 \text{ is zero where } x = 2.$$

To the left $f''(1)$ is negative (concave downward), and to the right ($x = 3$), $f''(3)$ is positive (concave upward) and we have an inflection point.

$$f(2) = 8 - 6(4) + 15(2) - 4 = 10.$$

41. $f(x) = 32x - (x + 7)^4 + 200$.

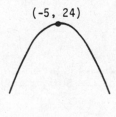

$f'(x) = 32 - 4(x + 7)^3$ is zero where

$$32 - 4(x + 7)^3 = 0$$

$$(x + 7)^3 = 8$$

$$x + 7 = 2$$

$$x = -5.$$

$f''(x) = -12(x + 7)^2$, and $f''(-5)$ is negative,

so we have a maximum at $x = -5$, $f(-5) = 24$. $f''(x)$ cannot be zero, so there are no inflection points.

43. $f(x) = x^4 - 16x^3 + 72x^2 - 128.$

$$f'(x) = 4x^3 - 48x^2 + 144x \text{ is zero where}$$
$$4x^3 - 48x^2 + 144x = 0$$
$$4x(x^2 - 12x + 36) = 0$$
$$4x(x - 6)(x - 6) = 0$$
$$x = 0 \text{ and } x = 6$$
$$f''(x) = 12x^2 - 96x + 144$$
$$f''(0) = 144 \qquad \text{(minimum)}$$
$$f''(6) = 0 \qquad \text{(test fails).}$$

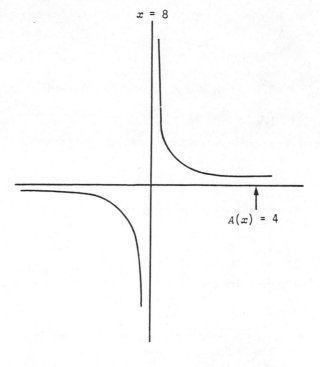

(6, 304)

(2, 48)

(0, -128)

To the left of $x = 6$, $f''(5) = -36$ (concave downward), and to the right $f''(7) = 60$ (concave upward), so there is a stationary inflection at $x = 6$. Checking for further inflections, we have found $x = 6$ to be at an inflection. To the left of $x = 2$, $f''(1) = 60$ (concave upward) and to the right $f''(3) = -36$ (concave downward), so we have an inflection. The desired function values are

$$f(0) = -128; \quad (0, -128), \qquad \text{minimum.}$$
$$f(6) = 304; \qquad (6, 304), \qquad \text{stationary inflection.}$$
$$f(2) = 48; \qquad (2, 48), \qquad \text{ordinary inflection.}$$

45. $f(x) = \dfrac{2x}{0.5x - 4}.$

$$f'(x) = \frac{(0.5x - 4)(2) - 2x(0.5)}{(0.5x - 4)^2}$$
$$= \frac{-8}{(0.5x - 4)^2}.$$

$x = 8$

$A(x) = 4$

We see that $f'(x)$ cannot equal zero, so there are no local extreme points. The denominator, but not the numerator, of $f(x)$ becomes zero when $0.5x - 4 = 0$, so $x = 8$ is a vertical asymptote. Moreover,

$$\lim_{x \to \infty} \frac{2x}{0.5x - 4} = 4$$

so $A(x) = 4$ is a horizontal asymptote. To the left of $x = 8$ (try $x = 7$) $f(x)$ is below $A(x) = 4$, and to the right of $x = 8$ (try $x = 9$), $f(x)$ is above $A(x) = 4$.

1.　$f(x) = 2e^x$

　　$f'(x) = 2e^x$

　　$f''(x) = 2e^x$

5.　$f(x) = 5e^{-0.2x}$

　　$f'(x) = 5(-0.2)e^{-0.2x}$

　　　　$= -1e^{-0.2x}$

　　　　$= -e^{-0.2x}$

　　$f''(x) = -0.2(-e)^{-0.2x}$

　　　　$= 0.2e^{-0.2x}$

9.　$f(x) = e^{x^2}$

　　$f'(x) = e^{x^2}(2x)$

　　　　$= 2xe^{x^2}$

　　$f''(x) = 2x(e^{x^2})(2x) + e^{x^2}(2)$

　　　　$= 4xe^{x^2} + 2e^{x^2}$

　　　　$= 2e^{x^2}(2x^2 + 1)$

13.　$f(x) = 1,000(1.06)^x$

　　$f'(x) = 1,000(\ln 1.06^x)$

　　　　$= 1,000x(\ln 1.06)$

　　　　$= 58.27(1.06)^x$

　　$f''(x) = 58.27(\ln 1.06)^x$

　　　　$= 58.27(x)(\ln 1.06)$

　　　　$= 3.395(1.06)^x$

17.　**FIGURE C**

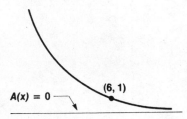

$A(x) = 0$ ⟶　　(6, 1)

21.　**FIGURE G**

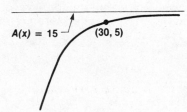

$A(x) = 15$ ⟶　(30, 5)

25. $r(t) = 0.25 - 0.25e^{-0.02t}$

$R(t) = (0.25 - 0.25e^{-0.02t})(1,000,000)(5)$

$C(t) = 15,000 + 1,000t$

$P(t) = R(t) - C(t)$

$[(0.25 - 0.25e^{-0.02t})(5,000,000)] - [15,000 + 1,000t]$

$1,250,000 - 1,250,000e^{-0.02t} - 15,000 - 1,000t$

$P'(t) = -(1,250,000)(-0.02)(e^{-0.02t}) - 1,000$

$\quad = +25,000e^{-0.02t} - 1,000$

$+25,000e^{-0.02t} - 1,000 = 0$

$\quad 25,000e^{-0.02t} = 1,000$

$$e^{-0.02t} = \frac{1,000}{25,000}$$

$e^{-0.02t} = .04$

$\ln(e^{-0.02t}) = \ln .04$

$-0.02t(\ln e) = \ln .04$

$-0.02t = \ln .04$

$\boxed{t = 160.94}$

$P(t) = P(160.94) = \$1,024,056$

29. $f(x) = 25x - e^x$

$f'(x) = 25 - e^x$

$25 - e^x = 0$

$25 = e^x$

$\ln 25 = x \ln e$

$3.218 = x$

$f''(x) = -e^x$

$f''(3.218) = -e^{(3.218)}$

$\quad = -24.97$

maximum @ $f(3.218) = 55.47$

33. $f(x) = 10x - e^{0.2x}$

$f'(x) = 10 - e^{0.2x}(.2)$

$\quad = 10 - .2e^{0.2x}$

Set $f'(x) = 0$

$0 = 10 - .2e^{0.2x}$

$10 = .2e^{0.2x}$

$50 = e^{0.2x}$

take the ln of both sides

$3.912 = .2x$

$19.56 = x$

$f(19.56) = 10(19.56) - e^{.2(19.56)} = 145.60$

$f''(x) = -.2e^{.2x}(.2)$

$= -.04e^{.2x}$

so maximum @ 145.60

Problem Set 12-2

1. $f(x) = \ln x$

   $f'(x) = \dfrac{1}{x}$

5. $f(x) = \ln e^x = x \ln e$

   $f'(x) = \ln e$

   $= 1$

9. $f(x) = \ln(3x + 2)^{1/2} = \dfrac{1}{2} \ln(3x + 2)$

   $f'(x) = \dfrac{1}{(3x + 2)(2)} \cdot 3$

   $= \dfrac{3}{2(3x + 2)}$

13. $f(x) = \ln(x^2 - 10x + 35)$

    $f'(x) = \dfrac{2x - 10}{x^2 - 10x + 35}$

    set $f'(x) = 0$ which occurs when

    $2x - 10 = 0$

    $x = 5$

    $f(5) = \ln(5^2 - 10(5) + 35)$

    $= 2.30$

    $f''(x) = \dfrac{(x^2 - 10x + 35)(2) - (2x - 10)(2x - 10)}{(x^2 - 10x + 35)^2}$

    $= \dfrac{2x^2 - 20x + 70 - 4x^2 + 40x - 100}{(x^2 - 10x + 35)^2}$

    $= \dfrac{-2x^2 + 20x - 30}{(x^2 - 10x + 35)^2}$

    $= -\dfrac{x^2 - 10x + 30}{(x^2 - 10x + 35)^2}$

    $f''(2.3) = -\dfrac{2.3^2 + 10(2.3) - 30}{(2.3^2 - 10(2.3) + 35)^2} = -\dfrac{-47.71}{149.38}$

    $f''(2.3) = +$ so minimum @ 2.3

17. max $f(x) = 30 \ln(2x + 1) - 2.5x$

$$f'(x) = \frac{30(2)}{(2x + 1)} - 2.5$$

set $f'(x) = 0$

$$\frac{60}{2x + 1} - 2.5 = 0$$

$$\frac{60}{2x + 1} = 2.5 \qquad 5x + 2.5 = 60$$

$$5x = 57.5 \qquad x = 11.5$$

$$f''(x) = 60(-1)(2x + 1)^{-2}(2)$$

$$= \frac{-120}{(2x + 1)^2} \qquad f''(11.5) = - \qquad \text{so maximum @ 11.5}$$

Problem Set 12-3

1. $c(x) = 2{,}000 + 2.50x$

$c'(x) = 2.5$

Cost increases at the (constant) rate of $2.50 per additional book made.

5. $c(x) = 16 + .20x$

$$a(x) = \frac{16}{x} + .20$$

$$a'(x) = 16x^{-1}$$

$$= -16x^{-2}$$

$$= \frac{-16}{x^2}$$

$$a'(40) = \frac{-16}{(40)^2}$$

$$= -.01$$

At 40 miles, the average cost per mile is decreasing at the rate of $0.01 per additional mile driven.

13. $A(t) = 5{,}000(1.07)^t$

$A'(t) = 5{,}000(1.07)^t \ln(1.07)$

$$\frac{A'(t)}{A(t)} = \frac{5{,}000(1.07)^t \ln(1.07)}{5{,}000(1.07)^t}$$

$$= \ln(1.07)$$

$$= 0.06766$$

$$= 6.76\%$$

At $t = 10$ (or any number of years), the amount in the account is increasing at the rate of 6.76 percent per additional year

17. a) $f(x) = \ln x$

$$f'(x) = \frac{1}{x}$$

$$f'(5) = \frac{1}{5}$$

$$= 0.2$$

At $x = 5$, ln x changes at the rate of 0.2 per unit change in x.

b) If ln x changes at the rate of 0.2 per unit change in x then a unit change of .001 (5 to 5.001) will increase x by .0002

$$(.001) \times (.2) = \boxed{.0002}$$

c) If ln 5 = 1.60944
    then ln 5.001 = 1.60944 + .0002

$$\boxed{= 1.60964}$$

Problem Set 12-4

1. $\dfrac{d}{dx} f(y) = \dfrac{df(y)}{dy} \cdot \dfrac{dy}{dx}$

5. $\dfrac{d}{dx}(y^4) = \dfrac{d(y^4)}{dy} \cdot \dfrac{dy}{dx}$

$$= 4y^3 \cdot \dfrac{dy}{dx}$$

9. $\dfrac{d}{dx} \ln(2y + 3) = \dfrac{d \ln(2y + 3)}{dy} \cdot \dfrac{dy}{dx}$

$$= \dfrac{2}{2y + 3} \cdot \dfrac{dy}{dx}$$

13. $y^3 - x^2 = 0$

$$y^3 = x^2$$

$$\dfrac{dy^3}{dx} = \dfrac{dx^2}{dx}$$

$$\dfrac{d}{dx}y^3 = 2x$$

$$3y^2 \cdot \dfrac{dy}{dx} = 2x$$

$$\dfrac{dy}{dx} = \boxed{\dfrac{2x}{3y^2}}$$

17. $x = y + e^{-y}$

$$\dfrac{d}{dx}x = \dfrac{d}{dx}y + \dfrac{d}{dx}e^{-y}$$

$$1 = 1\dfrac{dy}{dx} + e^{-y}(-1)\dfrac{dy}{dx}$$

$$1 = \dfrac{dy}{dx}(1 - e^{-y})$$

$$\dfrac{dy}{dx} = \dfrac{1}{(1 - e^{-y})} = \dfrac{e^y}{e^y - 1}$$

21. $xy^3 = x^2 + 5$

$$\frac{d}{dx}xy^3 = \frac{d}{dx}x^2 + \frac{d}{dx}5$$

$$y^3 + 3xy^2\frac{dy}{dx} = 2x$$

$$3xy^2\frac{dy}{dx} = 2x - y^3$$

$$\frac{dy}{dx} = \frac{2x - y^3}{3xy^2}$$

25. $C(Y) = 34 + 0.68Y$

a) $C'(Y) = 0.68 = $ mpc

b) 68 cents of an additional dollar of income is spent.

c) $\dfrac{1}{1 - \text{MPC}} = \dfrac{1}{1 - .68} = \dfrac{1}{.32} = \$3.125$

d) $C(200) = 34 + 0.68(200)$

$$= 170$$

$$\frac{170}{200} = .85 \quad \text{or} \quad 85\%$$

Problem Set 12-5

1. $f(x, y) = 3x - 2y + 6$

$f_x = 3$

$f_{xx} = 0$

$f_y = -2$

$f_{yy} = 0$

$f_{xy} = 0$

5. $f(x, y) = 3x^2 - 2xy + y^2 + 4$

$f_x = 6x - 2y$

$f_{xx} = 6$

$f_y = -2x + 2y$

$f_{yy} = 2$

$f_{xy} = -2$

9. $f(x, y) = 2xy^{1/2} - 3x^{1/3}y$

$$f_x = 2y^{1/2} - \frac{y}{x^{2/3}}$$

$$f_{xx} = 2y^{1/2} - yx^{-2/3}$$

$$= \left(\frac{-2}{3}\right)(-y)x^{-5/3}$$

$$= \frac{2y}{3x^{5/3}}$$

210

$$f_y = \left(\frac{1}{2}\right)2xy^{-1/2} - 3x^{1/3}$$

$$= \frac{x}{y^{1/2}} - 3x^{1/3}$$

$$f_{yy} = xy^{-1/2} - 3x^{1/3}$$

$$= \frac{-1}{2}(x)y^{-3/2}$$

$$= \frac{-\frac{1}{2}x}{y^{3/2}}$$

$$= \frac{-x}{2y^{3/2}}$$

$$f_{xy} = 2xy^{1/2} - 3x^{1/3}y$$

$$f_x = 2y^{1/2} - yx^{-2/3}$$

$$f_{xy} = \left(\frac{1}{2}\right)(2)y^{-1/2} - x^{-2/3}$$

$$f_{xy} = \left(\frac{1}{y^{1/2}}\right) - \left(\frac{1}{x^{2/3}}\right)$$

13. $f(x, y) = \dfrac{x - y}{x + y}$

$$f_x = \frac{(x + y)(1) - (x - y)(1)}{(x + y)^2}$$

$$= \frac{2y}{(x + y)^2}$$

$$f_{xx} = 2y(-2)(x + y)^{-3}(1)$$

$$= \frac{-4y}{(x + y)^3}$$

$$f_y = \frac{(x + y)(-1) - (x - y)(1)}{(x + y)^2}$$

$$= \frac{-2x}{(x + y)^2}$$

$$f_{yy} = -2x(-2)(x + y)^{-3}(1)$$

$$= \frac{-4x}{(x + y)^3}$$

$$f_{xy} = \frac{(x + y)^2(2) - 2y(2(x + y)^1(1))}{(x + y)^{2^2}}$$

$$= \frac{2(x + y)[(x + y) - 2y]}{(x + y)^4}$$

$$= \frac{2(x - y)}{(x + y)^3}$$

17. $\dfrac{\partial}{\partial z}(3z^2 - 2xz) = 6z - 2x$

21. $\dfrac{\partial^2}{\partial w \partial z}(w^3 - 3zw) = 3w^2 - 3z$

$$= -3$$

25. $f(x, y) = x^2 + xy - 3y^2 + 5$

   a) $\quad f(2, 1) = (2)^2 + (2)(1) - 3(1)^2 + 5$

$$= 4 + 2 - 3 + 5$$

$$= 8$$

   b) $\qquad f_x = 2x + y$

$$f_x(2, 1) = 2(2) + 1$$

$$= 4 + 1$$

$$= 5$$

   c) $\quad f_{xx}(2, 1) = 2$

   d) $\qquad f_y = x - 6y$

$$f_y(2, 1) = 2 - 6(1)$$

$$= 2 - 6$$

$$= -4$$

   e) $\quad f_{yy}(2, 1) = -6$

   f) $\quad f_{xy}(2, 1) = 1$

29. $p(x, y) = 50x - 0.05x^2 + 110y - 0.10y^2$

   a) $\qquad p_x = 50 - (2)(0.05)x$

$$p_x(400, 500) = 50 - (0.1)(400)$$

$$= 10$$

Profit is increasing at the rate of $10 per additional gallon of oats.

   b) $\qquad p_y = 110 - (2)(0.1)y$

$$p_y(400, 500) = 110 - 0.2(500)$$

$$= 10$$

Profit is increasing at the rate of $10 per additional gallon of hay

   c) $\quad p_x(600, 500) = 50 - (0.1)(600)$

$$= -10$$

At 600 gallons of oats and 500 gallons of hay profit is decreasing at the ratio of $10 per additional gallon of oats.

   d) $\quad p_y(400, 600) = 110 - (0.2)(600)$

$$= -10$$

At 400 gallons of oats and 600 gallons of hay profit is decreasing at the rate of $10 per additional gallon of hay.

1. $f(x, y) = 2x^2 + 3y^2 + 10$

    $f_x = 4x \qquad 4x = 0 \Rightarrow (x, y) = (0, 0)$ is a critical pt.

    $f_y = 6y \qquad 6y = 0$

    $f_{xx} = 4$

    $f_{yy} = 6$

    $f_{xy} = 0$

    $A = 4$

    $B = 0$

    $C = 6$

    $D = 0^2 - (4)(6)$

    $\quad = -24$

    minimum at $(0, 0, 10)$

    $f_{(x,y)} = x + y + \dfrac{9}{x} + \dfrac{4}{y}; \; x, y > 0$

5. $f_x = 1 - 9x^{-2} = 1 - \dfrac{9}{x^2}$

    $f_{xx} = -9(-2)x^{-3} = \dfrac{18}{x^3}$

    $f_y = 1 - 4y^{-2} = 1 - \dfrac{4}{y^2}$

    $f_{yy} = 1 - 4(-2)y^{-3} = \dfrac{8}{y^3}$

    $f_{xy} = 0$

    set f_x and $f_y = 0$

    $1 - \dfrac{9}{x^2} = 0 \qquad x^2 = 9 \qquad x = 3$

    $1 - \dfrac{4}{y^2} = 0 \qquad y^2 = 4 \qquad y = 2$

    $f(3, 2) = 3 + 2 + \dfrac{9}{3^2} + \dfrac{4}{2^2} = 10$

    $A = f_{xx}(3, 2) = \dfrac{18}{3^3} = \dfrac{2}{3}$

    $C = f_{yy}(3, 2) = \dfrac{8}{2^3} = 1$

    $B = 0$

    $D = 0^2 - \left(\dfrac{2}{3}\right)(1) = -\dfrac{2}{3}$

    minimum @ $(3, 2, 10)$

9. $f(x, y) = 3xy - 3x^2 - y^2 + 6x + 10y + 3$

    $\qquad f_x = 3y - 6x + 6$

213

$$f_{xx} = -6$$

$$f_y = 3x - 2y + 10$$

$$f_{yy} = -2$$

$$f_{xy} = 3$$

solve $f_x = 0$ and $f_y = 0$ using simultaneous equations

$$\begin{array}{r} 3y - 6x + 6 = 0 \\ -4y + 6x + 20 = 0 \\ \hline -y + 26 = 0 \end{array} \quad y = 26$$

$$3(26) - 6x + 6 = 0 \qquad -6x = -84 \qquad x = 14$$

$$f(14, 26) = 175$$

$$A = -6 \qquad B = 3 \qquad C = -2$$

$$D = 3^2 - (-6)(-2) = -3$$

so maximum @ (14, 26, 175)

13. $p(x, y) = 50x - .05x^2 + 110y - .10y^2$

$$p_x = 50 - .1x \qquad p_{xx} = -.1$$

$$p_y = 110 - .2y \qquad p_{yy} = -.2 \qquad p_{xy} = 0$$

set p_x and $p_y = 0$

a) $\quad 50 - .1x = 0 \qquad x = 500$

$\quad\quad 110 - .2y = 0 \qquad y = 550$

b) $\quad A = -.1 \qquad B = 0 \qquad C = -2$

$\quad\quad D = 0^2 - (-.1)(-.2) = -.02 \qquad 50$ maximum

c) $\quad p(500, 550) = 50(500) - .05(500^2) + 110(550) - .10(550^2)$

$\quad\quad\quad\quad = \$42,750$

17. $C(L, I) = 750{,}000L^{-1} + 20I^2L^{-1} + \dfrac{25}{2}L - 25I$

a) $\quad C_L = \dfrac{-750{,}000}{L^2} + \dfrac{-20I^2}{L^2} + \dfrac{25}{2}$

$\quad\quad C_{LL} = \dfrac{1{,}500{,}000}{L^3} + \dfrac{40I^2}{L^3}$

$\quad\quad C_I = \dfrac{40I}{L} - 25$

$\quad\quad C_{II} = \dfrac{40}{L} \qquad C_{LI} = \dfrac{-40I}{L^2}$

b) set C_L and $C_I = 0$ and, solve

$$\dfrac{40I}{L} = 25 \qquad 25L = 40I \qquad L = 1.6I$$

$$O = \dfrac{-750{,}000}{1.6^2I^2} + \dfrac{-20I^2}{1.6^2I^2} + \dfrac{25}{2}$$

$$\dfrac{750{,}000}{1.6^2I^2} = \dfrac{25}{2} - \dfrac{20}{1.6^2} = 4.6875$$

214

$$4.6875(1.6^2)l^2 = 750,000$$

$$l^2 = \frac{750,000}{4,6875(2.56)} = 62,500 \qquad l = 250$$

$$L = 1.6(250) = 400$$

$$C(400, 250) = \$3,750$$

Problem Set 12-7

1.

	x	y	x^2	y^2	xy	
	3	4	9	16	12	
	1	3	1	9	3	$n = 3$
	11	11	121	121	121	
Σ	15	18	131	146	136	

$$m = \frac{n\Sigma xy - (\Sigma x)(\Sigma y)}{n\Sigma x^2 - (\Sigma x)^2}$$

$$= \frac{3(136) - (15)(18)}{3(131) - (15^2)}$$

$$= \frac{408 - 270}{393 - 225} = \frac{138}{168} = 0.8214$$

$$b = \frac{\Sigma y - m\Sigma x}{n}$$

$$b = \frac{18 - (0.8214)(15)}{3} = \frac{5.679}{3} = 1.893$$

$$y = 1.893 + 0.8214x$$

1. $f(x) = 5e^{0.4x}$; $f'(x) = 5e^{0.4x}(0.4) = 2e^{0.4x}$.

$$f''(x) = 2[e^{0.4x}](0.4) = 0.8e^{0.4x}.$$

3. $f(x) = 4e^{0.5x-5}$; $f'(x) = 4e^{0.5x-5}(0.5) = 2e^{0.5x-5}$.

$$f''(x) = 2e^{0.5x-5}(0.5) = e^{0.5x-5}$$

5. $f(x) = 3e^{2x-x^2}$; $f'(x) = 3e^{2x-x^2}(2 - 2x) = 6(1 - x)e^{2x-x^2}$.

   By the product rule:

$$f''(x) = 6[(1 - x)e^{2x-x^2}(2 - 2x) + e^{2x-x^2}(-1)]$$
$$= 6[2(1 - x)^2e^{2x-x^2} - e^{2x-x^2}]$$
$$= 6e^{2x-x^2}[2(1 - x)^2 - 1].$$

7. $f(x) = e^{2x} - 10x + 4$

$$f'(x) = 2e^{2x} - 10 \text{ is zero where}$$
$$2e^{2x} - 10 = 0$$
$$e^{2x} = 5$$
$$\ln(e^{2x}) = \ln 5$$
$$2x \ln e = \ln 5$$
$$x = \frac{\ln 5}{2}$$
$$= \frac{1.60944}{2}$$
$$x = 0.80472.$$
$$f''(x) = 4e^{2x}.$$
$$f''(x) \text{ is positive (minimum).}$$

   Remembering that $e^{2x} = 5$, we find:

$$f(x) = f(0.80472) = 5 - 10(0.80472) + 4 = 0.9528.$$

   Answer: $f(x)$ has a local minimum value of 0.9528 at $x = 0.80472$.

9. $f(x) = xe^{-0.2x} + 3$.

   By the product rule:

$$f'(x) = x(e^{-0.2x})(-0.2) + e^{-0.2x}(1)$$
$$= e^{-0.2x}(-0.2x + 1) \text{ is zero where}$$
$$e^{-0.2x}(-0.2x + 1) = 0.$$

   Because $e^{-0.2x}$ is never zero, we have

$$-0.2x + 1 = 0, \text{ so } x = 5.$$
$$f''(x) = e^{-0.2x}(-0.2) + (-0.2x + 1)e^{-0.2x}(-0.2)$$
$$f''(x^*) = f''(5) = e^{-1}(-0.2) + 0, \text{ which is negative (maximum).}$$
$$f(x) = f(5) = 5e^{-1} + 3 = 5(0.3679) + 3 = 4.8395.$$

   Answer: $f(x)$ has a local maximum value of 4.8395 at $x = 5$. More accurately, by calculator, the maximum is 4.8394.

11. $f(x) = 30 + 20e^{3+0.2x}$.

The asymptote is $A(x) = 30$. The coefficient of x in the exponent is positive, and the base is greater than 1, so the asymptote is approached as $x \to -\infty$. The zero exponent point occurs where

$$3 + 0.2x = 0$$
$$x = -15.$$
$$f(-15) = 30 + 20e^0 = 50$$

and we have $(-15, 50)$ as the starting point.

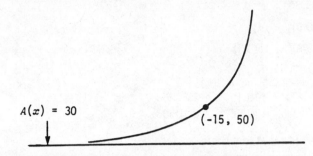

$A(x) = 30$

$(-15, 50)$

13. a) Profit is

$$P(t) = R(t) - C(t) = 3e^{0.05t} - 1.5e^{0.08t}.$$
$$P'(t) = 3e^{0.05t}(0.05) - 1.5e^{0.08t}(0.08).$$

Setting $P'(t)$ equal to zero, we have:

$$0.15e^{0.05t} - 0.12e^{0.08t} = 0$$
$$0.15e^{0.05t} = 0.12e^{0.08t}$$

$$\frac{0.15}{0.12} = \frac{e^{0.08t}}{e^{0.05t}} = e^{0.03t}$$

$$e^{0.03t} = 1.25$$
$$\ln(e^{0.03t}) = \ln 1.25$$
$$0.03t \ln e = \ln 1.25$$

$$t = \frac{\ln 1.25}{0.03}$$

$$= \frac{0.22314}{0.03}$$

$$= 7.4 \text{ years.}$$

The second derivative is

$$P''(t) = 0.0075e^{0.05t} - 0.0096e^{0.08t}$$
$$P''(7.4) = 0.0075e^{0.37} - 0.0096e^{0.59} = -0.006,$$

so we have a maximum.

b)
$$P(7.4) = 3e^{0.05(7.4)} - 1.5e^{0.08(7.4)}$$
$$= 3e^{0.37} - 1.5e^{0.59}$$
$$= 3(1.4477) - 1.5(1.8040)$$
$$= \$1.64 \text{ million}$$

More accurately, by calculator, the answer is \$1.6318 million.

15. a) Revenue $= R(t) = 2,000[1 - (0.9)^t](5)$.

Cost $= C(t) = 100 + 105.36t$.

Profit $= P(t) = 2,000[1 - (0.9)^t](5) - (100 + 105.36t)$.

$$P'(t) = 10,000[-(0.9)^t \ln(0.9)] + 105.36$$
$$= -10,000(0.9)^t(-0.10536) - 105.36$$
$$= 1,053.6(0.9)^t - 105.36.$$

Setting $P'(t)$ equal to zero, we have

$$1,053.6(0.9)^t - 105.36 = 0$$
$$(0.9)^t = 0.1$$
$$\ln(0.9)^t = \ln(0.1)$$
$$t \ln(0.9) = \ln(0.1)$$

$$t = \frac{\ln(0.1)}{\ln(0.9)} = \frac{-2.30259}{-0.10536}$$

$$t = 21.854 \text{ days}.$$

$$P''(t) = 1,053.6(0.9)^t \ln(0.9)$$

is always negative because $\ln(0.9)$ is negative, so we have a maximum.

b) Remembering that $(0.9)^t = 0.1$, the maximum profit is

$$P(t^*) = 2,000[1 - 0.1](5) - [100 + 105.36(21.854)]$$
$$= \$6,597.$$

17. $f(x) = \ln(5x - 4)$.

$$f'(x) = \frac{1}{5x - 4}(5) = \frac{5}{5x - 4}.$$

19. $f(x) = \ln(x^3 + x^2 + x - 5)$.

$$f'(x) = \frac{3x^2 + 2x + 1}{x^3 + x^2 + x - 5}.$$

21. Method 1: $f(x) = \ln xe^x$.

$$f'(x) = \frac{1}{xe^x} \frac{d}{dx}(xe^x)$$

$$= \frac{1}{xe^x}(xe^x + e^x)$$

$$= \frac{e^x(x + 1)}{xe^x}$$

$$= \frac{x + 1}{x}.$$

Method 2: $f(x) = \ln x + \ln e^x$

$$= \ln x + x \ln e$$

$$= \ln x + x.$$

$$f'(x) = \frac{1}{x} + 1$$

$$= \frac{x + 1}{x}.$$

23. $f(x) = x^2 - 4x - 16 \ln x + 30.$

$$f'(x) = 2x - 4 - \frac{16}{x} \text{ is zero where}$$

$$2x - 4 - \frac{16}{x} = 0$$

$$2x^2 - 4x - 16 = 0$$

$$x^2 - 2x - 8 = 0$$

$$(x - 4)(x + 2) = 0$$

$$x = 4.$$

Note that x cannot be -2 because the problem states $x > 0$.

$$f''(x) = 2 + \frac{16}{x^2}$$

$f''(4)$ is positive. (maximum)

$$f(4) = 16 - 16 - 16 \ln 4 + 30$$

$$= -16(1.38629) + 30$$

$$= 7.819.$$

Answer: $f(x)$ has a local minimum value of 7.819 at $x = 4$.

25. $f(x) = -0.5x^2 + 5x + 50 \ln x.$

$$f'(x) = -x + 5 + \frac{50}{x} \text{ is zero where}$$

$$-x^2 + 5x + 50 = 0$$

$$x^2 - 5x - 50 = 0$$

$$(x - 10)(x + 5) = 0$$

$$x = 10.$$

Note that $\underline{x}$ cannot be -5 because the problem states $x > 0$.

$$f''(x) = -1 - \frac{50}{x^2}.$$

$f''(10)$ is negative. (maximum)

$$f(10) = -0.5(100) + 5(10) + 50 \ln 10$$

$$= 50 \ln 10$$

$$= 50(2.30259)$$

$$= 115.13.$$

Answer: $f(x)$ has a local maximum of 115.13 at $x = 10$.

27. $\dfrac{d}{dh}p(q) = \dfrac{d}{dq}[p(q)] \cdot \dfrac{dq}{dh}.$

29. $\dfrac{d}{dx}\ln(y^2 - 2y) = \dfrac{1}{y^2 - 2y}(2y - 2) \cdot \dfrac{dy}{dx} = \dfrac{2y - 2}{y^2 - 2y} \cdot \dfrac{dy}{dx}.$

31. $\dfrac{d}{dx}(2y^{3/2} - x^2) = 2\left(\dfrac{3}{2}\right)y^{1/2} \cdot \dfrac{dy}{dx} - 2x = 3y^{1/2} \cdot \dfrac{dy}{dx} - 2x.$

219

33.
$$y^4 - x^2 = 0$$

$$4y^3 \frac{dy}{dx} - 2x = 0$$

$$\frac{dy}{dx} = \frac{2x}{4y^3} = \frac{x}{2y^3}.$$

35. $e^y \ln x = x^2$.

By the product and chain rules:

$$e^y \left(\frac{1}{x}\right) + (\ln x)e^y \cdot \frac{dy}{dx} = 2x$$

$$(\ln x)e^y \cdot \frac{dy}{dx} = 2x - \frac{e^y}{x}$$

$$\frac{dy}{dx} = \frac{2x - \dfrac{e^y}{x}}{(\ln x)e^y} = \frac{2x^2 - e^y}{x(\ln x)e^y}.$$

37. $y + e^y = x$.

$$\frac{dy}{dx} + e^y \frac{dy}{dx} = 1$$

$$\frac{dy}{dx}(1 + e^y) = 1$$

$$\frac{dy}{dx} = \frac{1}{1 + e^y}.$$

39. $C(Y) = 25 + 0.875Y$.

a) $C'(Y) = 0.875$ is the marginal propensity to consume.

b) Of an additional \$1 of income, the amount spent on consumption is 87.5 cents and the amount saved is 12.5 cents.

c) The multiplier is

$$\frac{1}{1 - MPC} \doteq \frac{1}{1 - 0.875} = \frac{1}{0.125} = \$8.$$

d) $C(500) = 25 + 0.875(500) = 462.5$ spent.

$$\text{Proportion spent} = \frac{462.5}{500} = 0.925 \text{ or } 92.5\%.$$

41.
$$C(Y) = a + bY.$$
$$C'(Y) = MPC(Y) = b.$$

$$\text{Multiplier} = \frac{1}{1 - MPC} = \frac{1}{1 - b}.$$

43.
$$P(x) = 4x - 200.$$
$$P'(x) = 4.$$
$$P'(500) = 4.$$

At sales of 500 gallons (or any number of galions), profit is increasing at the rate of \$4 per additional gallon made and sold.

45.

$$A(t) = 5,000(1.07)^t$$
$$A'(t) = 5,000(1.07)^t \ln(1.07)$$
$$= 5,000(1.07)^t(0.06766)$$
$$= 338.3(1.07)^t$$
$$A'(20) = 338.3(1.07)^{20}$$
$$= 338.3(3.86968)$$
$$= \$1,309.$$

More accurately, by calculator, $A'(20) = \$1,309.09$. At $t = 20$ years, the amount in the account is increasing at the rate of $\$1,309$ per year.

47.

$$C(x) = 2,500 + 2.5x.$$

a)

$$a(x) = \frac{2,500 + 2.5x}{x} = \frac{2,500}{x} + 2.5.$$

b)

$$a'(x) = -\frac{2,500}{x^2}.$$

$$a'(100) = -\frac{2,500}{(100)^2} = -0.25 \text{ dollars.}$$

At 100 books made, average cost is decreasing at the rate of 25 cents per additional book made.

49.

$$A(t) = 1,500(1.09)^t$$
$$A'(t) = 1,500(1.09)^t \ln(1.09)$$

The percent rate of change is

$$\frac{A'(t)}{A(t)} = \frac{1,500(1.09)^t \ln(1.09)}{1,500(1.09)^t}$$

$$= \ln 1.09 = 0.08618, \text{ or } 8.62\%.$$

The rate of change at any point in time is 8.62% per year.

51.

$$N(t) = \frac{200,000}{1 + 50e^{-0.1t}} = 200,000(1 + 50e^{-0.1t})^{-1}$$

$$N'(t) = -200,000(1 + 50e^{-0.1t})^{-2}(50e^{-0.1t})(-0.1)$$
$$= 1,000,000(1 + 50e^{-0.1t})^{-2}(e^{-0.1t}).$$

This percent rate of change is

$$\frac{N'(t)}{N(t)} = \frac{1,000,000(1 + 50e^{-0.1t})^{-2}(e^{-0.1t})}{200,000(1 + 50e^{-0.1t})^{-1}}$$

$$= \frac{5e^{-0.1t}}{1 + 50e^{-0.1t}}.$$

At $t = 5$,

$$\frac{N'(5)}{N(5)} = \frac{5e^{-0.5}}{1 + 50e^{-0.5}} = \frac{5(0.6065)}{1 + 50(0.6065)} = 0.0968,$$

so customer potential at $t = 5$ years is growing at a rate of 9.68% per year.

53. a) $y = \dfrac{10}{5} + 2(10) = 22.$

b) $y'(k) = -\dfrac{10}{k^2}.$

c) $y'(5) = -\dfrac{10}{25} = -0.4.$

Consequently, with $k = 5$, y is decreasing at the rate of 0.4 per increase of 1 in k, or by 0.2 per increase of 0.5 (5 to 5.5) in k, so y would decrease from 22 to about

$$22 - 0.2 = 21.8.$$

55. $f(x, y) = 2x^3 - 3xy + 4y^2 - 6.$

a) $f_x = 6x^2 - 3y.$ b) $f_{xx} = 12x.$ c) $f_y = -3x + 8y.$ d) $f_{yy} = 8.$ e) $f_{xy} = -3.$

57. $f(x, y) = 2y^5 - 6x^2y^3 + 3x - 2y.$

a) $f_x = -12y^3 + 3.$ b) $f_{xx} = -12y^3.$ c) $f_y = 10y^4 - 18x^2y^2 - 2.$

d) $f_{yy} = 40y^3 - 36x^2y.$ e) $f_{xy} = -36xy^2.$

59. $f(x, y) = xe^y.$

a) $f_x = e^y.$ b) $f_{xx} = 0.$ c) $f_y = xe^y.$ d) $f_{yy} = xe^y.$ e) $f_{xy} = e^y.$

61. $\dfrac{\partial}{\partial x}(x^2 - 3y^2) = -6y.$

63. $\dfrac{\partial^2}{\partial x \partial y}(x^3y^2) = \dfrac{\partial}{\partial x}(2x^3y) = 6x^2y.$

65. $f(x) = 5x - 4y.$

a) $f_x = 5;\ f_x(1, 2) = 5.$ b) $f_{xx} = 0.$

c) $f_y = -4;\ f_y(1, 2) = -4.$ d) $f_{yy} = 0.$

e) $f_{xy} = 0.$

67. $f(x, y) = xy - x^2 - y^2 + 15x$

$f_x = y - 2x + 15$

$f_y = x - 2y.$

Setting f_x and f_y equal to zero, we have

$$e_1: \quad -2x + y + 15 = 0$$
$$e_2: \quad x - 2y \qquad = 0$$
$$0 - 3y + 15 = 0 \qquad e_1 + 2e_2$$
$$y = 5$$

and, from e_2,

$$x = 10.$$
$$f_{xx} = -2; \qquad f_{yy} = -2; \qquad f_{xy} = 1.$$
$$D = 12 - (-2)(-2) = -3$$

D is negative, f_{xx} and f_{yy} are negative, so we have a local maximum which is

$$f_{max} = f(10, 5) = (10)(5) - (10)^2 - (5)^2 + 15(10) = 75.$$

69.
$$f(x, y) = 3x^2 - 3xy + y^2 - 6x + 32$$
$$f_x = 6x - 3y - 6$$
$$f_y = -3x + 2y.$$

Setting f_x and f_y equal to zero, we have

$$e_1: \quad 6x - 3y - 6 = 0$$
$$e_2: \quad -3x + 2y \quad 6 = 0$$
$$e_3: \quad 0 + y - 6 = 0 \qquad e_1 + 2e_2$$
$$y = 6$$

and from e_2

$$x = 4$$

so we have $x = 4$, $y = 6$ as a candidate point.

$$f_{xx} = 6; \qquad f_{yy} = 2; \qquad f_{xy} = -3.$$
$$D = (-3)^2 - (6)(2) = -3$$

D is negative, f_{xx} and f_{yy} are positive, so we have a local minimum value which is

$$f_{min} = f(4, 6) = 3(4)^2 - 3(4)(6) + (6)^2 - 6(4) + 32 = 20.$$

71.

$$f(x, y) = \frac{1,600,000}{x} + 2xy^2 + \frac{x(1 - y)^2}{2}$$

$$f_x = -\frac{1,600,000}{x^2} + 2y^2 + \frac{(1 - y)^2}{2}.$$

$$f_y = 4xy + \frac{x}{2}[2(1 - y)(-1)] = 4xy - x(1 - y).$$

Setting f_y equal to zero, we find

$$4xy - x(1 - y) = 0$$
$$x(4y - 1 + y) = 0.$$

Because $\underline{x}$ cannot be zero, we have

$$4y - 1 + y = 0$$
$$5y = 1$$
$$y = 0.2.$$

Setting f_x equal to zero, we find

$$-\frac{1,600,000}{x^2} + 2y^2 + \frac{(1 - y)^2}{2} = 0.$$

With $y = 0.2$, the last becomes

$$-\frac{1,600,000}{x^2} + 2(0.04) + 0.32 = 0$$

$$-\frac{1,600,000}{x^2} + 0.4 = 0$$

$$-1,600,000 + 0.4x^2 = 0$$

$$x^2 = \frac{1,600,000}{0.4} = 4,000,000$$

$$x = 2,000$$

and we have $x = 2,000$, $y = 0.2$ as a candidate point.

$$f_{xx} = \frac{3,200,000}{x^3};$$ $$\qquad f_{xx}(2,000; 0.2) = \frac{3,200,000}{(2,000)^3} = 0.0004.$$

$$f_{yy} = 4x + x = 5x;$$ $$\qquad f_{yy}(2,000; 0.2) = 10,000.$$

$$f_{xy} = 4y + \frac{1}{2}(2)(1-y)(-1) = 5y - 1;$$ $$\qquad f_{xy}(2,000; 0.2) = 0.$$

$$D = 0^2 - (0.0004)(10,000) = -4$$

D is negative, f_{xx} and f_{yy} are positive, so we have a local minimum value which is

$$f(2,000, 0.2) = \frac{1,600,000}{2,000} + 2(2,000)(0.2)^2 + \frac{2,000(0.8)^2}{2} = 1,600.$$

73. a)

x	y	xy	x^2
2	2	4	4
4	5	20	16
8	4	32	64
10	10	100	100
16	9	144	256
40	30	300	440

$n = 5$ points.

$$m = \frac{n\Sigma xy - (\Sigma x)(\Sigma y)}{n\Sigma x^2 - (\Sigma x)^2} = \frac{5(300) - (40)(30)}{5(440) - (40)^2} = \frac{300}{600} = 0.5.$$

$$b = \frac{\Sigma y - b\Sigma x}{n} = \frac{30 - 0.5(40)}{5} = \frac{10}{5} = 2.$$

$$y_f = 0.5x + 2.$$

b)

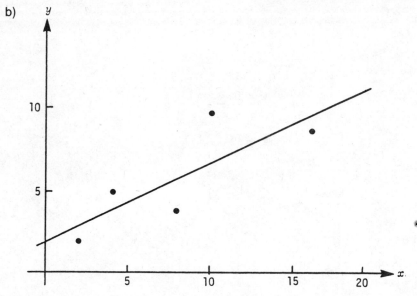

1. $\int dx$

   $x + C$

5. $\int (1 + x)dx$

   $x + \dfrac{x^2}{2} + C$

9. $\int p\,dq$

   $pq + C$

13. $\int (x^3 + x^4 - 1)dx$

   $\dfrac{x^4}{4} + \dfrac{x^5}{5} - x + C$

17. $\int x^{-2}dx$

   $-\dfrac{1}{x} + C$

21. $\int (5 - 2y^{-3})dy$

   $5y + \dfrac{1}{y^2} + C$

25. $\int p^{1/2}dp$

   $\dfrac{2p^{3/2}}{3} + C$

29. $\int \left(2 - \dfrac{1}{x^2} - \dfrac{2}{3x^{5/3}}\right)dx$

   $2x + \dfrac{1}{x} + \dfrac{1}{x^{2/3}} + C$

33. $\int 16(2x - 9)^3dx$

   $2(2x - 9)^4 + C$

37. $\int \dfrac{dx}{(5 - 3x)^{1/2}}$

   $\dfrac{-2(5 - 3x)^{1/2}}{3} + C$

Problem Set 13-2

1. $\int_2^5 2dx$

$\Big|_2^5 2x$

$[2(5)] - [2(2)]$

$10 - 4$

6

5. $\int_2^6 (x + 1)dx$

$\Big|_2^6 \left(\dfrac{x^2}{2} + x\right)$

$\left[\left(\dfrac{6^2}{2} + 6\right)\right] - \left[\left(\dfrac{2^2}{2} + 2\right)\right]$

$\left(\dfrac{36}{2} + 6\right) - \left(\dfrac{4}{2} + 2\right)$

$24 - 4$

20

9. $\int_1^2 (x^2 - 3x + 5)dx$

$\Big|_1^2 \left(\dfrac{x^3}{3} - \dfrac{3x^2}{2} + 5x\right)$

$\left(\dfrac{2^3}{3} - \dfrac{3(2)^2}{2} + 5(2)\right) - \left(\dfrac{1^3}{3} - \dfrac{3(1)^2}{2} + 5(1)\right)$

$\left(\dfrac{8}{3} - \dfrac{12}{2} + 10\right) - \left(\dfrac{1}{3} - \dfrac{3}{2} + 5\right)$

$\left(\dfrac{16}{6} - \dfrac{36}{6} + \dfrac{60}{6}\right) - \left(\dfrac{2}{6} - \dfrac{9}{6} + \dfrac{30}{6}\right)$

$\dfrac{40}{6} - \dfrac{23}{6}$

$\dfrac{17}{6}$

17. $\int_a^b 3x^2dx$

$\Big|_a^b \dfrac{3x^3}{3}$

$\Big|_a^b x^3$

$b^3 - a^3$

21. $f(x) = 2x; x = 1$ to $x = 2$

$$A = \int_1^2 2x\,dx$$

$$\left(\frac{2x^2}{2} + C\right)\Bigg|_1^2$$

$$\left(\frac{2(2)^2}{2} + C\right) - \left(\frac{2(1)^2}{2} + C\right)$$

$$\left(\frac{8}{2}\right) - \left(\frac{2}{2}\right) \qquad \text{3 square units}$$

25. $f(x) = \dfrac{6}{x^2}; x = 1$ to $x = 3$

$$A = \int_1^3 \frac{6}{x^2}\,dx$$

$$\left(\frac{-6}{x}\right)\Bigg|_1^3$$

$$\left(\frac{-6}{3}\right) - \left(\frac{-6}{1}\right)$$

$$(-2) - (-6) \qquad \text{4 square units}$$

29. Find the x values where $f(x)$ crosses the axes

$$\int_0^{20} (10 - 0.5x)\,dx = \left|_0^{20}\left(10x - \frac{0.5x^2}{2}\right)\right.$$

$$\left[10(20) - \frac{0.5(20^2)}{2}\right] - \left[10(0) - \frac{0.5(0)^2}{2}\right] = 100 - 0 = \boxed{100}$$

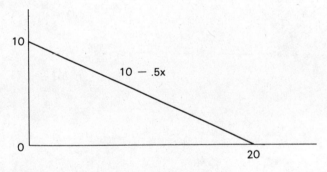

33. Set $f(x) = 0$ and solve for x

$0 = x^3 - 3x^2 - x + 3 = (x^2 - 1)(x - 3)$

solve for 2 parts $x = -1, 1, 3$

$$\int_{-1}^1 (x^3 - 3x^2 - x + 3)\,dx + \int_1^3 (x^3 - 3x^2 - x + 3)\,dx$$

$$\left|_{-1}^1 \frac{x^4}{4} - x^3 - \frac{x^2}{2} + 3x + \right|_1^3 \frac{x^4}{4} - x^3 - \frac{x^2}{2} + 3x$$

$$\left[\frac{1}{4} - 1 - \frac{1}{2} + 3\right] - \left[\frac{1}{4} - (-1) - \frac{1}{2} + (-3)\right] = 1.75 - (-2.25) = 4$$

$$\left[\frac{81}{4} - 27 - \frac{9}{2} + 9\right] - \left[\frac{1}{4} - 1 - \frac{1}{2} + 3\right] = -2.25 - 1.75 = |-4|$$

$4 + 4 = \boxed{8}$

227

1.

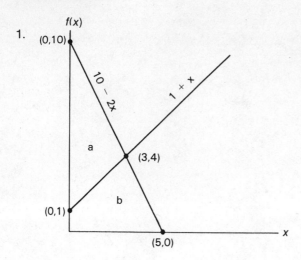

$$1 + x = 10 - 2x$$
$$3x = 9 \qquad x = 3$$

a) $\displaystyle\int_0^3 (10 - 2x)dx - \int_0^3 (1 + x)dx = \int_0^3 (9 - 3x)dx$

$$\Big|_0^3 \left(9x - \frac{3x^2}{2}\right)dx = \left[9(3) - \frac{3(3^2)}{2}\right] - [0] = \frac{27}{2}$$

b) $\displaystyle\int_0^3 (1 + x)dx + \int_3^5 (10 - 2x)dx$

$$\Big|_0^3 \left(x + \frac{x^2}{2}\right) = \left[3 + \frac{3^2}{2}\right] - [0] = 7.5$$

$$\Big|_3^5 (10x - x^2) = [10(5) - 5^2] - [10(3) - 3^2]$$

$$25 - 21 = 4 \qquad \boxed{11.5}$$

5.

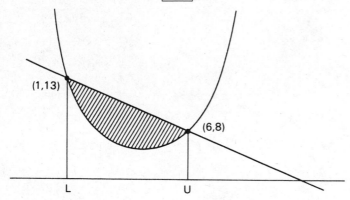

Find L and U by
$$x^2 - 8x + 20 = 14 - x$$
$$x^2 - 7x + 6 = 0 \qquad x = 1, 6$$

$$\int_1^6 (14 - x)dx - \int_1^6 (x^2 - 8x + 20)dx = \int_1^6 (-x^2 + 7x - 6)dx = \Big|_1^6 \left(\frac{-x^3}{3} + \frac{7x^2}{2} - 6x\right)$$

$$\left[\frac{-6^3}{3} + \frac{7(6^2)}{2} - 6(6)\right] - \left[\frac{-1^3}{3} + \frac{7(1^2)}{2} - 6(1)\right] = 18 - \left(-\frac{17}{6}\right) = 20\frac{5}{6}$$

228

9. Set functions equal and solve for x.

$x^3 = x \qquad x = -1, 0, 1$

$$\int_{-1}^{0} \left(x^3 dx - \int_{-1}^{0} x dx \right) = \int_{-1}^{0} (x^3 - x)dx = \left|_{-1}^{0} \left(\frac{x^4}{4} - \frac{x^2}{2} \right) \right.$$

$$\left[\frac{0^4}{4} - \frac{0^2}{4} \right] - \left[\frac{-1^4}{4} - \frac{-1^2}{2} \right] = 0 - \left(\frac{-1}{4} \right) = \frac{1}{4}$$

$$\int_{0}^{1} x dx - \int_{0}^{1} x^3 dx = \int_{0}^{1} (x - x^3)dx = \left|_{0}^{1} \frac{x^2}{2} - \frac{x^4}{4} \right.$$

$$\left[\frac{1^2}{2} - \frac{1^4}{4} \right] - \left[\frac{0^2}{2} - \frac{0^4}{4} \right] = \frac{1}{4} - 0 = \frac{1}{4}$$

$$\frac{1}{4} + \frac{1}{4} = \boxed{\frac{1}{2}}$$

Problem Set 13-4

1. a)
$$\int_{0}^{6} (2 + 0.1t)dt = \left|_{0}^{6} \left(2t + \frac{0.1t^2}{2} \right) \right.$$

$$\left[2(6) + \frac{0.1(6^2)}{2} \right] - \left[2(0) + \frac{0.1(0^2)}{2} \right] = 13.8 - 0 = \boxed{\$13,800}$$

b) M(t)

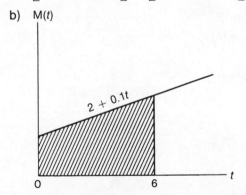

c) $\int_{6}^{12} (2 + 0.1t)dt = \left[2(12) + \frac{0.1(12^2)}{2} \right] - 13.8 = 17.4 \qquad \boxed{\$17,400}$

d) $\int_{0}^{t} (2 + 0.1t)dt = 60$

$$2t + \frac{0.1t^2}{2} = 60$$

$$0.05t^2 + 2t - 60 = 0$$

$$t = -60, 20 \qquad \boxed{20 \text{ years}}$$

5.
$$\int_0^t (2t + 9)^{1/2}dt = 63$$

$$\left.\frac{(2t + 9)^{3/2}}{(3/2)(2)}\right|_0^t = 63$$

$$\left[\frac{(2t + 9)^{3/2}}{3}\right] - \left[\frac{(2(0) + 9)^{3/2}}{3}\right] = 63$$

$$\frac{(2t + 9)^{3/2}}{3} - 9 = 63$$

$$(2t + 9)^{3/2} = 216$$

$$2t + 9 = 36$$

$$2t = 27 \qquad t = 13.5 \text{ years}$$

9. $$\int_0^{100} (0.006t^2 - 1.2t + 50)dt + 1,600$$

$$\left.\left(\frac{0.006t^3}{3} - \frac{1.2t^2}{2} + 50t\right)\right|_0^{100} + [1,600]$$

$$[0.002(100^3) - 0.6(100^2) + 50(100)] - [0] + 1,600$$

$$[2,000 - 6,000 + 5,000] - 0 + 1,600 = \boxed{\$2,600}$$

13. a) $$\int_0^{100} (75 - 0.6q)dq - [75 - 0.6(100)][100]$$

$$\left.\left(75q - \frac{0.6q^2}{2}\right)\right|_0^{100} - 1,500 = \left[75(100) - \frac{0.6(100^2)}{2}\right] - [0] - 1,500$$

$$= 4,500 - 0 - 1,500 = \boxed{\$3,000} \text{ million}$$

b) $p_d(q)$

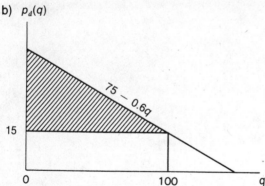

17. Set $p_s(q) = p_d(q)$ to find equilibrium

$$10 + 0.1q = 100 - 0.2q$$

$$0.3q = 90 \qquad \boxed{q = 300}$$

a) $$\int_0^{300} (100 - 0.2q)dq - [100 - 0.2(300)][300]$$

$$\left.\left(100q - \frac{0.2q^2}{2}\right)\right|_0^{300} - [12,000]$$

$$\left[100(300) - \frac{0.2(300^2)}{2}\right] - [0] - [12,000]$$

$$(30,000 - 9,000) - 0 - 12,000 = \boxed{\$9000} \text{ thousand}$$

230

b) $[10 + 0.1(300)][300] - \int_0^{300} (10 + 0.1q)dq$

$12,000 - \left|_0^{300} \left(10q + \frac{0.1q^2}{2}\right)\right.$

$12,000 - \left[10(300) + \frac{0.1(300^2)}{2}\right] - [0]$

$12,000 - 7,500 - 0 = \boxed{\$4,500}$ thousand

Problem Set 13-5

1. $\int x^{-1}dx = \ln x + C$

5. $\int x^{-2}dx = \frac{x^{-1}}{-1} + C = \frac{-1}{x} + C$

9. $\int \frac{dx}{(3 - 0.2x)} = \frac{\ln(3 - 0.2x)}{-0.2} + C = -5\ln(3 - 0.2x) + C$

13. $\int_1^{10} \frac{dx}{x} = \left|_1^{10}\right. \ln x = \ln 10 - \ln 1 = 2.303 - 0 = \boxed{2.303}$

17. $\int_0^{25} \frac{100}{0.2t + 1}dt = \left|_0^{25}\right. \frac{100\ln(0.2t + 1)}{12} = [500\ln(0.2(25) + 1)] - [500\ln(0.2(0) + 1)]$

$895.88 - 0 = \boxed{895.88}$ million barrels

Problem Set 13-6

1. $\int e^x dx = e^x + C$

5. $\int e^{0.5x}dx = \frac{e^{0.5x}}{0.5} + C = 2e^{0.5x} + C$

9. $\int 2e^{3 - 0.1x}dx = \frac{2e^{3 - 0.1x}}{-0.1} + C = -20e^{3 - 0.1x} + C$

13. $\int_0^5 2e^{1 - 0.2x}dx = \left|_0^5\right. \frac{2e^{1 - 0.2x}}{-0.2}$

$\left[\frac{2e^{1 - 0.2(5)}}{-0.2}\right] - \left[\frac{2e^{1 - 0.2(0)}}{-0.2}\right] = -10 - (-27.18) = \boxed{17.18}$

17. a) $\int_0^{20} 10e^{0.05t}dt = \left|_0^{20}\right. \frac{10e^{0.05t}}{0.05}$

$[200e^{0.05(2e)}] - [200e^{0.05(0)}] = 543.66 - 200 = \boxed{343.67}$ million barrels

b) $200e^{0.05t} - 200 = 1,000$

$e^{0.05t} = 6$ take ln of both sides

$0.05t = 1.7918$ $\boxed{t = 35.84 \text{ years}}$

21. $\int_0^5 (5 + 15e^{-0.2t})dt = \left|_0^5 \left(5t + \frac{15e^{-0.2t}}{-0.2}\right)\right.$

$[5(5) - 75e^{-0.2(5)}] - [5(0) - 75e^{-0.2(0)}]$

$-2.59 - 75 = 72.41$ million pounds

231

Problem Set 13-7

1. $\dfrac{x2^x}{\ln 2} - \dfrac{2^x}{(\ln 2)^2} + C$

5. $\dfrac{e^{2-0.5x}(0.5x - 1)}{0.5^2} + C$

   $-4(0.5x + 1)(e^{2-0.5x}) + C$

9. $2\left[\dfrac{x}{5} - \dfrac{-3}{5^2}\ln(5x - 3)\right] + C$

   $\dfrac{2x}{5} + \dfrac{6}{25}\ln(5x - 3) + C$

13. $\dfrac{0.5x - \ln(1 + 2e^{0.5x})}{(1)(0.5)} + C$

   $x - 2\ln(1 + 2e^{0.5x}) + C$

17. $\dfrac{1}{1}\ln\left|\dfrac{1 + \sqrt{1 - 9x^2}}{3x}\right| + C$

   $3\ln\left|\dfrac{x + 1}{3x}\right| + C$

Problem Set 13-8

1. $\left.\dfrac{4x^{-1/2}}{-1/2}\right|_1^\infty = \left.\dfrac{-8}{x^2}\right|_1^\infty$

   $\displaystyle\lim_{a\to\infty}\left[\dfrac{-8}{a^2}\right] - \left[\dfrac{-8}{-1^2}\right] = 0 - (-8) = \boxed{8}$

5. $\left.\dfrac{x^{1/2}}{1/2}\right|_1^\infty = \left.2x^{1/2}\right|_1^\infty$

   $\displaystyle\lim_{a\to\infty}[2a^{1/2}] - [2(1^{1/2})] = \infty$

9. $\left.\dfrac{-2x^{1/2}}{1/2}\right|_{25}^\infty = \left.-4x^{1/2}\right|_{25}^\infty$

   $\displaystyle\lim_{a\to\infty}[-4(a^{1/2})] - [-4(25^{1/2})] = \infty - (-20) = \infty$

13. $\left.\dfrac{x^{-98}}{-98}\right|_1^\infty = \left.\dfrac{-1}{98x^{98}}\right|_1^\infty = \lim_{a\to\infty}\left[\dfrac{-1}{98a^{98}}\right] - \left[\dfrac{-1}{98(1^{98})}\right] = 0 - \dfrac{-1}{98} = \boxed{\dfrac{1}{98}}$

17. $\left.\dfrac{4}{9}\dfrac{1}{1}\ln\left(\dfrac{x}{x + 1}\right)\right|_1^\infty = \left.\dfrac{4}{9}\ln\left(\dfrac{x}{x + 1}\right)\right|_1^\infty$

   $\displaystyle\lim_{a\to\infty}\dfrac{4}{9}\left[\ln\left(\dfrac{a}{a + 1}\right)\right] - \dfrac{4}{9}\left[\ln\left(\dfrac{1}{1 + 1}\right)\right]$

   $\dfrac{4}{9}[0] - \dfrac{4}{9}[-0.693] = \boxed{0.308}$

Problem Set 13-9

1.

x	$f(x)$		
1	0	$\times 0.5 =$	0
1.5	0.405		0.405
2	0.693		0.693
2.5	0.916		0.916
3	1.099		1.099
3.5	1.253		1.253
4	1.386	$\times 0.5 =$	0.693

$$w = \frac{4-1}{6} = \frac{1}{2} \qquad 5.059 \times \frac{1}{2} = \boxed{2.53}$$

5.

x	$f(x)$		
1	0	$\times 0.5 =$	0
1.2	0.091		0.091
1.4	0.167		0.167
1.6	0.231		0.231
1.8	0.286		0.286
2	0.333	$\times 0.5 =$	0.167

$$w = \frac{2-1}{5} = \frac{1}{5} \qquad 0.941 \times \frac{1}{5} = \boxed{0.188}$$

9.

x	$f(x)$		
1	0.368	$\times 0.5 =$	0.184
1.5	0.335		0.335
2	0.271		0.271
2.5	0.205		0.205
3	0.149	$\times 0.5 =$	0.075

$$w = \frac{3-1}{4} = \frac{1}{2} \qquad 1.070 \times \frac{1}{2} = \boxed{0.535}$$

Problem Set 13-10

1. $3x(\ln x - 1) + C$

5. $\dfrac{(2x + 1)[\ln(2x + 1) - 1]}{2} + C$

9. $\displaystyle\int_0^7 4 \ln(2t + 6)\,dt$

$$\left|_0^7 \frac{4(2t + 6)[\ln(2t + 6) - 1]}{2} + \right.$$

$$\left[\frac{4(2(7) + 6)[\ln(2(7) + 6) - 1]}{2}\right] - \left[\frac{4(2(0) + 6)[\ln(2(0) + 6) - 1]}{2}\right]$$

$$= 4\left[\frac{20[\ln(20) - 1]}{2} - \frac{6[\ln(6) - 1]}{2}\right]$$

$$= 4[10[1.9957] - 3[0.7918]] = 17.5816(4) = \boxed{\$70.334} \text{ thousand}$$

17. $\displaystyle\int x(1 - x)^{1/2}\,dx$

$$u = x \qquad \frac{du}{dx} = \frac{d(x)}{dx} = 1 \qquad du = dx$$

$$dv = (1 - x)^{1/2}\,dx$$

$$\int dv = \int (1 - x)^{1/2}dx$$

$$v = \frac{-(1 - x)^{3/2}}{3/2} = \frac{-2(1 - x)^{3/2}}{3}$$

$$u = x \qquad v = \frac{-2}{3}(1 - x)^{3/2}$$

$$du = 1 \qquad dv = (1 - x)^{1/2}$$

$$\int u\,dv = \int x(1 - x)^{1/2}dx$$

$$-x\left(\frac{2}{3}(1 - x)^{3/2}\right) - \int -\frac{2}{3}(1 - x)^{3/2}(1)dx$$

$$\frac{2x}{3}(1 - x)^{3/2} - \frac{4}{15}(1 - x)^{5/2} + C$$

$$\left(\frac{-2}{15}\right)(1 - x)^{3/2}(7x - 2) + C$$

Problem Set 13-11

1. $y + C_1 - (x + C_2) = 0$

   $y = x + C_2 - C_1 \qquad y = x + C$

5. $y = Kx$

9. $dy = \dfrac{dx}{(0.2x + 3)}$

   $y = \dfrac{\ln(0.2x + 3)}{0.2} + C$

   $y = 5 \ln(0.2x + 3) + C$

13. $y - \left(\dfrac{x^2}{2} + x\right) + 26 - \left(\dfrac{6^2}{2} + 6\right)$

    $y = \dfrac{1}{2}x^2 + x + 2$

17. $\displaystyle\int \frac{dy}{(0.2y + 3)} = \int dx$

    $\dfrac{\ln(0.2y + 3)}{0.2} = x + C_1$

    $\ln(0.2y + 3) = 0.2x + 0.2C = 0.2x + C$

    take the "e" of both sides

    $0.2y + 3 = e^{0.2x + C}$

    $0.2y = K_1 e^{0.2x} - 3$

    $y = \dfrac{K_1 e^{0.2x} - 3}{0.2}$

    $y = Ke^{0.2x} - 15$

    $y = 4 \qquad x = 0$

    $4 = Ke^{0.2(0)} - 15$

    $19 = K$

    thus $y = 19Ke^{0.2x} - 15$

Problem Set 13-12

1. a) $dS = (150 + 6t)dt$

   b) $S = 0$ when $t = 0$

   c) $S(t) = 150t + \dfrac{6t^2}{2} = 150t + 3t^2$

   d) $[150(50) + 3(50^2)] - [150(0) + 3(0^2)]$
      $15,000 - 0 = 15,000$

   e) $\qquad 150t + 3t^2 = 45,000$
      $t^2 + 50t - 15,000 = 0 \qquad t = 100$ days

5. a) $dS = 0.08Sdt + 500dt$

   b) $S(t) = 8,250e^{0.08t} - 6,250$

   c) $[8,250e^{0.08(10)} - 6,250] = \$12,110.71$

   d) $18,500 = 8,250e^{0.08t} - 6,250$

   $$e^{0.08t} = \frac{18,500 + 6,250}{8,250} = 3 \qquad \text{take ln of both sides}$$

   $$0.08t = \ln 3 = 1.0986 \qquad t = \frac{1.0986}{0.08} = 13.73 \text{ years}$$

1. $q + C$

3. $Kx + C$

5. $y + \dfrac{y^3}{3} + C$

7. $ax + \dfrac{bx^2}{2} + C$

9. $12\left(2\dfrac{x^3}{3} - \dfrac{x^4}{4} + \dfrac{3x^2}{2} + 2x\right) + C = 8x^3 - 3x^4 + 18x^2 + 24x + C.$

11. $\dfrac{x^{5/3}}{\dfrac{5}{3}} + \dfrac{2x^{-1/2}}{-\dfrac{1}{2}} + C = \dfrac{3}{5}x^{5/3} - \dfrac{4}{x^{1/2}} + C.$

13. $\displaystyle\int\left(1 + \dfrac{2}{x^3} + \dfrac{4}{x^{1/2}}\right)dx = \int(1 + 2x^{-3} + 4x^{-1/2})dx$

$$= x + \dfrac{2x^{-2}}{-2} + \dfrac{4x^{1/2}}{\dfrac{1}{2}} + C$$

$$= x - \dfrac{1}{x^2} + 8x^{1/2} + C.$$

15. $\dfrac{30(3x - 5)^5}{5(3)} + C = 2(3x - 5)^5 + C.$

17. $\displaystyle\int\dfrac{6dx}{(8 - 3x)^{4/3}} = 6\int(8 - 3x)^{-4/3}dx$

$$= 6\left(\dfrac{(8 - 3x)^{-1/3}}{-\dfrac{1}{3}(-3)}\right) + C$$

$$= \dfrac{6}{(8 - 3x)^{1/3}} + C.$$

19. $x\Big|_1^5 = 5 - 1 = 4.$

21. $\dfrac{4}{7}(x^{7/4})\Big|_1^{16} = \dfrac{4}{7}[(16)^{7/4} - (1)^{7/4}] = \dfrac{4}{7}[2^7 - 1] = \dfrac{4}{7}(127) = \dfrac{508}{7}.$

23. $\displaystyle\int_2^3\dfrac{12dx}{(3x - 5)^3} = 12\int_2^3(3x - 5)^{-3}dx$

$$= \dfrac{12(3x - 5)^{-2}}{-2(3)}\Big|_2^3$$

$$= \dfrac{-2}{(3x - 5)^2}\Big|_2^3$$

$$= -2\left[\dfrac{1}{4^2} - \dfrac{1}{1}\right]$$

$$= -2\left(-\dfrac{15}{16}\right) = \dfrac{15}{8}.$$

25. $\displaystyle\int_a^{2a}\left(\frac{x}{a}+\frac{a}{x^2}\right)dx = \int_a^{2a}\left(\frac{x}{a}+ax^{-2}\right)dx$

$$= \left(\frac{x^2}{2a}+\frac{ax^{-1}}{-1}\right)\Bigg|_a^{2a}$$

$$= \left(\frac{x^2}{2a}-\frac{a}{x}\right)\Bigg|_a^{2a}$$

$$= \left(\frac{4a^2}{2a}-\frac{a}{2a}\right)-\left(\frac{a^2}{2a}-\frac{a}{a}\right)$$

$$= 2a-\frac{1}{2}-\frac{a}{2}+1$$

$$= \frac{3a+1}{2}.$$

27. $\displaystyle\int_0^4(8x+4)^{1/2}dx = \frac{(8x+4)^{3/2}}{\left(\dfrac{3}{2}\right)(8)}\Bigg|_0^4$

$$= \frac{(8x+4)^{3/2}}{12}\Bigg|_0^4$$

$$= \frac{1}{12}[(36)^{3/2}-(4)^{3/2}]$$

$$= \frac{1}{12}(216-8)$$

$$= \frac{208}{12}$$

$$= \frac{52}{3}.$$

29. Area $\displaystyle= \int_0^{50}(10-0.2x)dx$

$$= (10x-0.1x^2)\Big|_0^{50}$$

$$= (500-250)$$

$$= 250.$$

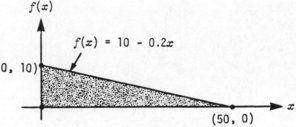

30. $f(x)$

$f(x) = 10 - 0.2x$

$(0, 10)$

$(50, 0)$

31. Area $\displaystyle= \int_{-3}^6(3x-x^2+18)dx$

$$= \left(\frac{3x^2}{2}-\frac{x^3}{3}+18x\right)\Bigg|_{-3}^6$$

$$= \left[\frac{3(36)}{2}-\frac{216}{3}+18(6)\right]$$

$$-\left[\frac{3(9)}{2}+\frac{27}{3}+18(-3)\right]$$

$$= 54-72+108-\frac{27}{2}-9+54$$

$$= 121.5.$$

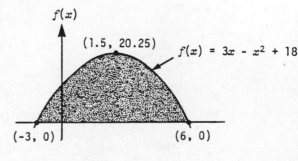

$f(x)$

$(1.5, 20.25)$

$f(x) = 3x - x^2 + 18$

$(-3, 0)$

$(6, 0)$

33. The intersections occur where

$$f(x) = g(x)$$

$$x^2 = \frac{x^2}{2} + 2; \quad \frac{x^2}{2} = 2; \quad x^2 = 4; \quad x = 2.$$

We seek only the first quadrant area:

$$\text{Area} = \int_0^2 [g(x) - f(x)]dx$$

$$= \int_0^2 \left(2 - \frac{x^2}{2}\right)dx$$

$$= \left(2x - \frac{x^3}{6}\right)\Big|_0^2$$

$$= \left(4 - \frac{8}{6}\right) - (0)$$

$$= \frac{8}{3}.$$

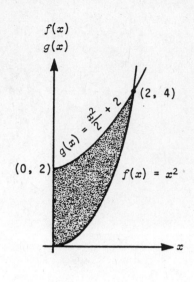

35. $\int_0^9 (1 + 0.3t)dt = (t + 0.15t^2)\Big|_0^9$

$$= [9 + 0.15(81)] - 0$$

$$= 21.15 \text{ million barrels.}$$

37. The variable component is

$$\int_0^4 (10 + 0.1t)dt = (10t + 0.05t^2)\Big|_0^4$$

$$= (40 + 0.8) - (0) = 40.8.$$

The fixed component for four years is $4(5) = 20$, so the total is

$$40.8 + 20 = \$60.8 \text{ thousand.}$$

39. $\int_0^{30} (0.9t + 9)^{1/2}dt = \dfrac{(0.9t + 9)^{3/2}}{\left(\dfrac{3}{2}\right)(0.9)}\Bigg|_0^{30}$

$$= \frac{2}{2.7}(0.9t + 9)^{3/2}\Big|_0^{30}$$

$$= \frac{2}{2.7}[(36)^{3/2} - (9)^{3/2}]$$

$$= \frac{2}{2.7}(216 - 27)$$

$$= 140 \text{ thousand tons.}$$

41. The integral of marginal cost is total variable cost. This is

$$\int_0^{200} (0.003t^2 - 0.4t + 25)dt = (0.001t^3 - 0.2t^2 + 25t)\Big|_0^{200}$$

$$= (8{,}000 - 8{,}000 + 5{,}000) - (0)$$

$$= \$5{,}000.$$

Adding the $1,000 fixed cost to the variable cost, $5,000, total cost is $6,000.

43.

$$p_d(q) = \frac{100}{(0.2q + 1)^2}$$

$$p_d(20) = \frac{100}{25} = \$4 \text{ per gallon.}$$

$$\text{Consumers' surplus} = \int_0^{q_m} p_d(q)dq - (q_m\, p_m)$$

$$= \int_0^{20} 100(0.2q + 1)^{-2}dq - (20)(4)$$

$$= \left.\frac{100(0.2q + 1)^{-1}}{-1(0.2)}\right|_0^{20} - 80$$

$$= \left.\frac{-500}{(0.2q + 1)}\right|_0^{20} - 80$$

$$= -500\left[\frac{1}{5} - 1\right] - 80$$

$$= 400 - 80$$

$$= \$320 \text{ million.}$$

45. $3 \ln x + C$

47. $\dfrac{2 \ln(5x + 4)}{5} + C = 0.4 \ln(5x + 4) + C.$

49.

$$\int_0^{10} 6(2x + 3)^{-1}dx = \left.3 \ln(2x + 3)\right|_0^{10}$$

$$= 3(\ln 23 - \ln 3)$$

$$= 3(3.13549 - 1.09861)$$

$$= 6.11064.$$

More accurately, by calculator, the answer is 6.11065.

51.

$$\int_0^{20}\left(\frac{40}{0.25t + 1}\right)dt = \left.40\,\frac{\ln(0.25t + 1)}{0.25}\right|_0^{20}$$

$$= \left.160 \ln(0.25t + 1)\right|_0^{20}$$

$$= 160(\ln 5 - \ln 1)$$

$$= 160 \ln 5$$

$$= 160(1.60944)$$

$$= 257.51 \text{ million tons.}$$

53. $3e^{2x+5} + C$

55. $\dfrac{2^x}{\ln 2} + C$

57. $\int_5^{10} e^{0.2x-1}dx = \left.5e^{0.2x-1}\right|_5^{10} = 5(e^1 - e^0) = 5(2.7183 - 1) = 8.5915.$

More accurately, by calculator, the answer is 8.5914.

59.

$$\int 10(0.5)^x dx = \frac{10(0.5)^x}{\ln (0.5)} + C$$

$$= -14.427(0.5)^x + C.$$

239

61. a) $\int_0^{10} 2e^{0.08t}dt = \dfrac{2e^{0.08t}}{0.08}\bigg|_0^{10}$

$$= 25(e^{0.08t})\bigg|_0^{10}$$

$$= 25(e^{0.8} - e^0)$$

$$= 25(2.2255 - 1)$$

$$= 30.6375 \text{ billion barrels.}$$

More accurately, by calculator, the answer is 30.6385 billion barrels.

b) Fuel will last until 200 billion barrels have been consumed.

$$\int_0^t 2e^{0.08t}dt = 200$$

$$25e^{0.08t}\bigg|_0^t = 200$$

$$25(e^{0.08t} - e^0) = 200$$

$$e^{0.08t} - 1 = 8$$

$$e^{0.08t} = 9$$

$$\ln(e^{0.08t}) = \ln 9$$

$$0.08t \ln e = \ln 9$$

$$t = \dfrac{\ln 9}{0.08}$$

$$= 27.47 \text{ years.}$$

63. $p_s(q) = 2 + e^{0.01q}$

$p_s(100) = 2 + e = p_m.$

Producer's surplus $= 100(2 + e) - \int_0^{100}(2 + e^{0.01q})dq$

$$= 100(2 + e) - (2q + 100e^{0.01q})\bigg|_0^{100}$$

$$= 100(2 + e) - [(200 + 100e) - (0 + 100e^0)]$$

$$= 200 + 100e - 200 - 100e + 100$$

$$= \$100 \text{ million.}$$

65. $x(\ln 5x - 1) + C$

67. $\dfrac{(10x + 3)[\ln(10x + 3) - 1]}{10} + C.$

69. $\int_0^4 \ln(5x + 7)dx = \dfrac{(5x + 7)[\ln(5x + 7) - 1]}{5}\bigg|_0^4$

$$= 0.2[27(\ln 27 - 1) - 7(\ln 7 - 1)]$$

$$= 0.2[27(3.29584 - 1) - 7(1.94591 - 1)]$$

$$= 11.07326.$$

More accurately, by calculator, the answer is 11.07324.

71. By formula 19, Table XII-B, with $a = -0.25, b = 1$:

$$\int 4xe^{1-0.25x^2}dx = 4\dfrac{e^{1-0.25x^2}}{2(-0.25)} + C = -8e^{1-0.25x^2} + C.$$

73. By formula 12, Table XII-B, with $m = 0.4$, $b = 3$:

$$\int \frac{4dx}{x(0.4x + 3)} = \frac{4}{3}\ln\left(\frac{x}{0.4x + 3}\right) + C.$$

75. By formula 17, Table XII-B, with $m = -0.1$, $b = 5$:

$$\int 3xe^{5-0.1x}dx = 3\left[\frac{e^{5-0.1x}(-0.1x - 1)}{(-0.1)^2}\right] + C$$

$$= -300e^{5-0.1x}(0.1x + 1) + C.$$

77. By formula 11, Table XII-B, with $m = 3$, $b = 2$:

$$\int \frac{9xdx}{(3x + 2)^2} = 9\left[\frac{2}{9(3x + 2)} + \frac{\ln(3x + 2)}{9}\right] + C$$

$$= \frac{2}{(3x + 2)} + \ln(3x + 2) + C.$$

79. $\int_0^\infty 10e^{-0.5x}dx = -20e^{-0.5x}\Big|_0^\infty$

$$= -20\left(\frac{1}{e^{0.5x}}\right)\Big|_0^\infty$$

$$= -20\left[\lim_{x \to \infty}\left(\frac{1}{e^{0.5x}}\right) - \left(\frac{1}{e^0}\right)\right]$$

$$= -20(0 - 1)$$

$$= 20.$$

81. $\int_0^\infty \frac{2dx}{(0.2x + 1)^2} = 2\int_0^\infty (0.2x + 1)^{-2}dx$

$$= -10(0.2x + 1)^{-1}\Big|_0^\infty$$

$$= -10\left[\lim_{x \to \infty}\left(\frac{1}{0.2x + 1}\right) - \frac{1}{1}\right]$$

$$= -10(0 - 1)$$

$$= 10.$$

83. $f(x) = \ln(x^2 + 1)$; $w = \dfrac{b - a}{n} = \dfrac{3 - 0}{6} = 0.5.$

$$\frac{1}{2}f(0) \quad = \frac{1}{2}\ln 1 \quad = 0.00000$$

$$f(0.5) = \ln 1.25 = 0.22314$$
$$f(1) \quad = \ln 2 \quad = 0.69315$$
$$f(1.5) = \ln 3.25 = 1.17865$$
$$f(2) \quad = \ln 5 \quad = 1.60944$$
$$f(2.5) = \ln 7.25 = 1.98100$$

$$\frac{1}{2}f(3) \quad = \frac{1}{2}\ln(10) = \underline{1.15129}$$
$$6.83667$$

$\int_0^3 \ln(x^2 + 1)dx \doteq w(6.83667) = 0.5(6.83667) = 3.418.$

85. $f(x) = \ln(x^2 + 1)$; $w = \dfrac{b - a}{n} = \dfrac{3 - 0}{6} = 0.5$. By <u>hand calculator</u>,

$$
\begin{array}{llll}
f(0) & = \ln 1 & = & 0.00000 \\
4f(0.5) & = 4 \ln 1.25 & = & 0.89257 \\
2f(1) & = 2 \ln 2 & = & 1.38629 \\
4f(1.5) & = 4 \ln 3.25 & = & 4.71462 \\
2f(2) & = 2 \ln 5 & = & 3.21888 \\
4f(2.5) & = 4 \ln 7.5 & = & 8.05961 \\
f(3) & = \ln 10 & = & \underline{2.30259} \\
& & & 20.57456
\end{array}
$$

$$\int_0^3 \ln(x^2 + 1)dx \doteq \frac{w}{3}(20.57456) = \frac{0.5}{3}(20.57456) = 3.429.$$

87. $\int x^2 e^x dx$.

$$
\begin{array}{ll}
\text{Let:} \quad u = x^2 & dv = e^x \\
du = 2xdx & v = e^x.
\end{array}
$$

$$\int x^2 e^x dx = \int udv = uv - \int vdu$$

$$= x^2 e^x - \int e^x(2x)dx.$$

$$x^2 e^x - 2e^x(x - 1) + C = e^x(x^2 - 2x + 2) + C.$$

89. $dy + dx = 0$:

$$dy = -dx$$

$$\int dy = -\int dx$$

$$y = -x + C.$$

91. $x^2 dy - dx = 0$:

$$x^2 dy = dx$$

$$dy = \frac{dx}{x^2}$$

$$\int dy = \int x^{-2}dx$$

$$y = -x^{-1} + C = -\frac{1}{x} + C.$$

93. $xdy + 2dx = 0$:

$$xdy = -2dx$$

$$dy = -2\frac{dx}{x}$$

$$\int dy = -2 \int \frac{dx}{x}$$

$$y = -2 \ln x + C.$$

95. $dy - 0.4x(5y + 4)dx = 0$.

$$dy = 0.4x(5y + 4)dx$$

$$\frac{dy}{5y + 4} = 0.4xdx$$

$$\int \frac{dy}{5y + 4} = \int 0.4xdx$$

$$\frac{\ln(5y + 4)}{5} = 0.2x^2 + K_1$$

$$\ln(5y + 4) = x^2 + K_2$$

$$\ln(5y + 4) = e^{x^2} + K_2 = K_3 e^{x^2}$$

$$5y = K_3 e^{x^2} - 4$$

$$y = Ce^{x^2} - 0.8.$$

97. $x^2dy - y^2dx$; $y = 1.8$ when $x = 18$.

$$x^2dy = y^2dx$$

$$\frac{dy}{y^2} = \frac{dx}{x^2}$$

$$\int \frac{dy}{y^2} = \int \frac{dx}{x^2}$$

$$-y^{-1} = -x^{-1} + C \qquad\qquad (1)$$

$$-\frac{1}{1.8} = -\frac{1}{18} + C$$

$$\frac{1}{18} - \frac{1}{1.8} = C$$

$$\frac{1}{18} - \frac{10}{18} = C$$

$$-\frac{1}{2} = C.$$

Returning to (1)

$$-\frac{1}{y} = -\frac{1}{x} - \frac{1}{2}$$

$$\frac{1}{y} = \frac{1}{x} + \frac{1}{2}$$

$$\frac{1}{y} = \frac{2 + x}{2x}$$

$$y = \frac{2x}{2 + x}.$$

99. $dy - (0.4y + 3)dx = 0$; $y = 2.5$ when $x = 0$.

$$dy = (0.4y + 3)dx$$

$$\frac{dy}{0.4y + 3} = dx$$

$$\int \frac{dy}{0.4y + 3} = \int dx$$

$$\frac{\ln(0.4y + 3)}{0.4} = x + K_1$$

$$\ln(0.4y + 3) = 0.4x + K$$

$$0.4y + 3 = e^{0.4x+K} = K_2 e^{0.4x}$$

$$0.4y = K_2 e^{0.4x} - 3$$

$$y = Ce^{0.4x} - 7.5$$

$$2.5 = Ce^0 - 7.5$$

$$10 = C$$

$$y = 10e^{0.4x} - 7.5.$$

101.   a) $dA = 0.06A\,dt + 300\,dt$

$dA = (0.06A + 300)dt$.

b) $\dfrac{dA}{(0.06A + 300)} = dt$

$$\int \frac{dA}{(0.06A + 300)} = \int dt$$

$$\frac{\ln(0.06A + 300)}{0.06} = t + K_1$$

$$\ln(0.06A + 300) = 0.06t + K_2$$

$$0.06A + 300 = Ke^{0.06t}$$

$$0.06A = Ke^{0.06t} - 300$$

$$A(t) = Ce^{0.06t} - 5,000.$$

Using the initial conditions, $A(0) = 1,000$

$$1,000 = Ce^0 - 5,000$$

$$6,000 = C$$

$$A(t) = 6,000e^{0.06t} - 5,000.$$

c) $A(10) = 6,000e^{0.6} - 5,000$

$$= 6,000(1.8221) - 5,000$$

$$= \$5,932.6.$$

More accurately, by calculator, the answer is $5,932.71.

CHAPTER 14
Problem Set 14-1

1. a) $\int_0^{10} 20dx = \Big|_0^{10} 20x$

    $[20(10)] - [20(0)] = 200 - 0 = 200$

    $p(x) = \dfrac{20}{200} = 0.1$ $\boxed{p(x) = 0.1}$

    b) $\int_4^7 0.1dx = \Big|_4^7 0.1x = [0.1(7)] - [0.1(4)] = \boxed{0.3}$

5. a) $\int_0^4 (12x - 3x^2)dx = \Big|_0^4 \left(\dfrac{12x^2}{2} - \dfrac{3x^3}{3} \right)$

    $[6(4^2) - (4^3)] - [6(0^2) - 0^3] = 32 - 0 = 32$

    $p(x) = \dfrac{12x - 3x^2}{32}$

    b) $\int_0^{20} \dfrac{1}{32}(12x - 3x^2)dx = \Big|_0^2 \dfrac{1}{32}\left(\dfrac{12x^2}{2} - \dfrac{3x^3}{3} \right)$

    $\left[\dfrac{1}{32}(6(2^2) - 2^3) \right] - \left[\dfrac{1}{32}(6(0^2) - 0^3) \right]$

    $0.5 - 0 = \boxed{0.5}$

Problem Set 14-2

1. a) $\int_0^{20} x(0.05)dx = \Big|_0^{20} \dfrac{0.05x^2}{2} - \Big|_0^{20} 0.025x^2$

    $[(0.025(20^2)] - [0.025(0^2)] = 10 - 0 = 10$ $\boxed{\mu = 10}$

    b) $\sigma^2 = \int_0^{20} (x - 10)^2(0.05)dx = \Big|_0^{20} \dfrac{0.05(x - 10)^3}{3}$

    $\left[\dfrac{0.05(20 - 10)^3}{3} \right] - \left[\dfrac{0.05(0 - 10^3)^3}{3} \right] = \dfrac{50}{3} - \left(\dfrac{-50}{3} \right) = \dfrac{100}{3} = \sigma^2$

    c) $\sigma = \sqrt{\sigma^2} = \sqrt{\dfrac{100}{3}} = \boxed{5.77}$

5. a) $E(x) = \int_0^5 x(0.04x + 0.1)dx$

    $= \int_0^5 (0.04x^2 + 0.1x)dx = \Big|_0^5 \dfrac{0.04x^3}{3} + \dfrac{0.1x^2}{2}$

    $\left[\dfrac{0.04(5^3)}{3} + \dfrac{0.1(5^2)}{2} \right] - \left[\dfrac{0.04(0^3)}{3} + \dfrac{0.1(0^2)}{2} \right]$

    $\left(\dfrac{5}{3} + \dfrac{2.5}{2} \right) - 0 = \dfrac{35}{12}$ hundred gallons

    b) $\dfrac{35}{12} \times 72 = 210$ hundred gallons

Problem Set 14-3

1. a) $p(0 \text{ to } 3) = 1 - e^{-3/2} = 1 - 0.223 = \boxed{0.777}$

   b) $p(2 \text{ to } 4) = p(0 \text{ to } 4) - p(0 \text{ to } 2)$

   $$= [1 - e^{-4/2}] - [1 - e^{-2/2}]$$

   $0.865 - 0.632 = \boxed{0.233}$

   c) $p(5 \text{ to } \infty) = 1 - p(0 \text{ to } 5)$

   $$= p(0 \text{ to } 5) = 1 - e^{-5/2} = 0.918 \qquad 1 - 0.918 = \boxed{0.082}$$

5. a) 8 calls in 40 hours $= 1$ call in 12 minutes

   $$p(0 \text{ to } 60 \text{ min.}) = 1 - e^{-60/12} = 1 - 0.0067 = \boxed{0.9933}$$

   b) $p(30 \text{ to } \infty) = 1 - p(0 \text{ to } 30)$

   $p(0 \text{ to } 30) = 1 - e^{-30/12} = 1 - 0.0821 = 0.9179$

   $p(30 \text{ to } \infty) = 1 - 0.9179 = \boxed{0.0821}$

Problem Set 14-4

1. a) $p(150 \text{ to } 160) = \boxed{0.1915}$

   $$z = \frac{160 - 150}{20} = 0.5 \qquad p(0.5) = 0.1915$$

   b) $p(150 \text{ to } 160) = \boxed{0.1915}$

   $$z = \frac{160 - 150}{20} = 0.5 \qquad p(0.5) = 0.1915$$

   c) $p(170 \text{ to } \infty) = 5 - p(150 \text{ to } 170)$

   $$= p(150 \text{ to } 170) = \frac{170 - 150}{20} = 1 \qquad p(1) = 0.3413$$

   $0.5 - 0.3413 = \boxed{0.1587}$

   d) $p(160 \text{ to } 170) = p(150 \text{ to } 170) - p(150 \text{ to } 160)$

   $$= 0.3413 - 0.1915$$

   $$= \boxed{0.1498}$$

   e) $p(-\infty \text{ to } 135) = 0.5 - p(135 \text{ to } 150)$

   $$p(135 \text{ to } 150) = \frac{135 - 150}{20} = -0.75 \qquad p(-0.75) = 0.2734$$

   $p(-\infty \text{ to } 135) = 0.5 - 0.2734 = \boxed{0.2266}$

   f) $p(145 \text{ to } 160) = p(145 \text{ to } 150) + p(150 \text{ to } 165)$

   $$p(145 \text{ to } 150) = \frac{145 - 150}{20} = -0.25 p(-0.25) = 0.0987$$

   $$p(150 \text{ to } 165) = \frac{165 - 150}{20} = 0.75 p(0.75) = 0.2734 \qquad \boxed{0.3721}$$

g) $p(142 \text{ to } 150) = \dfrac{142 - 150}{20} = -0.4$

$p(-0.4) = \boxed{0.1554}$

h) $p(138 \text{ to } 146) = p(138 \text{ to } 150) - p(146 \text{ to } 150)$

$p(138 \text{ to } 150) = \dfrac{138 - 150}{20} = -0.6 \, p(-0.6) = 0.2257$

$p(146 \text{ to } 150) = \dfrac{146 - 150}{20} = -0.2 \, p(-0.2) = 0.0793 \qquad \boxed{0.1464}$

Problem Set 14-5

1.

x	$x - \bar{x}$	$(x - \bar{x})^2$
8	1	1
8	1	1
9	2	4
6	−1	1
4	−3	9
35		16

$\bar{x} = \dfrac{35}{5} = 7$

$s = \sqrt{\dfrac{16}{4}}$

$\boxed{s = 2}$

5.

x	$x - \bar{x}$	$(x - \bar{x})^2$
.64	.06	.0036
.58	.00	0
.57	−.01	.0001
.57	−.01	.0001
.52	−.06	.0036
.58	.00	0
.60	.02	.0004
.58	.00	0
4.64		.0078

$\bar{x} = \dfrac{4.64}{8} = 0.58 \qquad s = \sqrt{\dfrac{0.0078}{7}} = \boxed{0.0334}$

Problem Set 14-6

1. a) z for $0.17 = 0.44$ therefore

$$\dfrac{x - 50}{5} = 0.44 \qquad x - 50 = 2.2 \qquad \boxed{x = 52.2}$$

b) Find z for $0.5 - 0.1 = 0.4$ or $z = 1.28$

$$\dfrac{x - 50}{5} = 1.28 \qquad x - 50 = 6.4 \qquad \boxed{x = 56.4}$$

c) Find z for $0.5 - 0.05 = 0.45$ or -1.645 negative because x is less than the number

$$\dfrac{x - 50}{5} = -1.645 \qquad x - 50 = -8.225 \qquad \boxed{x = 41.775}$$

d) Find z for $0.5/2 = 0.25$ or $z = 0.67$

$$\dfrac{x - 50}{5} = \pm 0.67 \qquad x - 50 = \pm 3.35 \qquad \boxed{x = 46.65 \text{ and } 53.35}$$

e) Find $z = 0.95 - 0.45 = 0.05$ $z = 1.645$

$$\frac{x - 50}{5} = 1.645 \quad x - 50 = 8.225 \quad \boxed{x = 58.225}$$

5. a) $$z = \frac{275 - 200}{25} = 3.00$$

$p(>275) = 0.5 - 0.4987 = 0.13\%$

b) $$z = \frac{160 - 200}{25} = -1.60$$

$p(<160) = 0.5 - 0.4452 = 5.48\%$

c) z for $0.2500 = 0.67$ therefore

$$\pm 0.67 = \frac{x - 200}{25} \quad \pm 16.75 = x - 200 \quad \boxed{x = 183.25 \text{ and } 216.75}$$

d)   Find negative z for $0.4500 = -1.645$

$$-1.645 = \frac{x - 200}{25} \quad -41.125 = x - 200 \quad \boxed{x = 158.875}$$

e) $$z = \frac{260 - 200}{25} = 2.40$$

Percentile for $260 = 0.4918 + 0.5 = 99.18\%$

1. a) $\int_0^{10} (x + 1)dx = \left(\frac{x^2}{2} + x\right)\Big|_0^{10} = 60. \quad p(x) = \frac{x + 1}{60}.$

    b) $\int_0^1 \left(\frac{x + 1}{60}\right)dx = \frac{1}{60}\left(\frac{x^2}{2} + x\right)\Big|_0^1 = \frac{1}{60}\left(\frac{3}{2}\right) = 0.0250.$

    $\int_5^6 \left(\frac{x + 1}{60}\right)dx = \frac{1}{60}\left(\frac{x^2}{2} + x\right)\Big|_5^6 = \frac{1}{60}\left[24 - \left(\frac{25}{2} + 5\right)\right] = 0.1083.$

3. a) $\int_{20}^{45} 50dx = 50x\Big|_{20}^{45} = 1{,}250; \quad p(x) = \frac{50}{1{,}250} = 0.04.$

    b) $\int_{30}^{40} 0.04dx = 0.04x\Big|_{30}^{40} = 0.4.$

5. $\int_0^1 \frac{12x - 3x^2}{32}dx = \frac{1}{32}(6x^2 - x^3)\Big|_0^1 = \frac{5}{32}.$

    The same integral evaluated from 0 to 2 $= \frac{1}{2}.$

    The same integral evaluated from 2 to 3 $= \frac{11}{32}.$

7. a) $\mu = E(x) = \int_0^{50} xp(x)dx = \int_0^{50} x(0.02)dx = 0.01x^2\Big|_0^{50} = 25.$

    b) $\sigma^2 = \int_0^{50} (x - \mu)^2 p(x)dx = \int_0^{50} (x - 25)^2(0.02)dx$

    $$= (0.02)\frac{(x - 25)^3}{3}\Big|_0^{50}$$

    $$= \frac{0.02}{3}[25^3 - (-25)^3]$$

    $$= \frac{625}{3}$$

    $$= 208.33.$$

    c) $\sigma = \left(\frac{625}{3}\right)^{1/2} = 14.43.$

9. $\mu = E(x) = \int_1^\infty xp(x)dx = \int_1^\infty x\frac{3}{x^4}dx = \int_1^\infty 3x^{-3}dx = -\frac{3}{2}x^{-2}\Big|_1^\infty$

    $$= -1.5\left[\lim_{x \to \infty}\frac{1}{x^2} - \frac{1}{1}\right] = -1.5(0 - 1) = 1.5.$$

11. a) $1 - e^{-4/10} = 1 - e^{-0.4} = 1 - 0.6703 = 0.3297.$

    b) $(1 - e^{-5/10}) - (1 - e^{-1/10}) = e^{-0.1} - e^{-0.5} = 0.9048 - 0.6065 = 0.2983.$

    c) $1 - (1 - e^{-8/10}) = e^{-0.8} = 0.4493.$

13. The average interval between customers is $\mu = 4$ minutes.

a) $1 - e^{-5/4} = 1 - e^{-1.25} = 1 - 0.2865 = 0.7135.$

b) $1 - (1 - e^{-3/4}) = e^{-0.75} = 0.4724.$

15. a) The area over 90 to 100 is the area for $z = (100 - 90)/5 = 2$, which Table XI gives as 0.4772. The area over 100 to 105 is the area for $z = (105 - 100)/5 = 1$, which Table XI gives as 0.3413. The desired (shaded) area is the sum, $0.4772 + 0.3413 = 0.8185.$

b) The area over 100 to 115 is the area for $z = (115 - 100)/5 = 3$, which Table XI gives as 0.4987. The area over 100 to 105 is the area for $z = (105 - 100)/5 = 1$, which Table XI gives as 0.3413. The desired (shaded) area is the difference, $0.4987 - 0.3413 = 0.1574.$

c) The area over 92 to 100 is the area for $z = (100 - 92)/5 = 1.6$, which Table XI gives as 0.4452. The area over 96 to 100 is the area for $z = (100 - 96)/5 = 0.8$, which Table XI gives as 0.2881. The desired (shaded) area is the difference, $0.4452 - 0.2881 = 0.1571.$

d) The area over 100 to 103 is the area for $z = (103 - 100)/5 = 0.6$, which Table XI gives as 0.2257. The desired (shaded) area is $0.5000 + 0.2257 = 0.7257.$

e) The area over 88 to 100 is the area for $z = (100 - 88)/5 = 2.4$, which Table XI gives as 0.4918. The desired (shaded) area is $0.5000 + 0.4918 = 0.9918.$

f) The area over 100 to 112 is the area for $z = (112 - 100)/5 = 2.4$, which Table XI gives as 0.4918. The area over 100 to 115 is the area for $z = (115 - 100)/5 = 3$, which Table XI gives as 0.4987. The desired (shaded) area is the difference, $0.4987 - 0.4918 = 0.0069.$

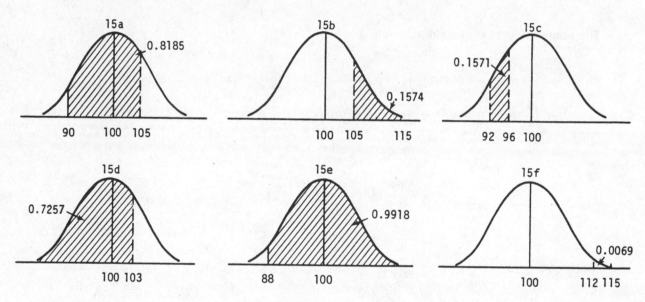

17. a) The value of z which gives an area of 0.2000 is found in Table XI to lie between 0.52 and 0.53. Interpolating, we find $z = 0.524$ which means ? is 0.524 standard deviations to the right of 20. Hence, ? is $20 + 0.524(4) = 22.096.$

b) The area to the right of ? is 0.1600, leaving 0.3400 from 20 to ?. The value of z which gives an area of 0.3400 is found in Table XI to lie between 0.99 and 1.00. Interpolating, we find $z = 0.995$, which means ? is 0.995 standard deviations to the right of 20. Hence, ? is $20 + (0.995)(4) = 23.98.$

c) The area to the left of ? is 0.0250, leaving 0.4750 between ? and 20. The value of z which gives an area of 0.4750 is found in Table XI to be 1.96, which means ? is 1.96 standard deviations to the left of 20. Hence, ? is $20 - 1.96(4) = 12.16.$

d) The value of z which gives an area of 0.2500 is found in Table XI to lie between 0.67 and 0.68. Interpolating, we find $z = 0.675$, which means the question marks are 0.675 standard deviations away from 20. We find $20 \pm (0.675)(4)$ yields the range from 17.3 to 22.7.

e) The area to the right of ? is 0.05, leaving 0.4500 between 20 and ?. The value of z which gives an area of 0.4500 is found in Table XI to lie between 1.64 and 1.65. Interpolating, we find z = 1.645 which means ? is 1.645 standard deviations to the right of 20. Hence, ? is 20 + 1.645(4) = 26.58.

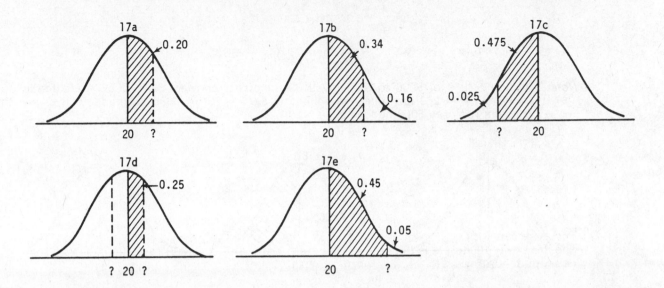

19. a) The area over 50 to 65 is the area for z = (65 − 50)/5 = 3 which Table XI gives as 0.4987. The desired area is in the tail to the right of 65 and is 0.5000 − 0.4987 = 0.0013 or 0.13%.

    b) As in (a), the area to the right of 65 is 0.0013, and the area to the left of 35 is also 0.0013. The total is 0.0026.

    c) The area over 50 to 60 is the area for z = (60 − 50)/5 = 2 which Table XI gives as 0.4772. The desired area is 2(0.4772) = 0.9544 = 95.44%.

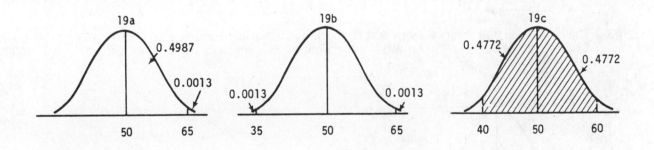

21. a) The standard deviation is 0.2. The area over the interval from 19.7 to 20 is the area for a z value of (20.0 − 19.7)/0.2 = 1.5 which Table XI gives as 0.4332. The desired area (probability) is the area to the left of 19.7, which is 0.5000 − 0.4332 = 0.0668.

    b) The standard deviation is 0.5. The area over the interval from 50 to 51 is the area for a z value of (51 − 5)/0.5 = 2 which Table XI gives as 0.4772. The desired area is twice this amount = 2(0.4772) = 0.9544, so that 954 cans out of 1000 would contain amounts of fill between 49 and 51 ounces.

    c) The standard deviation is 0.49. The area over the interval from 48 to 49 is the area for a z value of (49 − 48)/0.49 = 2.041 which Table XI gives as 0.4793. The desired area (to the left of 48) is 0.5000 − 0.4793 = 0.0207.

    d) The standard deviation is 1.01. The area over the interval from 100 to 101 is the area for a z value of (101 − 100)/1.01 = 0.9900 which Table XI gives as 0.3389. The desired area (to the right of 100) is 0.5000 + 0.3389 = 0.8389 or 83.89%.

    e) The area over the interval 101 to 102.3 is the area for a z value of (102.3 − 101)/1.01 = 1.287 which Table XI gives as 0.4010. The desired area (to the right of 102.3) is 0.5000 − 0.4010 = 0.0990 or 9.9%.

251

f) The standard deviation is 0.5. The area over the interval from 50 to 50.8 is the area for a z value of $(50.8 - 50)/0.5 = 1.6$ which Table XI gives as 0.4452. The area to the right of 50.8 (overflows) is $0.5000 - 0.4452 = 0.0548$. Hence, the fraction of overflows is 0.0548 (or 5.48%) and the fraction not defective is 0.9452 (or 94.52%). To get 5000 nondefectives, we must fill x cans, where

$$0.9452x = 5000 \qquad \text{so that}$$

$$x = \frac{5000}{0.9452} = 5290.$$

Note: Adding 5.48% of 5000 to 5000 gives the incorrect answer, 5274. If 5274 are made and 5.48%(5274) = 289 are defective, then only 5274 − 289 = 4985 are nondefective, and the problem requires 5000 nondefective.

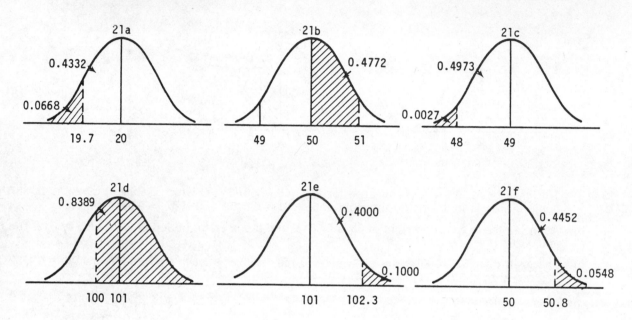

23. The area over the interval from 100 to 150 is the area for a z value of $(150 - 100)/20 = 2.5$ which Table XI gives as 0.4938. The area to the right of 150, which is the desired probability, is $0.5000 - 0.4938 = 0.0062$.

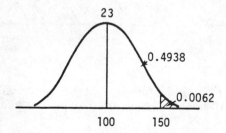

1. a) "*B* is the set whose numbers are 2, 4 and 6."

    b) "*C* is the set whose element is 0."

    c) "*Q* is the set whose members are the odd numbers 1 through 29."

    d) "*F* is the set whose elements are the lower case English vowels."

    e) "*L* is the set whose members are George and Charles."

    f) "*K* is the set of positive even integers starting with 2."

5. a) $1/2 \notin \{1, 2, 3, \ldots\}$.

    b) $64 \in \{4, 8, 12, \ldots\}$.

    c) $a \in \{a, e, i, o, u\}$.

    d) $4 \notin \{1, 3, 5, \ldots\}$.

    e) $\$ \notin \{a, b, c, \ldots, z\}$.

    f) $9 \notin \{a, b, c, d, e, f\}$.

9. ϕ, the empty set.

13. Yes, because for each point on the horizontal line there is one and only one point on the slant line.

17. $\{y: y = 2x + 7\}$

Problem Set A1-2

1. a) $\{a, b, c, d, e, f, g, h\}$.

    b) $\{a, b, c, d, e, i, j\}$.

    c) $\{d, e\}$

    d) ϕ

    e) $\{d, e, f, g, h, i, j\}$

    f) ϕ

5. a) ϕ

    b) $M \cap N$ is the point at which the lines intersect.

1. a) "*A* is the set whose elements are 5, 6, 7, and 9."

   b) "*B* is the set whose elements are Amherst, Babson, Colgate, and Dartmouth."

   c) "*C* is the set whose elements are 1, 3, 5, 7, and so on."

   d) "*D* is the set whose elements are A, B, C, and so on through Z."

   e) "*E* is the set whose elements are 1, 1/2, 1/4, 1/8, and so on."

   f) "*F* is the set whose elements are Tom, Dick, and Harry."

3. a) $A = \{H, A, R, V, D\}$.

   b) $B = \{1, 2, 3, 5, 7, 11, 13, 17, 19\}$.

   c) $C = \{4, 12, 20, 28, \ldots\}$.

   d) $D = \{6, 12, 18, 24, 30\}$.

5. a) $\{t: t + 1 = 20\} = \{19\}$.

   b) The set of *y*'s such that three times *y* plus five is eleven is the set with the single element, 2.

7. There is no value for *t* which will make $t = t + 1$ true. Hence, $\{t: t = t + 1\} = \varnothing$, the empty or null set.

9. a) $\{2, 5, 10, 12, 13, 14, 15\}$.

   b) $\{10, 13\}$.

   c) ϕ.

   d) $\{5, 12, 15\}$.

   e) $\{12\}$.

   f) ϕ.

11. a) $\{3, 5, 10, 12, 15, 19\}$.

    b) $\{10, 15\}$.

    c) $\{12\}$.

    d) ϕ.

    e) $\{5, 7, 10, 12, 15, 19\}$.

    f) $\{3, 7, 10, 12, 15\}$.

13. Concentric circles are disjoint; that is, they have no points in common. Hence, $M \cap N = \phi$, the empty or null set.

15. a) $\{y: y + 5 = 15\} = \{10\}$.

    b) The set of *x*'s such that $x - 2 = 10$ is the set with the single element, 12.

17. Yes, because the set of *x*'s which contains all numbers less than 10 has 5 as one of its elements.

19. a) No, because for a given secretary there is more than one corresponding executive.

    b) Yes, because for a given executive there is one, and only one, corresponding secretary.

21. $\{y: y = 12x + 6\}$.

23. An infinite number, which means the number of ordered pairs is unlimited.

49. $\dfrac{\dfrac{2a}{3b} - \dfrac{1}{6} + 2}{\dfrac{1}{6} - \dfrac{2}{bc}}$ Convert everything to common denominator of $6bc$

$\dfrac{\dfrac{4ac}{6bc} - \dfrac{6b}{6bc} + \dfrac{12bc}{6bc}}{\dfrac{bc}{6bc} - \dfrac{12}{6bc}} = \dfrac{4ac - 6b + 12bc}{bc - 12}$

Problem Set A2-5

1. $2^4 = 16$

5. $(-3)^{-2}(2)^{-3} = \left(\dfrac{1}{9}\right)\left(\dfrac{1}{8}\right) = \dfrac{1}{72}$

9. $3^{-2} = \dfrac{1}{9}$.

13. $\dfrac{10^{-4}}{10^{-5}} = \dfrac{10^1}{1} = 10$

17. $2^4(25)^{-3} = \dfrac{25^4}{25^3} = 25$

21. $125^{1/3} = 5$

25. $\dfrac{1}{3^2}\left(\dfrac{1}{1} + \dfrac{1}{3^1}\right) = \dfrac{1}{9}\left(\dfrac{4}{3}\right) = \dfrac{4}{27}$

29. $(abc^2)(a^2cb) = a^3b^2c^3$

33. $\dfrac{xy^3b^3}{x^3yb} = \dfrac{y^2b^2}{x^2}$

37. $\dfrac{(a^1b)^2(ab)}{a} = \dfrac{a^3b^3}{a} = a^2b^3$

41. $(xy^2)\left(\dfrac{a}{y^2}\right) = \dfrac{axy^2}{y^2} = ax$

45. $\left(\dfrac{1}{x^2}\right)\left(\dfrac{1}{ax}\right) = \dfrac{1}{ax^3}$

49. $\left(\dfrac{2}{3}\right)\left(\dfrac{1}{(3x)^{1/2}}\right) = \dfrac{2}{3^{3/2}x^{1/2}}$

53. $x^{-2}\left(\dfrac{x+1}{3}\right) = \dfrac{x+1}{3x^2}$

57. $(a - 3b)^2 = a^2 - 3ab - 3ab + 9b^2 = a^2 - 6ab + 9b^2$

61. $(a^{1/2} - 1)^2 = a^1 - a^{1/2} - a^{1/2} + 1 = a - 2a^{1/2} + 1$

1. $-3.$

3. $+11.$

5. $0.$

7. $-5.$

9. $-1.$

11. a) $+3 + (-4).$

    b) $+(-1) + (+2) + (-3).$

    c) $+(-1) + (-2) + (-4) + (+5).$

    d) $+(+2) + (+3).$

13. a) Cummutative, multiplication.

    b) Associative, multiplication.

    c) Conventions; no sign means assume $+$, and addition of a negative is indicated by a minus sign.

    d) Distributive property.

    e) Commutative, addition.

    f) Associative, addition.

    g) Associative, addition.

    h) Commutative, multiplication.

    i) Addition of negative indicated by a minus sign.

    j) Convention; absence of coefficient means coefficient of 1.

    k) Distributive property.

    l) Commutative, addition.

    m) Distributive property.

    n) Distributive property.

15. a) Associative, addition.

    b) Commutative, multiplication.

    c) Associative, multiplication.

    d) Commutative, addition.

    e) Associative, addition.

    f) Distributive property.

17. a) $x - a - 2ax.$

    b) $12z - 37.$

    c) $3 - 10x + 4a.$

    d) $3x - ax - 3b + ab + 6 - 2a.$

    e) $3a - 3ax.$

19. a) $x(2 + a).$

    b) $xy(1 + 3 + a) = xy(4 + a).$

    c) $2(1 + 2a + 3b).$

    d) $x(5y + 4).$

e) $3a(x + 2y + 3)$.

f) $(2 + a)(x - 1)$.

g) $(a + b)(1 + x)$.

h) $(x + 2)(x - 1)$.

i) $(5x - 1)(2x + 1)$.

j) $(2x + 5)(3x - 4)$.

k) $(4x + 2)(2x + 3) = 2(2x + 1)(2x + 3)$.

21. a) $\dfrac{4ax}{b}$.

b) $\dfrac{-2x + 6}{a}$.

c) $6a - x + y$.

d) $2x - 5a$.

23. a) $\dfrac{11}{12}$.

b) $\dfrac{a + b}{b}$.

c) $\dfrac{3}{4x}$.

d) $\dfrac{2ay - 2ax + xy}{2ax}$.

e) $\dfrac{1 + 8xy - 60y}{12xy}$.

f) $\dfrac{3 + 2bx - 3b}{3(2x - 3)}$.

g) $\dfrac{az - b(x + y) + 5z(x + y)}{z(x + y)} = \dfrac{az - bx - by + 5zx + 5zy}{z(x + y)}$

h) $\dfrac{3(2)(x + y) - ba(x + y) + c(2a) - d(a)(2)(x + y)}{2a(x + y)}$

$= \dfrac{6x + 6y - abx - aby + 2ac - 2adx - 2ady}{2a(x + y)}$.

i) $\left(\dfrac{3}{4}\right)\left(\dfrac{5}{2}\right) = \dfrac{15}{8}$.

j) $\dfrac{21}{4} - \dfrac{7}{3} = \dfrac{21(3) - 7(4)}{12} = \dfrac{63 - 28}{12} = \dfrac{35}{12}$.

k) $\dfrac{\dfrac{15}{8}}{\dfrac{5}{2}} = \dfrac{\dfrac{15}{8}(8)}{\dfrac{5}{2}(8)} = \dfrac{15}{20} = \dfrac{3}{4}$.

25. a) 9.

b) $2(1) = 2$.

c) 1.

d) $\dfrac{1}{(0.9)^2} = \dfrac{1}{0.81} = 1.235.$

e) $\left(\dfrac{2}{3}\right)^{-2} = \dfrac{1}{\left(\dfrac{2}{3}\right)^2} = \dfrac{1}{\dfrac{4}{9}} = \dfrac{9}{4}.$

f) $\left(\dfrac{1}{4}\right)(4) = 1.$

g) $(75)^{100+(-98)} = (75)^2 = 5{,}625.$

h) $1 - 1 = 0.$

i) $\dfrac{1}{2}.$

j) $\dfrac{1}{\dfrac{1}{2}} = 2.$

k) $\dfrac{4}{5}.$

l) The 1/3rd power of 27 is 3, and 3 to the second power is the answer, 9.

m) The 1/3rd power of 125 is 5, and 5 to the fourth power is the answer, 625.

n) This is $\dfrac{1}{(8)^{2/3}}$. The 1/3rd power of 8 is 2, and the second power of 2 is 4. The answer is $\dfrac{1}{4}$.

o) This is $\dfrac{1}{\left(\dfrac{2}{3}\right)^1} = \dfrac{3}{2}.$

p) Applying the rules for exponents in multiplication and division, the expression is equivalent to

$$10^{-5+2-3-(-8)} = 10^2 = 100.$$

q) This is

$$\dfrac{1}{2^3}\left(4 + \dfrac{1}{2}\right) = \dfrac{9}{16}.$$

r) Multiply by $\dfrac{3^3}{3^3}$ to obtain $\dfrac{3^2 - 3}{1} = 6.$

s) 4.

t) $(1.03)^3 = 1.092727.$

u) The square root of a negative number is not a real number.

v) $\dfrac{\dfrac{3}{2}}{\left(\dfrac{2}{3}\right)^2} = \dfrac{27}{8}.$

w) $\dfrac{2}{5}$ and $-\dfrac{2}{5}.$

x) The cube root of 27 is 3, and 3 to the second power is 9.

y) The square root of 16 is 4, and 4 to the third power is 64. The square root of 16 could also be taken as -4, in which case the third power would be -64. Answer, ± 64.

z) The expression is equivalent to $(9)^{-3/2}$. The 1/2 power of 9 is ± 3, and ± 3 to the -3 power is $\pm\dfrac{1}{27}$.

1. $2x - 3 = x + 4$ add 3

       $2x = x + 7$ subtract x

       $x = 7$

5. $7x - 5 = 3 - 4x$ add 5

       $7x = 8 - 4x$ add $4x$

       $11x = 8$ divide by 11

       $x = \dfrac{8}{11}$

9. $\dfrac{2x}{5} - \dfrac{3x}{2} = 4$ multiply by 10

       $4x - 15x = 40$ combine like terms

       $-11x = 40$ divide by -11

       $x = \dfrac{-40}{11}$

13. $\dfrac{x + 3}{2} = x - \dfrac{1}{4}$ multiply by 4

        $2(x + 3) = 4x - 1$ apply distributive property

        $2x + 6 = 4x - 1$ subtract 6

        $2x = 4x - 7$ subtract $4x$

        $-2x = -7$ divide by -2

        $x = \dfrac{7}{2}$

17. $bx + 2 = c$ subtract 2

        $bx = c - 2$ divide by b

        $x = \dfrac{c - 2}{b}$

21. $a(x - a) = 2x$ apply distributive property

        $ax - a^2 = 2x$ add a^2

        $ax = 2x + a^2$ subtract $2x$

        $ax - 2x = a^2$ factor

        $x(a - 2) = a^2$ divide by $(a - 2)$

        $x = \dfrac{a^2}{a - 2}$

25. $\dfrac{3}{4} - \dfrac{2x}{3} = 2x(a - 1)$ multiply by 12

        $9 - 8x = 24x(a - 1)$ apply distributive property

        $9 - 8x = 24ax - 24x$ add $8x$

        $9 = 24ax - 16x$ factor

        $9 = x(24a - 16)$ divide by $(24a - 16)$

        $\dfrac{9}{24a - 16} = x$

29.
$$\frac{b}{a} - x = 2a(b - x) \qquad \text{multiply by } a$$

$$b - ax = 2a^2(b - x) \qquad \text{apply distributive property}$$

$$b - ax = 2a^2b - 2a^2x \qquad \text{add } 2a^2x$$

$$2a^2x + b - ax = 2a^2b \qquad \text{subtract } b$$

$$2a^2x - ax = 2a^2b - b \qquad \text{factor}$$

$$x(2a^2 - a) = 2a^2b - b \qquad \text{divide by } (2a^2 - a)$$

$$x = \frac{2a^2b - b}{2a^2 - a}$$

Problem Set A3-2

1. $y = \dfrac{(12)(5)}{4} = \dfrac{60}{4} = 15$

5. $y = (4 - 5)[4 - 12(5 + 4)]$
   $= (-1)(4 - 108) = (-1)(-104) = 104$

9. $y = \left(5^2 - \dfrac{3(12)}{4}\right)^{5/4} = (25 - 9)^{5/4} = 16^{5/4} = 32$

13. $y = \dfrac{\dfrac{5}{3}\left(\dfrac{1}{7} + \dfrac{2}{9}\right)}{3} = \dfrac{\dfrac{5}{3}\left(\dfrac{9}{63} + \dfrac{14}{63}\right)}{3}$

   $= \dfrac{\dfrac{5}{3}\left(\dfrac{23}{63}\right)}{3} = \dfrac{\dfrac{115}{189}\left(\dfrac{1}{3}\right)}{3\left(\dfrac{1}{3}\right)} = \dfrac{115}{567}$

17. $y = \left(1 - \dfrac{\dfrac{5}{3}}{\dfrac{5}{12}}\left(\dfrac{12}{12}\right)\right) = \left(1 - \dfrac{20}{5}\right)^3$

   $= (1 - 4)^3 = -3^3 = -27$

21. $y = .1667(140,000) + .15(140,000 - 75,000)$
   $y = 23,333.38 + 9,750 = \$33,083.38$

25. a) $100 = \dfrac{5}{9}(f - 32) \qquad \text{multiply by } \dfrac{9}{5}$

   $180 = f - 32 \qquad \text{add 32}$
   $212^0 = f$

   b) $0 = \dfrac{5}{9}(f - 32)$

   $0 = f - 32$
   $32^0 = f$

   c) $-10.6 = \dfrac{5}{9}(f - 32)$

   $-19.08 = f - 32 \qquad f = 12.92^0$

APPENDIX 3
Review Problems (Odds)

1. $3x - 2 = 2x + 5$ Subtract $2x$

    $x - 2 = 5$ Add 2

        $x = 7.$

3. $\dfrac{(3 + 2x)}{4} - 2 = x$ Multiply by 4

    $3 + 2x - 8 = 4x$ Subtract $4x$

    $3 - 2x - 8 = 0$ Add 8

       $3 - 2x = 8$ Subtract 3

          $-2x = 5$ Divide by -2

             $x = -\dfrac{5}{2}.$

5. $2a = \dfrac{x}{3 - cx}$ Multiply by $3 - cx$

    $2a(3 - cx) = x$ Apply distributive property

      $6a - 2acx = x$ Subtract x

  $6a - 2acx - x = 0$ Subtract $6a$

     $-2acx - x = -6a$ Factor

    $x(-2ac - 1) = -6a$ Divide by $-2ac - 1$

           $x = \dfrac{-6a}{-2ac - 1}$ Multiply numerator and denominator by -1

           $x = \dfrac{6a}{2ac + 1}.$

7. $5(x - b) = a + b[3 - 2(x + 1)]$ Apply distributive property

    $5x - 5b = a + b[3 - 2x - 2]$ Apply distributive property

    $5x - 5b = a + 3b - 2bx - 2b$ Add $2bx$, add $5b$

      $5x + 2bx = a + 6b$ Factor

    $x(5 + 2b) = a + 6b$ Divide by $5 + 2b$

         $x = \dfrac{a + 6b}{5 + 2b}.$

9. $x - \dfrac{c}{d} = a - \dfrac{3[2 - b(x - 1)]}{4}$ Multiply by $4d$

  $4dx - 4c = 4ad - 3d[2 - b(x - 1)]$ Apply distributive property

  $4dx - 4c = 4ad - 3d[2 - bx + b]$ Apply distributive property

  $4dx - 4c = 4ad - 6d + 3bdx - 3bd$ Subtract $3bdx$, add $4c$

  $4dx - 3bdx = 4ad + 4c - 6d - 3bd$ Factor

  $x(4d - 3bd) = 4ad + 4c - 6d - 3bd$ Divide by $4d - 3bd$

          $x = \dfrac{4ad + 4c - 6d - 3bd}{4d - 3bd}.$

11. $x = \dfrac{6(2) - 10}{2} = \dfrac{2}{2} = 1.$

13. $x = \dfrac{50}{6} = \dfrac{25}{3}.$

15. $x = (30 - 3)^{1/3} = (27)^{1/3} = 3.$

17. $x = 2(4 - 0) = 8.$

19. $y = \dfrac{\frac{1}{8}}{\frac{2}{7}} = \dfrac{7}{16}.$

21. $y = \dfrac{5}{12} - \dfrac{1}{\frac{2}{7}} = \dfrac{5}{12} - \dfrac{7}{2} = -\dfrac{37}{12}.$

23. $y = \left[1 - \left(\dfrac{1}{3}\right)\left(\dfrac{12}{5}\right) \right]^3 = \left(1 - \dfrac{4}{5} \right)^3 = \left(\dfrac{1}{5}\right)^3 = \dfrac{1}{125}.$

25. $y = \sqrt{\dfrac{4}{9} - \dfrac{1}{3}} = \sqrt{\dfrac{1}{9}} = \pm\dfrac{1}{3}.$

27. $4\,1/7\% = \dfrac{29}{7}\% = \dfrac{29}{700}.$ Substituting, we have $y = \dfrac{29}{700}(28{,}000) + 0.22(10{,}000) = \$3{,}360.$

29. $y = \dfrac{(1.05)^{-3} + 1}{0.05} = \dfrac{1 + (1.05)^3}{0.05(1.05)^3} = \dfrac{1 + 1.157625}{0.05(1.157625)} = \dfrac{2.157625}{0.05788125} = 37.2767 = 37.277.$

31. Solving the formula for C, we find

$$C = \frac{5}{9}(F - 32).$$

   a) $\dfrac{5}{9}(-32) = -\dfrac{160}{9}.$

   b) $\dfrac{5}{9}(68) = \dfrac{340}{9}.$

   c) $\dfrac{5}{9}(19) = \dfrac{95}{9}.$

   d) $\dfrac{5}{9}(-64) = -\dfrac{320}{9}.$

33. a) $B = 150$, $C = 28.50$, $n = 18$, $y = 12$. Hence,

$$r = \frac{(2)(12)(28.5)}{150(19)} = 0.24 \text{ or } 24\%.$$

   b) $B = 300$, $r = 0.3$, $n = 12$, $y = 12$. Hence,

$$0.3 = \frac{2(12)C}{(300)(13)} \text{ from which } C = \frac{0.3(300)(13)}{2(12)} = \$48.75.$$

35. a)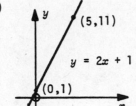

b)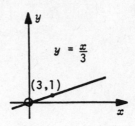

c)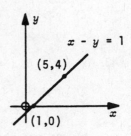

d)

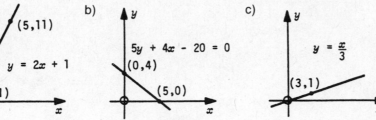

e)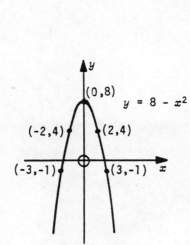

f)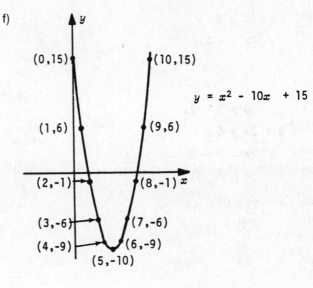

37. a) $6x^2 - 5x + 1 = 0$ factors to $(3x - 1)(2x - 1) = 0$.

Setting $3x - 1 = 0$ and $2x - 1 = 0$, we have $x_1 = \frac{1}{3}$; $x_2 = \frac{1}{2}$.

b) $16x^2 - 40x + 25 = 0$ factors to $(4x - 5)(4x - 5) = 0$.

Setting $4x - 5 = 0$, we have $x_1 = x_2 = \frac{5}{4}$.

c) $3x^2 - 48x = 0$ factors to $3x(x - 16) = 0$.
Setting $3x = 0$ and $x - 16 = 0$, we have $x_1 = 0$; $x_2 = 16$.

d) $x^2 - 100 = 0$ factors to $(x + 10)(x - 10) = 0$.
Setting $x + 10 = 0$ and $x - 10 = 0$, we have $x_1 = -10$; $x_2 = 10$.

39. $x + y > 3$; $x = 1$

a) $y > 3 - x$

b) above the line

c) $y > 3 - 1 \quad y > 2$

41. $-2x + 5y > 2$; $x = 4$

a) $5y > 2 + 2x$

$y > .4 + .4x$

b) above the line

c) $y > .4 + .4(4)$

    $y > 2$

43. $x - y \leq 0;\ x = 5$

    a) $-y \leq -x$

       $y \geq x$

    b) on and above the line

    c) $y > 5$

45. $2x + 7 \geq 4$

    $2x \geq -3$

    $x \geq -\dfrac{3}{2}$

47. $3 \geq 5 - 2x$

  $3 + 2x \geq 5$

    $2x \geq 5 - 3$

    $x \geq 1$

49. $x - y \geq 0$

    $x \geq 4$

c) $y \leq \frac{7}{5}(20) - 9$

   $y \leq 28 - 9$

   $y \leq 19$

25. $y - 2x \geq -1$
    $0 - 2(0) \geq -1$
        $0 \geq -1;$ *Yes*

29. $5x + 2y \geq 40$
    $5(0) + 2(0) \geq 40$
            $0 \geq 40;$ No

on or above line

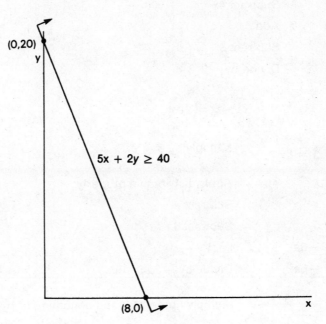

33. $x \geq 0$

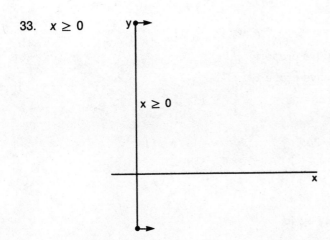

APPENDIX 3
Review Problems (Odds)

1. $3x - 2 = 2x + 5$ Subtract $2x$

    $x - 2 = 5$ Add 2

        $x = 7$.

3. $\dfrac{(3 + 2x)}{4} - 2 = x$ Multiply by 4

    $3 + 2x - 8 = 4x$ Subtract $4x$

    $3 - 2x - 8 = 0$ Add 8

      $3 - 2x = 8$ Subtract 3

         $-2x = 5$ Divide by -2

$$x = -\frac{5}{2}.$$

5. $2a = \dfrac{x}{3 - cx}$ Multiply by $3 - cx$

       $2a(3 - cx) = x$ Apply distributive property

      $6a - 2acx = x$ Subtract x

   $6a - 2acx - x = 0$ Subtract $6a$

     $-2acx - x = -6a$ Factor

    $x(-2ac - 1) = -6a$ Divide by $-2ac - 1$

$$x = \frac{-6a}{-2ac - 1} \quad \text{Multiply numerator and denominator by } -1$$

$$x = \frac{6a}{2ac + 1}.$$

7. $5(x - b) = a + b[3 - 2(x + 1)]$ Apply distributive property

   $5x - 5b = a + b[3 - 2x - 2]$ Apply distributive property

   $5x - 5b = a + 3b - 2bx - 2b$ Add $2bx$, add $5b$

     $5x + 2bx = a + 6b$ Factor

    $x(5 + 2b) = a + 6b$ Divide by $5 + 2b$

$$x = \frac{a + 6b}{5 + 2b}.$$

9. $x - \dfrac{c}{d} = a - \dfrac{3[2 - b(x - 1)]}{4}$ Multiply by $4d$

   $4dx - 4c = 4ad - 3d[2 - b(x - 1)]$ Apply distributive property

   $4dx - 4c = 4ad - 3d[2 - bx + b]$ Apply distributive property

   $4dx - 4c = 4ad - 6d + 3bdx - 3bd$ Subtract $3bdx$, add $4c$

 $4dx - 3bdx = 4ad + 4c - 6d - 3bd$ Factor

$x(4d - 3bd) = 4ad + 4c - 6d - 3bd$ Divide by $4d - 3bd$

$$x = \frac{4ad + 4c - 6d - 3bd}{4d - 3bd}.$$

11. $x = \dfrac{6(2) - 10}{2} = \dfrac{2}{2} = 1.$

13. $x = \dfrac{50}{6} = \dfrac{25}{3}.$

15. $x = (30 - 3)^{1/3} = (27)^{1/3} = 3.$

17. $x = 2(4 - 0) = 8.$

19. $y = \dfrac{\frac{1}{8}}{\frac{2}{7}} = \dfrac{7}{16}.$

21. $y = \dfrac{5}{12} - \dfrac{1}{\frac{2}{7}} = \dfrac{5}{12} - \dfrac{7}{2} = -\dfrac{37}{12}.$

23. $y = \left[1 - \left(\dfrac{1}{3}\right)\left(\dfrac{12}{5}\right) \right]^3 = \left(1 - \dfrac{4}{5}\right)^3 = \left(\dfrac{1}{5}\right)^3 = \dfrac{1}{125}.$

25. $y = \sqrt{\dfrac{4}{9} - \dfrac{1}{3}} = \sqrt{\dfrac{1}{9}} = \pm\dfrac{1}{3}.$

27. $4\,1/7\% = \dfrac{29}{7}\% = \dfrac{29}{700}.$ Substituting, we have $y = \dfrac{29}{700}(28,000) + 0.22(10,000) = \$3,360.$

29. $y = \dfrac{(1.05)^{-3} + 1}{0.05} = \dfrac{1 + (1.05)^3}{0.05(1.05)^3} = \dfrac{1 + 1.157625}{0.05(1.157625)} = \dfrac{2.157625}{0.05788125} = 37.2767 = 37.277.$

31. Solving the formula for C, we find

$$C = \dfrac{5}{9}(F - 32).$$

    a) $\dfrac{5}{9}(-32) = -\dfrac{160}{9}.$

    b) $\dfrac{5}{9}(68) = \dfrac{340}{9}.$

    c) $\dfrac{5}{9}(19) = \dfrac{95}{9}.$

    d) $\dfrac{5}{9}(-64) = -\dfrac{320}{9}.$

33.   a) $B = 150$, $C = 28.50$, $n = 18$, $y = 12$. Hence,

$$r = \dfrac{(2)(12)(28.5)}{150(19)} = 0.24 \text{ or } 24\%.$$

    b) $B = 300$, $r = 0.3$, $n = 12$, $y = 12$. Hence,

$$0.3 = \dfrac{2(12)C}{(300)(13)} \text{ from which } C = \dfrac{0.3(300)(13)}{2(12)} = \$48.75.$$

35. a)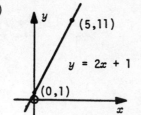

b)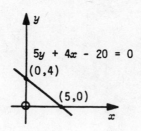

c)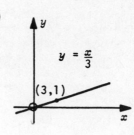

d)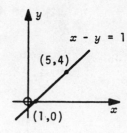

e)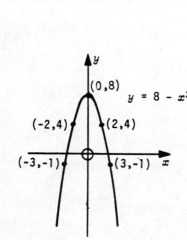

f)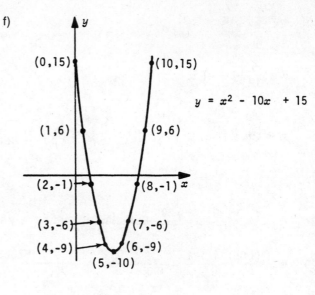

37. a) $6x^2 - 5x + 1 = 0$ factors to $(3x - 1)(2x - 1) = 0$.

Setting $3x - 1 = 0$ and $2x - 1 = 0$, we have $x_1 = \frac{1}{3}$; $x_2 = \frac{1}{2}$.

b) $16x^2 - 40x + 25 = 0$ factors to $(4x - 5)(4x - 5) = 0$.

Setting $4x - 5 = 0$, we have $x_1 = x_2 = \frac{5}{4}$.

c) $3x^2 - 48x = 0$ factors to $3x(x - 16) = 0$.

Setting $3x = 0$ and $x - 16 = 0$, we have $x_1 = 0$; $x_2 = 16$.

d) $x^2 - 100 = 0$ factors to $(x + 10)(x - 10) = 0$.

Setting $x + 10 = 0$ and $x - 10 = 0$, we have $x_1 = -10$; $x_2 = 10$.

39. $x + y > 3$; $x = 1$

a) $y > 3 - x$

b) above the line

c) $y > 3 - 1$ $y > 2$

41. $-2x + 5y > 2$; $x = 4$

a) $5y > 2 + 2x$

$y > .4 + .4x$

b) above the line

268

c) $y > .4 + .4(4)$

    $y > 2$

43. $x - y \leq 0; x = 5$

    a) $-y \leq -x$

         $y \geq x$

    b)   on and above the line

    c) $y > 5$

45. $2x + 7 \geq 4$

       $2x \geq -3$

        $x \geq -\dfrac{3}{2}$

47. $3 \geq 5 - 2x$

    $3 + 2x \geq 5$

       $2x \geq 5 - 3$

        $x \geq 1$

49. $x - y \geq 0$

      $x \geq 4$